The Roots of *Lo Mexicano*

SELF AND SOCIETY IN MEXICAN

THOUGHT, 1900-1934

by

Henry C. Schmidt

TEXAS A&M UNIVERSITY PRESS

College Station and London

Library of Congress Cataloging in Publication Data

Schmidt, Henry C   1937–
   The roots of lo mexicano.

   Bibliography: p.
   Includes index.
   1. Mexico—Intellectual life. 2. Ramos, Samuel.
3. Mexico—Civilization. 4. National characteristics,
Mexican. I. Title.
F1210.S35   972.08   77-99280
ISBN 0-89096-048-8

Manufactured in the United States of America

First edition

To Gretchen

Contents

Preface

THE search for identity is characteristic of peoples bound in some common way and compelled to understand themselves in terms of their history and their relationship to the rest of the world. Tradition is transformed from daily events into myth, and a symbolic experience of colony, nation, region, or locale emerges. The roots of identity may reach back to a culture hero—a Moses or Quetzalcóatl—as the message of social genesis is communicated by tribal guardians: medicine men, prophets, savants, bards, scholars, and statesmen. The sacred books of the Mayas, the Old Testament, and Pericles' "Funeral Oration" illustrate the use of origins to ensure continuity with the future. The anxiety of collective purpose may be linked to development, as in Latin America, or it may indicate failure, as in Spain and the "generation of '98."[1]

This study seeks to substantiate the growth of Mexican self-awareness as an intellectual foundation of nationalism. From 1900 to 1934, Mexicans made the transition from a culture largely foreign in spirit to one created in the aftermath of the 1910 Revolution, insistently and proudly Mexican. Peoples who for centuries were yoked to a paternalistic socioeconomic system now struggled for self-expression, making their voices heard in constitutional reform and fixing their images in the iconography of the pueblo. The Mexican intellectual has a special capacity to perceive his identity. Heir to the Ibero-Latin American humanistic tradition, he has an *"innerweltlich* orientation"[2] and views history internally.[3] Methodology must bypass conventional topicality and facilitate an intimate approach to history.[4] In such an atmosphere the application of a Mexicanist cri-

[1] See Octavio Paz, *Posdata*, p. 14, and Fredrick B. Pike, *Hispanismo, 1898–1936: Spanish Conservatives and Liberals and Their Relations with Spanish America*, pp. 48–64.

[2] See François Bourricaud, "The Adventures of Ariel," *Daedalus* 101 (Summer, 1972), 113.

[3] See Luis Villoro, "The Historian's Task: The Mexican Perspective," in *The New World Looks at Its History*, ed. Archibald R. Lewis and Thomas F. McGann, pp. 176–179.

[4] See especially Josefina Vázquez de Knauth, "Sobre la síntesis de la historia de México," *Historia Mexicana* 21 (October–December, 1971), 221–222,

tique to self and society has contributed one of the most interesting chapters to the history of ideas; for, as one author writes, Mexico is a dangerous and impassioned country because of its need to know itself as it really is—"like a *calavera* of Posada or a monster of Cuevas."[5]

But this reasoning alone does not account for the Mexican's zeal in self-analysis. Negative assessment of a political incumbent can jeopardize one's career, and this circumstance may be one of the keys to the country's well-developed tradition in philosophical history and moralistic sociology. The strictures on attacking current leadership are so severe that the intellectual often has to flee into a baroque world of guilt and salvation where his commentary is dissolved in harmless alienation. At this level he can point up the flaws in the Mexican system, but he may not doubt or even be indifferent to any activity that has a personalistic source of power. Moreover, the media may have party ties, and educational institutions are usually agencies of the state. As a rule, Latin American governments try to co-opt their intellectuals; thus cultural life is shaped in no small measure by the tension of idealism and the sinecure. If this gives us insights into some of the complexities of Latin American civilization, it also puts many forms of criticism on par with a symbolic game.

During the period 1920 to 1952, when the Revolution engendered the appraisal of Mexico, the term *lo mexicano* became a "sacred phrase" and assumed popular as well as academic meanings as the question of what is Mexico and the Mexican was asked. *Lo mexicano* referred to the Mexican ethos as well as to its study and became a driving principle for the growth of knowledge relating to Mexico. With its allied terms, *mexicanidad, mexicanismo,* and *el mexicano,* it cut across disciplines and engaged historians as well as philosophers and psychologists. In part a manifestation of post-Revolutionary cultural nationalism, the movement was analogous in the history of ideas to the quest for Mexican authenticity in painting, music, the novel, and education. The study of Mexican identity peaked from

---

for suggestions concerning an approach to history beyond chronology, and Luis González, "Microhistoria para multi-México," *Historia Mexicana* 21 (October–December, 1971), 225, in which local history is linked to the poetical method in order to achieve the necessary intimate re-creation of daily life.

[5] Carlos Fuentes, *Tiempo mexicano,* p. 26.

1949 to 1952, when it was centered in the National University's Faculty of Philosophy and Letters, then directed by Samuel Ramos, and when it saw an independent expression in Octavio Paz's *El laberinto de la soledad* (1950).

However, it was Samuel Ramos who launched the modern analysis of Mexican identity with the publication of *Perfil del hombre y la cultura en México* (1934). Historiography only hints at the genesis of this book and the cultural context in which it was written. Did this work, which shifted Mexican problems from a physical base to a psychological plane,[6] spring full-blown, or were its ideas shared by other intellectuals? Credited as the initiator of *lo mexicano*,[7] Ramos emphasized his seminal role in the study of the Mexican character. He stated that he was the first to treat the "psychology of the Mexican," yet the theme was anticipated by Antonio Caso in 1925.[8] And while philosophers are usually regarded as having introduced Orteguian perspectivism into Mexico,[9] it is noteworthy that a historian, Daniel Cosío Villegas, began his lifelong critique of Mexican history in 1925 with the Spanish thinker as his point of departure.[10] Research has not removed this confusion, although one scholar notes the prevalence of *lo mexicano* in 1900.[11] Thus it is suggested that Ramos's work crystallized a current of thought discernible from the 1920's on with roots in even earlier periods. Ramos must therefore be considered in light of the ideas that preceded him, for only then may he be seen as a witness to his age as well as a creator preserving but modifying his intellectual heritage.

However, *lo mexicano* encompasses more than the theme of national character. Rather, it speaks of the passion to understand things Mexican, in evidence from Cortés to today's professional Mexicanist at El Colegio de México. Well known is the curiosity Mexico has

---

[6] Abelardo Villegas, *La filosofía de lo mexicano*, pp. 135–136.

[7] *Diccionario Porrúa de Historia, Biografía y Geografía de México*, II, 1723.

[8] Samuel Ramos, *Historia de la filosofía en México*, p. 153; Ramos quoted in Rosa Castro, "¿Qué es y cómo es lo mexicano?" *Hoy*, April 14, 1951, p. 36; Antonio Caso, "Psicología del pueblo mexicano," *Excélsior*, June 8 and 15, 1925.

[9] Ramos, *Historia de la filosofía en México*, pp. 149–151.

[10] Daniel Cosío Villegas, "La riqueza de México," *La Antorcha* 1 (May 30, 1925), 8.

[11] Juan Hernández Luna, "Primeros estudios sobre lo mexicano en nuestro siglo," *Filosofía y Letras* 20 (October–December, 1950), 327–354.

stimulated for four centuries among its own and foreign scholars. Mexico's nationalism is usually regarded as the most powerful in Latin America, owing to the country's contiguity to the United States and to its recognition of its rich Spanish-Indian culture. The student of Mexico feels immersed in mythical time, not unlike that of the Nahua poets or the literary personage, José Trigo.

In this special cultural space, the Mexican's desire to know himself, to create a truer self-image by disposing of stereotypes, has a didactic purpose. If, for example, machismo is no longer an acceptable standard for male behavior, it is partly because for some time both elite and popular writers have condemned the complex as counterproductive to social progress. This book, therefore, may be viewed as an attempt to understand one aspect of a country's spiritual history.

Attaining a Mexican identity has been as difficult as achieving an equitable economy, social justice, or a responsible polity, and it may be the most significant result of the 1910 Revolution, although its roots antedate that event. Thus the ideational process becomes another medium through which history is enacted. While this study does not deny the interdependence of all historical phenomena, ideas are given a partial autonomy and placed in their relative context. Hence ideas are employed to register the course of a civilization, as symbols of an attitudinal relationship between intellectuals and their country's history. Whether or not they have a direct bearing on political life does not alter their historicity. Political events are discussed only to offer a background to the problems of identity; hence portraits of Porfirian and Revolutionary Mexico are largely dispensed with, since they have been done often in other books. Cultural forms like the novel, music, and painting, which were infused with Mexican identity, remain outside the scope of this study and are mentioned only as ancillary data. The first chapter surveys the growth of a Mexican consciousness in the colonial period and in the nineteenth century in order to identify *lo mexicano* trends prior to 1900. Chapter two treats *lo mexicano* in an era of waning positivism, while chapter three analyzes the 1910 Revolution as an intensifier of older currents of Mexicanism. Chapters four and five provide the ambience for intellectual nationalism in the 1920's and place in relief the immediate precursors of Ramos. Chapter six examines the intellectual

growth of Samuel Ramos as the culmination of the *lo mexicano* tradition that preceded him. Sources include the essential essays found in books, journals, and newspapers; personal materials, such as letters and memoirs; and institutional data, such as reports, memorandums and minutes. Chapter five appeared in a different form as "Antecedents to Samuel Ramos: Mexicanist Thought in the 1920's," *Journal of Interamerican Studies and World Affairs* 18 (May, 1976), 179–202.

To Nettie Lee Benson, Lewis Hanke, and John P. Harrison I am thankful for initially stimulating my interest in Mexican thought. I am indebted to Arturo Arnáiz y Freg, Fernando Benítez, Ana María Rosa Carreón, Daniel Cosío Villegas, Rogelio Díaz Guerrero, Luis González, José Guzmán, Juan Hernández Luna, Wigberto Jiménez Moreno, Carlos Monsiváis, Alejandra Moreno de Florescano, Edmundo O'Gorman, Juan Antonio Ortega y Medina, Octavio Paz, Rodolfo Usigli, Luis Villoro, Leopoldo Zea, and Josefina Vázquez, who patiently led me into the by-ways of Mexican intellectual life. For reading sections of this book in an earlier form and offering suggestions for revision, I wish to thank William H. Goetzmann, Thomas F. McGann, Américo Paredes, and Richard N. Sinkin. My appreciation goes to Gretchen Schmidt for research assistance; David Bailey, Jack Dabbs, Linda Hall, and David Maciel for sharing their research with me; Lysander Kemp for his support of my work; and Dan Aynesworth for resolving problems of interpretation. I wish to express my special gratitude to Stanley R. Ross for guiding me through this study. Research was undertaken with grants from the Mexican Ministry of Foreign Relations, the Institute of Latin American Studies of the University of Texas at Austin, and Texas A&M University.

The Roots of *Lo Mexicano*

1.
The Growth of a Mexican Consciousness

BY the twentieth century, when *mestizaje* was promoted as the anthropological basis of Mexican national identity, the roots of Mexicanness had become a fashionable topic as scholars studied the origins of contemporary society, in some instances pushing the beginnings back to the first evidence of native sensibility or to the first peninsular codes regulating the relationship between vassal and king. Thus one scholar has focused on the Olmec-Totonac genesis of modern popular art, another on the continuity between Judeo-Christian eschatology and indigenous religion, and another on medieval law and the seeds of a Mexican consciousness in the early colonial period.[1] Indeed, a chronology cannot be imposed on some elements in the Mexican consciousness. Written sources undergo marked changes during the sixteenth, eighteenth, and nineteenth centuries, so that the problem of twentieth-century identity often rests on older ideas transmuted by the mythology of national regeneration in the post-Revolutionary period.

Colonial Factors

The New World compelled the imagination of western man and stood as an allegory of identity. A more or less empty land, discovered and settled in modern times by different nationalities who commingled or separated, evolved with or without miscegenation, the New World became both an extension of European civilization and the determinant of new cultures that could oppose and even transcend the forces of their making. The dynamic of interrelated yet

[1] See Octavio Paz, "Risa y penitencia," in *Magia de la risa*, by Octavio Paz, Alfonso Medellín Zenil, and Francisco Beverido, p. 27; Jacques Lafaye, *Quetzalcóatl et Guadalupe: La formation de la conscience nationale au Mexique (1531–1813)*, pp. 90, 120–122; Peggy K. Liss, *Mexico under Spain, 1521–1556: Society and the Origins of Nationality*, p. xi.

separate traditions that underlay New World history refocused the objectives of Euro-Christian pluralism and suggested relativist approaches to the problems born of established responses adjusting to the unknown. Thus the New World as colony was an experience in historical transition. The new civilizations, built on the wreckage of the native ones and the incomplete culture brought by the conquerors, gave only embryonic signs of the ideologies that one day would characterize their struggles for nationhood. Yet from Columbus's paradisiacal rendering of the Caribbean to Humboldt's rationalist preoccupation with New Spain, the European conscience troubled itself with questions about life in the New World. Ultimately, the problem of man and environment led to a great polemic and set the stage for the play of meaning that was to accompany the evolution of Latin American history.

The seeds of Mexican identity germinated in the European ideas of the New World formed during the period between discovery and colonial consolidation. When Columbus wrote of his voyages, he reflected the culture of his age, his special mission, and the environment he encountered.[2] He had navigated the feared "green sea of darkness," and although his geography was confused, his writings expressed a dissipation of doubt and conjecture, which was an important element in exploration's contribution to western civilization. Possession, knowledge, progress, and wealth formed the sequence of Columbus's metaphors, and the European intentions were apparent in such terms as "convenience," "excellence," "abundance," and "surpass." He promised the Old World gold, rhubarb, spices, and drugs. His letters convey the tension between mobility and permanence that characterizes the western ethos, and in his rational, if at times visionary, approach to nature, Columbus revealed himself a modern European. Yet coasting northern South America on his third voyage, he lapsed into an older, though no less contemporary, chiliasm and described the comely natives, the benign climate, and his version of the "earthly paradise."[3] The formulation of the Columbian context was

[2] See Paolo Toscanelli to Fernando Martínez, June 25, 1474, in C. Edwards Lester and Andrew Foster, *The Life and Voyages of Americus Vespucius*, pp. 331–335, for the attitudinal and geographical framework Columbus would in part replicate in his journal.

[3] Christopher Columbus, *Four Voyages to the New World: Letters and Selected Documents*, trans. and ed. R. H. Major, pp. 1–17, 104–168. Perhaps, as

clear: expansion, prosperity, and salvation. But the synthesis of Renaissance and medieval experience collapsed when Columbus's earthly schemes failed, and, weakened in body and spirit, he could only retreat further into his milennarian dream.

Where Columbus failed, Cortés triumphed—as molder of men and master of machinations.[4] His conquest correspondence, written with the determinism of a government report, suggested the imperial system that was to provide the standards of existence in the New World. The watchwords were "serve" and "obey"; the sword was used for the glory of gold and "God our Savior." And true to the Euro-Iberian requirements for prestige and the cosmographical anxieties that shaped the course of exploration, Cortés could not stop with his Mexican domain but looked westward to the "Southern sea."[5] God, king, wealth, and the world. This was the initial European vision through which New World man would be seen—Spaniard, creole, Indian, Negro, and caste—each integrated into the attitudinal pattern developed during centuries of georeligious growth and now tested by the enlarged and dynamic parameters of a once-obscure historical theory. If Columbus and Cortés embodied the New World as European idea, from their first encounters with the strange lands their perceptual capacity was broadened by the new experience, and the repetition of this act by those who followed would provide the basis for Euro-American identity.[6]

It is always stated that the exploits of Columbus and Cortés were manifestations of a complex historical development. Spain had been expanding in the centuries-long Reconquest of Moslem-held territories, and under Ferdinand and Isabella, the concerns of Renaissance Europe were fused with the problems of administering con-

---

two scholars suggest, Columbus was a carrier of the "paradise cult" of Judeo-Christian civilization (Frank and Fritzie P. Manuel, "Sketch for a Natural History of Paradise," *Daedalus* 101 [Winter, 1972], 83–128).

[4] For a discussion of Cortés as Machiavellian man, see Howard Mumford Jones, *O Strange New World: American Culture, the Formative Years*, pp. 137–139.

[5] Hernán Cortés, *Letters from Mexico*, trans. and ed. A. P. Pagden, p. 267.

[6] For the idea of discovery as an act of perception, see Thomas Goldstein, "Impulses of Italian Renaissance Culture behind the Age of Discoveries," in *First Images of America: The Impact of the New World on the Old*, ed. Fredi Chiapelli, I, 29.

quered and alien peoples. After Granada fell, it is argued, the religious and military momentum of the Reconquest was transferred in the same year to the New World when Columbus set sail from Palos. Ocean rivalry with Portugal, the colonization of the Canaries, the growth of the wool trade, and the rise of Castile were other factors in the imperial evolution of Spain that marked its advance from an "inferior" nation to an "equal" one.[7] *Pureza de sangre* (blood purity) contributed, however nefariously, to the new Castilian eminence, and, assuming the role of cross-bearer of Christianity and upholding the fighting tradition of his infantry, the Spaniard of the sixteenth century launched into a neo-medieval venture in which the attitudes of *dignidad, honor,* and *señorearse* would be drawn in the new secular profile of the Renaissance.[8] The caste of the New World, the foundling Mexican, would buy certificates of *gracias a sacar* to simulate the Spanish status. Identity was to be derived from a social hierarchy contingent on religious incentives and economic realities.

If, through its discovery and colonization of the New World, Spain was able to revivify the medieval notions of feudalism and Catholicism, it also reinforced Renaissance Europe in its rise to world hegemony. Expansion had shaped the European experience since the Crusades, and by the fifteenth century, with the Turks pressing in, the way for Christianity was to encircle Islam by going around Africa, until the voyages of Columbus made the western route feasible. Now the cooperation of individual enterprise with institutional authority, commerce, and banking found an outlet as Europe turned to broader horizons, found its passages to India, and ploughed its New World silver into warfare and capitalism.

Together with the material transfer in the culture of conquest went the religio-mythic baggage of the Renaissance. As one scholar has noted, Europe was never sure that its institutions perfectly embodied the Christian revelation. A golden age lay in the past and utopia

---

[7] See J. H. Elliott, *Imperial Spain, 1469–1716,* pp. 33–119; Otis H. Green, *Spain and the Western Tradition: The Castilian Mind in Literature from El Cid to Calderón,* III, 250–279; and J. H. Parry, *The Spanish Seaborne Empire,* pp. 27–52.

[8] One scholar defines the influence of the New World conquest on Spain as a "compensatory side-effect" of the political ideology of Charles V and notes that Cortés embodies various intellectual traditions. See Carlos G. Noreña, *Studies in Spanish Renaissance Thought,* p. 108.

either far away or in the future. The Renaissance "ventured forth on a quest to objectify" the golden age, which "became an attainable goal and a challenge to the explorers." The mythos of a divine well-head rewarding perseverance and faith was contained in a dual response—the one formal, scholastic, and intellectual, and the other mystical, emotional, and pragmatic. Both traditions originated in a Europe imbued with "humanist optimism" that could purify the Christian religion and extend its benefits to foreign lands. As the Franciscan chronicler Motolinía confidently concluded, the New World providentially had awaited discovery by the men of his age. Thus the Christian humanism of More, Erasmus, and Jiménez de Cisneros brought about religious reform in New Spain, less a process of conversion than an ingenious cultural transfer from the Old World to the New, generating the adaptive mechanisms necessary for the growth of a Mexicanist mentality.[9]

The religious impulse was linked to the Renaissance convergence of geographical knowledge and the myth of a western sea route to the Orient. Here the fifteenth-century Italian cosmographers were largely responsible, although their heritage had classical origins. As one scholar wrote, the "journey pattern of modern western history" began with the "paradisiac yearning" of the Renaissance that sent the European westward. These were only the psychological reasons in the logic of exploration: in the physical realm the age saw the marriage of hull and sail that carried the European onward in his dream of Cathay.[10] Thus the Renaissance and the discovery of sea routes and new lands must be mutually conceived. Both reflected European expansion in science, commerce, philosophy, government, and religion. With the Renaissance experience superimposed on the older medieval one, the New World became a metaphor of European

---

[9] See Myron P. Gilmore, *The World of Humanism, 1453–1517*, pp. 34–35, 2–4; Harry Levin, *The Myth of the Golden Age in the Renaissance*, p. 59; Motolinía [Fray Toribio de Benavente], *Memoriales o libro de las cosas de la Nueva España y de los naturales de ella*, ed. Edmundo O'Gorman, p. 199; Marcel Bataillon, *Erasmo y España: Estudios sobre la historia espiritual del siglo XVI*, trans. Antonio Alatorre, II, p. 429.

[10] See Boies Penrose, *Travel and Discovery in the Renaissance, 1420–1620*, pp. 3–19; Charles E. Sanford, *The Quest for Paradise: Europe and the American Moral Imagination*, pp. 36–46; J. H. Parry, *The Age of Reconnaissance*, pp. 67–83.

design in its multiple and often conflicting forms—the power of state and enterprise and the bucolic-utopian quest of reformers and mendicants. Yet these energies were unified by forces both powerful and persuasive—the spread of Christianity and the attainment of wealth.

The European idea of New World man alternated between the pagan-Aristotelian attitude of measurable becoming and the Platonic-Christian ideal of spiritual being. Administratively, this meant conquest and community—the orderly worldliness of Renaissance materialism and the transcendence of Christian humanism.[11] Church and state: time was to be circular or linear if there was to be redemption or progress. Hence the polarization of the New World experience as empire and salvation, the legalistic and the apocalyptic, the narrative and the prophetic, the imperialistic and the messianic, the papal and the spiritual church. Yet in no wise was this dichotomy absolute. The spiritual conquest of the New World could extend to the worldly, while the paper rationale of material conquest was underlaid with religious purpose.

Inevitably the New World was to be viewed at first within a European framework. The new lands fell within the scope of European knowledge, since they were geographical proof of the fullness of God and nature and tested man as "modifier of his environment," while the discovery of man in the New World posed questions concerning human rights. Thus the integrity of the western teleology was at stake, and the Indian would have to be incorporated into the chain of being or, at the lowest level, he could be put on display for the curious.[12] The Renaissance now acquired an anthropological dimension, and the identity of New World Man was infused with western intellectualism and praxis. Attitudes built up during the medieval and Renaissance periods and fueled by travel, adventure, fraterniza-

---

[11] For a discussion of how the crown oscillated between spiritual and temporal policies during the first half of the sixteenth century, see José Miranda, *Las ideas y las instituciones políticas mexicanas, 1521–1820*, p. 41.

[12] See Clarence J. Glacken, *Traces on the Rhodian Shore: Nature and Culture in Western Thought from Ancient Times to the End of the Eighteenth Century*, p. 358; Lewis Hanke, *The Spanish Struggle for Justice in the Conquest of America*, pp. 1, 175; Margaret T. Hodgen, *Early Anthropology in the Sixteenth and Seventeenth Centuries*, pp. 386–433, 111–112; J. A. Fernández-Santamaria, *The State, War and Peace: Spanish Political Thought in the Renaissance, 1516–1559*, pp. 58–96, 196–236.

tion, and Erasmian humanism, had now made their way to New Spain. There interaction with indigenous influences produced a cycle of mental transformations that set in motion the evolution of the idea of Mexico.[13]

In New Spain the image of man was forged in the Renaissance-Hispanic theory of governmental and religious administration. The Thomist-inspired universal order sanctified the linkage between crown and subject, the colonies rendering nominally greater homage to the king than did the willful Iberian provinces. Thus the notion of New World man was developed through the historical circumstances of the rulers. Knowledge was put at the service of Spanish imperial interests and the universal ideal of Christianity. For example, mathematics and astronomy were taught in geographical treatises and navigation manuals by the cosmographer who channeled the flow of information from the New World into royal policymaking; the viceroy viewed the Indian in terms of his service to Christianity and the crown, while the Franciscan friar often looked upon the Indian community as a refuge from a corrupt Europe.[14] For the *arriviste*, man was explained by his relationship to power. That the Spanish imperial system did not preclude divergent responses to the New World, however, testified to the competing interests of royal administration as well as to a changing colonial experience. Thus the growth of Mexican identity followed a shifting cultural and political pattern whose signals marked the evolution of Mexico from colony to state. Here the dynamic rather than the static factors of New Spain became the indicators of an incipient Mexican consciousness, as when Cortés created an infrastructure by rejecting crown policy inapplicable to local conditions.[15]

The Indian constituted a special class or was declassed alto-

---

[13] Colonial Mexican historiography is organized around the permutations of civil and religious life as New Spain received and adopted European culture. For an example, see José M. Gallegos Rocafull, *El pensamiento mexicano en los siglos XVI y XVII*, pp. 169–213.

[14] See Francisco de la Maza, *Enrico Martínez: cosmógrafo e impresor de Nueva España*, pp. 22–23; Lesley Byrd Simpson, *The Encomienda in New Spain*, pp. 116–120; John Leddy Phelan, *The Millenial Kingdom of the Franciscans in the New World*, pp. 59–68.

[15] See Mario Góngora, *Studies in the Colonial History of Spanish America*, trans. Richard Southern, pp. 18–19.

gether within the prevailing Euro-Spanish values. The mestizo—who some say is the key factor in Mexican identity—became the pariah of colonial society,[16] while the creole emerged subservient to the peninsular. On the other hand, the corporate identity of the colonial social structure revealed both Spanish and indigenous origins, and on this basis one may argue that colonial society demonstrated embryonic Mexican characteristics. Nevertheless, the documents edited by Richard Konetzke for a social history of colonial Latin America clearly show the Indian, the mestizo, and the creole under the Hispanic tutelage, while Benjamin Keen has observed that the conquistadors saw the Indians as peoples either gifted or guilty of crimes against God and Nature. Scholars of colonial Mexico agree that the Black Legend of Spanish cruelty to the Indian was essentially true.[17] Exploited by the Spaniard, the Indian was stripped of his identity and often reduced to a caricature before the western advance.

Spanish governmental and religious policies of conciliation and beneficence toward the Indian were at best academic niceties amid the greater cultural forces at work. Christian humanism smacked of intellectual faddism, and its moral outcry could be a veiled form of conquest.[18] The principles of the Spanish colonization, including the humanitarian protests against the abuses of the Conquest, presupposed the Europeanization of the earth. Europe had become "history's paradigm" and the New World "could acquire historical significance only by becoming another Europe"; hence the image of Mexico in large measure was controlled by the imposition of Euro-Christian values on the native populace.[19] However, in spite of the

[16] For discussions of the emergence of the mestizo in colonial Mexican and Latin American society, see Eric Wolf, *Sons of the Shaking Earth*, pp. 233–246; and Magnus Mörner, *Race Mixture in the History of Latin America*, pp. 75–102.

[17] See *Colección de documentos para la historia de la formación social de Hispanoamérica, 1493–1810*, ed. Richard Konetzke; Benjamin Keen, *The Aztec Image in Western Thought*, p. 63; François Chevalier, *Land and Society in Colonial Mexico: The Great Hacienda*, trans. Alvin Eustis, p. 309; Charles Gibson, *The Aztecs under Spanish Rule: A History of the Indians of the Valley of Mexico, 1519–1810*, p. 403; and Josefina Zoraida Vázquez, *La imagen del indio en el español del siglo XVI*, p. 157.

[18] For a discussion of the material motives of New World Christianization, see Marvin Harris, *Patterns of Race in the Americas*, p. 16.

[19] Edmundo O'Gorman, *The Invention of America*, pp. 137–139; see José Miranda, *Vida colonial y albores de la independencia*, p. 25.

catastrophic biological decline of the Indian in the sixteenth century, he persisted as the one foil to the transplanted Euro-Hispanic society. Thus the Indian was thrust into the paradoxical role of being displaced before the spread of European civilization but at the same time providing a cohesive symbol of New World identity. It was still the indigenous culture that elicited the greatest awe from Cervantes de Salazar's hypothetical visitor to Mexico City in 1554.[20]

In spite of the formal values that underlay man's relationship to the New World environment and determined his perception of it, the first observers recorded different impressions of a society emerging from tumult into order. The clerical writers in particular never fully agreed about the meaning of the confrontation between Christian and heathen. Although Bartolomé de las Casas strenuously objected to the inhumane nature of the Europeanization of the New World, the mendicant writers early opened a fissure in Mexican identity by rejecting aspects of pre-Hispanic religion and justifying the Conquest to which, after all, they owed their livelihood. Moreover, in the comparisons of culture that resulted from the contact of the Old World with the New, the testimony often betrayed a defensive bias regarding the colonies, which, if it hindered critical historical detachment, also established a characteristic trend in the search for identity in the national period of Latin America.[21] These early writers usually reflected their official positions, and if their subject matter was circumscribed by the problems of conquest and the conversion of Indians, it was precisely these tasks which impelled them to collect first-rate ethnographic data and convey the Mexican presence in the form of the landscape and the Indian. Thus colonial literature is a key source for establishing the dichotomy between the Spaniards as the active, Europeanizing agents and the indigenous culture, defeated but readapting—the cultural cross-fertilization that foreshadowed the birth of a new hybrid civilization.

In reporting the interaction between the Euro-Hispanic ruling structure and the native population, the observer bore testimony to a

[20] For the impact of the Indian on the ideology of conquest, see Lee E. Huddleston, *Origins of the American Indian: European Concepts, 1492–1729*, pp. 14–15; and Lewis Hanke, "El significado teológico del descubrimiento de América," *Diálogos* 12 (January–February, 1976), 21–26. Francisco Cervantes de Salazar, *México en 1554*, p. 98.

[21] See Góngora, *Colonial History of Spanish America*, p. 230.

new cultural synthesis, and his insights constituted the beginnings of a Mexicanist awareness. The first viceroy to New Spain, Antonio de Mendoza, placed the Indians and mestizos in a socioracial context based on historical circumstances and crown policy for treating the two classes. Gerónimo de Mendieta's description of Indian art demonstrated a preoccupation with popular culture, while visitor Jerónimo Valderrama's discussion of the character of the Indian in relation to labor and administration illustrated a nascent consciousness of Mexican social problems.[22]

A salient example of the changing intellectual perspective is the historiography of Ixtlilxóchitl (Fernando de Alva). Of native royal lineage, he wrote with the introspection, if not the guilt, of his family's role in the controversy over Texcoco's aid to Cortés. For him Mexican history was conceived locally, yet it had to be incorporated into a universal design; hence the awkward but logical emphasis on analogies between classical and Christian culture and the autochthonous ambit of Texcoco. Basically, Ixtlilxóchitl's frame of reference is neither Spanish nor indigenous, and his social bias was determined by cultural *mestizaje* that allowed him to articulate a Mexicanist position.[23]

However, the evidence for a creole, or native, world view emerging in sixteenth-century Mexico invites controversy. From affirmation based on intuitive approaches to doubt resulting from political analysis, consensus is unobtainable.[24] Nevertheless, by the end of the century, writers had begun to differentiate the quality of life in the Old World and the New, and most scholars agree that the first signs

---

22 Antonio de Mendoza to Luis Velasco, in *Instrucciones que los virreyes de Nueva España dejaron a sus sucesores*, I, 14, 16–17; Gerónimo de Mendieta, *Historia eclesiástica indiana*, pp. 403–407; Jerónimo Valderrama, *Cartas del Licenciado Jerónimo Valderrama y otros documentos sobre su visita al gobierno de Nueva España, 1563–1565*, pp. 46–47, 58–60.

23 See the interpretation by Gloria Grajales, *Nacionalismo incipiente en los historiadores coloniales: estudio historiográfico*, pp. 25–27.

24 For examples of the emergence of the creole based on a literary approach, see Fernando Benítez, *In the Footsteps of Cortés*, pp. 244–245, and *The Century after Cortés*, p. 275. For an expression of doubt regarding the putative Mexican identity of the sixteenth-century creole, see Peggy Liss, "A Cosmic Approach Falls Short: A Review of Jacques Lafaye's *Quetzalcóatl and Guadalupe: The Formation of Mexican National Consciousness, 1531–1813*," *Hispanic American Historical Review* 57 (November, 1977), 708.

of a Mexican consciousness had appeared.[25] As part of the New World, Mexico was subject to the on-going debate over its significance; thus indirectly it must have benefitted when José de Acosta challenged the European premises and provided a watershed for thought about Latin American identity in 1590. Arguing with eloquence and a surprising degree of reason for the age, Acosta refuted the long accumulation of European prejudice against the New World by skillfully dismantling the chain of ideas originating with the ancients that human life did not exist outside the then known universe. Discovery of the New World, Acosta stated, had helped prove that the world was round; it existed and even had the same sky that covered Spain.[26] The importance of Acosta's work lies in the fact that it presented the New World as a philosophical problem, but one that had become integral to western notions of the cosmos.

Although Acosta was writing with Peru in mind, his efforts were similar to those of Mexican intellectuals like Juan de Cárdenas and Enrico Martínez, whose sensitivity to geohistorical contexts enhanced the incipient Mexican identity.[27] Mexico was now asserting its presence in the universal order and during the seventeenth century it witnessed a cultural flowering at the elite and popular levels that, in effect, pulled the colony away from the Spanish metropolis toward a serene and independent Mexican matrix. Ranch lore, the *pulquería*, and the cult of Guadalupe were producing the materials of a Mexican iconography;[28] literary history emphasizes the Mexicanness implicit in some writers of the period. New Spain had obtained a level of cultural development comparable to Spain's, and in 1603 Bernardo de Balbuena sang of the fullness and brilliance of Anáhuac. Yet the importance of Balbuena's work lay not in the author's paean to Mexico City but in the fact that the apotheosis of pagan

[25] Luis González, "En torno de la integración de la realidad mexicana," in *Estudios históricos americanos: homenaje a Silvo Zavala*, p. 424; José Miranda, *España y Nueva España en la época de Felipe II*, p. 127; and Liss, *Mexico under Spain, 1521–1556*, p. 152.

[26] José de Acosta, *Historia natural y moral de las Indias*, pp. 11–27, 93.

[27] See Juan de Cárdenas, *Primera parte de los problemas y secretos maravillosos de las Indias*, pp. 154–160; and Francisco de la Maza, Introduction to Henrico Martínez, *Repertorio de los tiempos e historia natural de Nueva España*, p. xxv.

[28] See J. I. Israel, *Race, Class and Politics in Colonial Mexico, 1610–1670*, p. 270.

and Christian civilizations was transferred to the New World.[29] Thus, as the experience based on conquest and consolidation waned, New Spain entered the baroque period, marked by the tension of the older medieval Catholic and Renaissance world confronting the initial impact of the age of reason, a conflict classically embodied in the life and work of the poet Sor Juana Inés de la Cruz.[30]

Most of the later themes of the Mexicanist inquiry were articulated in a seventeenth-century version that pointed to the maturing intellectual life of New Spain. One noteworthy effort was the history by Juan de Torquemada, who, writing during the decline of the Indian church, harped on the stock comparison between Mexican and European antiquity, although in typical mendicant fashion he justified the Conquest. On the other hand, identity with Mexico was by no means common, as Carlos Sigüenza y Góngora demonstrated when he charged that Mexicans ignored their history, disdained the native, and admired the European. The images of colonial character, by now widespread in the Hispanic world and common to such diverse writers as the Spanish apologist Juan de Solórzano and the creole-oriented Francisco Vetancurt, revealed both a crystallizing social configuration of Indian, mestizo, and creole and an increasing conceptualization of the Mexican experience. These trends were evident in the writings of Bishop Juan de Palafox, who substantially advanced the meditation on the Indian by cogently proceeding from a factual to an ideational synthesis.[31] Represented in the great pageantry of the era and invoked in the scholar's study, the Indian remained a prominent fixture in the Mexican mythology, yet he was hardly a contemporary figure but rather the abstract, at times idealized, creature of history used for this or that political end. It was the shift from the mendicant to the creole awareness of pre-Hispanic civilization during the course of the seventeenth century that initiated a new phase in the evolution of Mexicanism, one that would

---

[29] See Bernardo de Balbuena, *Grandeza mexicana*, pp. 70–71.

[30] See the discussion by Lafaye, *Quetzalcóatl et Guadalupe*, pp. 101–108.

[31] On Torquemada and Sigüenza, see Keen, *The Aztec Image*, pp. 180–184, 190–191; on the Mexicanism of Don Carlos, see Irving A. Leonard, *Baroque Times in Old Mexico: Seventeenth Century Persons, Places, and Practices*, pp. 126, 225; Juan de Solórzano y Pereyra, *Política indiana*, I, 172, 442–447; and Agustín de Vetancurt, *Teatro mexicano*, f. 1, p. 3; Juan de Palafox y Mendoza, *Ideas políticas*, pp. 53–122.

assume a political dimension as the idea of Mexico became associated with independence and with the mandate to develop cultural autonomy and to create the symbols of nationhood.

The eighteenth century saw the decline of the baroque era of identity with its allegorical universe, dynamic of conquest, and ethnically determined social hierarchy. The new phase of Mexican consciousness was concerned with science; it also significantly framed Mexico in a relationship to the non-Hispanic world and sought to dissolve the antinomy of the Christian Conquest and pre-Columbian paganism through a broader acceptance of the Indian past and by positing the apostolic origins of Aztec religion and the direct intervention of God in Mexico as reflected in the Guadalupe cult. Articulated largely by the creoles, whose community of interests and shared attitudes toward their history had been germinating since the late sixteenth century, these themes are usually associated with the politics and ethos of that native elite and were evident from the 1740's, when the Jesuits introduced modernist thought into Mexico, until 1808, when the first movement for independence placed creole thought in a larger political framework.[32] To the extent that the creoles provided a unified vision of Mexico, they did so through anti-Spanish bias and a tendency to ascribe uniqueness to Mexican culture.[33] Thus when Juan José de Eguiara y Eguren published *Biblio· teca mexicana* in 1755 in defense of Mexican culture, it was obvious that New Spain was leaning toward an implicit nationalism.

The Liss thesis holds that the Jesuits gave the creoles an exaggerated sense of their intellectual abilities, converting them into "trained aristocrats" who were cognizant of their intellectual autonomy but who could not assume a corresponding social position in the colony. However, the creoles' hyperbolic identity with Mexico—a manifestation of the Jesuit rationale of cultural pluralism within

[32] See especially Bernabé Navarro, *La introducción de la filosofía moderna en México*, pp. 40–41; Xavier Tavera Alfaro, *El nacionalismo en la prensa mexicana del siglo XVIII*, p. xxii; Hugh M. Hamill, Jr., *The Hidalgo Revolt: Prelude to Mexican Independence*, p. 43; and Doris M. Ladd, *The Mexican Nobility at Independence, 1780–1826*, pp. 95–96.

[33] For a survey of the scholarship on creole identity see Peggy K. Korn, "Topics in Mexican Historiography, 1750–1810: The Bourbon Reforms, the Enlightenment, and the Background of Revolution," in *Investigaciones contemporáneas sobre historia de México*, pp. 159–195.

the empire—was an early expression of the inferiority complex Samuel Ramos would study.[34]

If the Jesuits were partly responsible for the methodological advances that activated the creole consciousness, their expulsion in 1767 only furthered the growth of a nationalistic ideology. Some of the Jesuits went in exile to Italy, where, for a variety of reasons— nostalgia for their homeland, anti-Spanish expediency, and polemics against European denigrators of the New World—they wrote treatises on Mexican history and culture that reinforced the Mexicanism of the age.[35] Impelled by intensely political motives, these writers absorbed some of the major preoccupations of colonial thought and, giving them a crucial contemporary focus, transmitted to later generations a body of fresh and vigorous Mexican themes. Some, like Andrés Cavo, saw the need for miscegenation in Mexico; others, like Pedro José Márquez, echoed Las Casas and Torquemada and called on the Mexican to regard pre-Hispanic civilization the way the Europeans did the Greeks. The most important exiled Jesuit intellectual was Francisco Xavier Clavijero, whose book *Storia Antica del Messico* (1780–1781) is regarded as a seminal work in Mexican nationalism. His noteworthy essay on the "Aztec character" outlines opposing behavioral traits, a concept of character polarization that would appear in *lo mexicano* analysis into the twentieth century.[36]

The Enlightenment renewed the debate over the meaning of New World man, and the fact that both Indian and creole were often treated as inferior caused the Mexican to spring to life in defense of his land and people.[37] Under Bourbon tutelage, New Spain

---

[34] Peggy K. Liss, "Jesuit Contributions to the Ideology of Spanish Empire in Mexico," *The Americas* 29 (April, 1973), 464–465.

[35] See the discussion by Gabriel Méndez Plancarte, ed., "Introducción," *Humanistas del siglo XVII*, p. xi.

[36] Andrés Cavo, "La necesidad del mestizaje," in *Humanistas del siglo XVIII*, ed. Méndez Plancarte, pp. 105–106; Pedro José Márquez, "Los mexicanos y los griegos," ibid., pp. 140–141; Antonello Gerbi, *The Dispute of the New World: The History of a Polemic*, trans. Jeremy Moyle, pp. 195–208; Antonio Gómez Robledo, "La conciencia mexicana en la obra de Francisco Xavier Clavijero," *Historia Mexicana* 19 (January–March, 1970), 347–364; Francisco Xavier Clavijero, "El carácter de los mexicanos," in *Humanistas del siglo XVIII*, ed. Méndez Plancarte, p. 7.

[37] See the discussions by Keen, *The Aztec Image*, p. 219; and John Leddy

received the reformist spirit of the Enlightenment, and the principles of rational criticism began to loosen the grip of scholasticism on the Mexican mind and to bring the Mexican into contact with his environment.[38] Regalism became the political corollary to the new intellectual emphasis on the physical world and encouraged the state to centralize royal power and gather information on the colonial sources of wealth. The natural sciences now vied with theology for scholarly attention. Botany, medicine, and mining became paramount as it was realized that the physical resources of Mexico, improperly understood, could not be efficiently utilized. As one scholar writes, the scientific inquiry of the Enlightenment in the New World began the process of "introspection" and the "rediscovery of America." Chronicles, reports, poetry, and geographical treatises pointed to the increasing interest in Mexican archaeology and history.[39]

Science, however, generated not only a new methodology with which to spur the formation of a national consciousness, but also a new cosmopolitan matrix for Mexican intellectual growth. In the eighteenth century European science, exclusive of the Spanish, discovered Latin America. Its most distinguished representative was the German naturalist Alexander von Humboldt, whose *Essai politique sur le royaume de la Nouvelle Espagne* (1810) became the most important book of its time on Mexico and influenced Mexican and European intellectuals for several generations.

Humboldt's book changed the concept of Mexico and inaugurated the nineteenth century in Mexico, an era that would stimulate the desire for progress and nationalism. The work embraced both the Enlightenment curiosity about the physical realm and the awakened interest in foreign cultures derived from Herder's romantic cultural pluralism. Humboldt acted as a catalyst for potential Mexican de-

---

Phelan, "Neo-Aztecism in the Eighteenth Century and the Genesis of Mexican Nationalism," in *Culture in History: Essays in Honor of Paul Radin*, ed. Stanley Diamond, p. 762.

38 Not all scholars agree about the positive effects of the Enlightenment on Mexicanism. For a viewpoint that supports this thesis, see Monelisa Lina Pérez Marchand, *Dos etapas ideológicas del siglo XVIII en México: a través de los papeles de la Inquisición*, p. 142. For an opposing view, see Shirley Brice Heath, *La política del lenguaje en México: de la colonia a la nación*, pp. 92–93.

39 José Joaquín Izquierdo, *Montaña y los orígenes del movimiento social y científico de México*, pp. 167–168; Germán Arciniegas, *Latin America: A Cultural History*, p. 314; Miranda, *Vida colonial*, pp. 210–211.

velopment; and sanctioning the creole self-image, he lent his prestige to the counterattack on the European critics of the New World.[40] Insofar as he posited Mexico as autonomous historical entity at the same time removing it from its Spanish context and opening it to the wider western world, Humboldt laid the conceptual basis for national identity that would be elaborated by intellectuals well into the twentieth century. In the tradition of colonial characterology Humboldt analyzed the Indian and saw the "national character" revealed in the indigenous fiesta, while the mestizo he viewed as one who "lived in a constant state of irritation against the whites." In the environmentalism common to his age he linked the problem of New Spain to its physical geography, ultimately reaching his famous conclusion that Mexico was a "land of inequality." And in a judgment that would endear him to nineteenth-century devotees of liberal progress, he stated that the European felt oppressed by the colonial mentality of Mexico.[41]

The creole influence on Mexican identity culminated with the movements for independence (1808–1821), an experience that gave the intellectual nationalism germinating since the 1740's an overt political context. Significantly, by 1800 such signs of modernity as the new scientific rationale and a surprising expression of Spanish women's rights had found a forum in the *Gaceta de México*, the official news organ of the colony.[42] And if the New World had been shaped by the strange fixations of empire, by the latter part of the eighteenth century there was in the air, from the North Atlantic seaboard to the Rio de la Plata, a sense of Americanness, newness, and enterprise, of a way of life different from that of Europe.[43] It was the intensified political focus of independence, however, that brought

[40] For discussions of the "Humboldtization" of Mexico, see Juan Antonio Ortega y Medina, *Humboldt desde México*, p. 22; Leopoldo Zea, "Humboldt y la independencia de América," in *Ensayos sobre Humboldt*, pp. 104–120; and Luis González, "Humboldt y la revolución de independencia," ibid., pp. 201–216.

[41] Alexander von Humboldt, *Political Essay on the Kingdom of New Spain*, I, 194, 52–53, 184, 258.

[42] See "Oración que para abrir los exámenes públicos de las niñas que se educan en la Casa de Misericordia de la Ciudad de Cádiz . . . ," *Gaceta de México*, September 13, 1803.

[43] Humboldt noted that creoles preferred to be called Americans (*Political Essay*, I, 205).

the long evolution of the issue of cultural separation from Europe to a crucial juncture. For now the attitudes articulated by a handful of illuminati had filtered down into the language of everyday discourse. Initially the Mexicans thought only of creole leadership within the empire, but even then the forces of psychological autonomy were present, suggesting "something of the idea of America representing the future of Europe."[44] As the process of independence unfolded, according to one existentialist interpretation, the Mexican began to analyze the elements that hid him from his "authenticity."[45]

Yet in spite of the emergent identity of the creole at both the elite and popular levels, a sense of national identity was by no means well developed or widespread. The term *Mexican* might refer to a region or a locale, but not to a nation. In discrete situations, however, a shifting framework of allegiance is clear. There is no mistaking the comprehensive identity implicit in the speeches of the impassioned *norteño* deputy to the Cortes of Cádiz, Miguel Ramos Arizpe, which gave political voice to social inequities. That the relationship between independence and Mexican identity remains problematical may be seen in the way present-day analysis has polarized around antithetical concepts. According to one viewpoint, independence was the crowning achievement of forces set in motion by creolism, Bourbonism, and the Enlightenment; another regards it negatively, as a desire to destroy baroque culture, seeing development only as a possible long-term result of imminent political separation.[46]

The contemporary summary of Mexican identity that offered the most persuasive index of later topical growth in the national consciousness was provided by the iconoclastic patriot Servando Teresa de Mier. Influenced by Thomas Paine's idea of New World autono-

[44] Peggy Ann Korn, "The Beginnings of Mexican Nationalism: The Growth of an Ideology" (Ph.D. diss., University of Pennsylvania, 1965), p. 211.

[45] Luis Villoro, *El proceso ideológico de la revolución de independencia,* pp. 148–149.

[46] Raúl Cardiel Reyes, *Del modernismo al liberalismo: la filosofía de Manuel María Gorriño,* p. 253; Miguel Ramos Arizpe, *Discursos, memorias, e informes,* pp. 7–10; Luis González, "El optimismo nacionalista como factor de la independencia de México," in *Estudios de historiografía americana,* pp. 153–215; and Jorge Alberto Manrique, "El pesimismo como factor de la independencia de México," in *Conciencia y autenticidad históricas: escritos en homenaje a Edmundo O'Gorman,* pp. 177–196.

my, Mier argued that Mexico must face the task of taking its place in the world. He saw society in the context of miscegenation; hence, he emphasized the mestizo, the Afro-American, and the Indian, whom he optimistically viewed as inhabiting a land of plenty. Independence, Mier thought, marked the coming of age for Mexico, whose history and national character he contrasted with that of the United States. Yet Mier warned that the Mexican political system must conform to the social realities of the country and not to foreign models.[47] Mier thus absorbed and reworked the colonial lore of identity, giving it insight and force, and left a legacy that still seems refreshingly modern.

The Nineteenth Century

In the New World of the late eighteenth and early nineteenth centuries, the question, What is an American? began to be asked. Whereas in the United States it was answered by relatively smooth national development, in the republics to the south the answers often did not take root and shape the societies that gave them utterance. Humboldt might have inferred sovereignty from the term *America*, but the revolutionaries who waged the wars of independence and the prophets of national values found it difficult to generate the powerful energies necessary to sustain nationhood. Chaos prevailed, and sometimes the leaders despaired; Bolívar remarked that America was ungovernable. The colonial heritage remained an incubus on the nascent nationalism of Latin America,[48] and savage conflict ensued that saw conservatives, liberals, nationalists, cosmopolitans, Catholics, and capitalists pour forth their individual rhetorics of national salvation. When most of the colonies were gone, the old and new civilizations stood more starkly opposed, and if there were not actual-

47 Servando Teresa de Mier, *Escritos inéditos*, ed. J. M. Miguel Vergés and Hugo Díaz-Thomé, p. 104; idem, *Carta de un americano al español sobre su número XIX*, p. 68; idem, *Escritos inéditos*, p. 312. See the discussion by David A. Brading, *Los orígenes del nacionalismo mexicano*, pp. 143–144.

48 Leopoldo Zea notes that Latin America in the nineteenth century struggled against a nefarious Spanish past (Black Legend) in seeking "mental emancipation." See *The Latin American Mind*, trans. James H. Abbott and Lowell Dunham, pp. 78–79.

ly new social forces at work, there were implicit in the independence movements new ways of thinking and living. A new metaphorical and existential dimension was being added to western civilization as the New World deepened its search for meaning. In Mexico formal history articulates the end of the wars of independence (1821) as the beginning of nationhood. Yet the growth of national awareness was not the result of a monogenetic process, but was instead temporally diffuse and, throughout much of the nineteenth century, associated precariously with an intellectual elite. To the masses Mexican identity at best might have been restricted to the patria chica. The question now was the extent to which the European idea of Mexico had become a Mexican one.

As some scholars have indicated, independence was frequently a nominal rather than a substantive factor in national identity. Never neatly coterminous with national self-awareness, most of the New World independence movements signified the separation of the American republics from Spain at the formal political level but not at the institutional and psychological ones. Raúl Cardiel Reyes pointed out that an intellectual could speak for liberalism and independence without implying the idea of nationality. If Mexican identity at the beginning of the nineteenth century was not an all-pervasive concept, as Luis Villoro noted, independence nevertheless helped usher in nationalism and encouraged a reevaluation of Mexican history. And independence propaganda was successful in underscoring the indigenous origins of the patria.[49]

The changing course of Mexican history in the nineteenth century gave a new context to the search for nationhood through the interplay of three forces: the conservative Hispanic tradition, the liberal heritage that now included direct influences from the developing western world, and foreign imperialism. If the Díaz regime closed the century with a synthesis of the three experiences, chaos was the stage on which "conservatives" and "liberals" vied for the privileges of nation-making after independence in 1821. The conservative mind, as articulated by one of its chief ideologues, Lucas Alamán, sought to identify Mexico with its Spanish past and desig-

---

[49] Cardiel Reyes, *Del modernismo al liberalismo*, p. 253; Villoro, *El proceso ideológico*, pp. 148–149; Keen, *The Aztec Image*, p. 317.

nated Cortés as the founder of Mexican nationalism.[50] Conservatives supported the colonial corporate identity, clericalism, the military establishment, and the landed oligarchy, and were centralist in governmental administration and European-oriented in foreign affairs. Some were proponents of monarchy.

Mexican liberalism is more difficult to trace, partly because of its broad genesis and partly because many of its theories were often inapplicable to the Mexican circumstances.[51] Harking back to the birth of classical liberalism in seventeenth- and eighteenth-century England and France and eighteenth- and nineteenth-century Spain, the Mexican version reflected the secular trends fashioned out of the Enlightenment, the American and French revolutions, and the ideas of material progress articulated by utilitarians, positivists, and Spencerians. Liberal thought opposed the power of the church and state and espoused republican notions, individual property rights, and secular education. Inspired by the Spanish Constitution of 1812, Mexican liberals sought to implement many of these ideals in a series of reform programs that included the Constitutions of 1814, 1824, and 1857, the Gómez Farías decrees of 1833, and the constitutionalization of reform laws in 1873. Yet as Charles A. Hale has observed, "equality" and "democracy" were not consubstantial to Mexican liberalism, and José María Luis Mora, the leading liberal intellectual in the prereform era, thought the Indian inferior to the white and suggested that European colonization might solve the Indian problem. Ultimately, the liberals chased a chimera: the United States model of seemingly enlightened success.[52] A more precise relationship between ideas and society awaited a later age.

Partially the result of the conflict between liberals and conservatives, the non-Hispanic influence in the nineteenth century provided a focus for national identity. Legally separated from Spanish domination, Mexico grappled with the problems of nationhood and, unsure of itself, gravitated eclectically toward the western powers,

---

[50] See Charles A. Hale, *Mexican Liberalism in the Age of Mora*, pp. 295–296, 17–18.

[51] Jesús Reyes Heroles argues that Mexican liberalism must be viewed in its political and institutional manifestations and always as the opposite face of conservatism. See *El liberalismo mexicano*, I, x, xiv, and II, xiii–xiv.

[52] Hale, *Mexican Liberalism*, pp. 38, 223, 247, 298; see ibid., pp. 200–204, for Hale's treatment of Lorenzo de Zavala.

especially England, France, and the United States, who were casting their shadows on the fabled land. Purely Hispanic values no longer applied, yet Mexico's native values, slowly being discovered, were too weak as yet to shape a national consciousness. What to do? Borrow, recast, imitate.

In his study of popular attitudes at the time of independence, Javier Ocampo has shown that Mexico faced the century not knowing whether to rely on itself or on foreign paradigms.[53] Technology and classical economic theory were proving useful to northern Europe and the United States, so here the Mexican dilemma could perhaps be resolved. Moreover, the presence of the United States, which underscored the younger nation's weakness and instilled a fear of annexation, led to a precipitous dumping of Mexican values and a flight either to the conservative order of Europe or to newer liberal ideals emanating in part from the northern neighbor. Thus Mexicans fashioned a national image from ideas outside the Hispanic orbit. If Mexico feared its new exposure in the wider western sphere, it could nonetheless experiment from a broader cultural base than ever before and, significantly, use the foreign model as a critical point of departure for its problems. One of the classic examples came with Gabino Barreda, who in his "Oración cívica" (1867) formally introduced positivism in Mexico,[54] apparently unaware of the effects of a philosophy that suppressed subjectivity.[55] Yet positivism, especially as taught at the National Preparatory School, was to provide a new transcendent order that would supersede the older, racially structured society by delivering the country from chaos and cultural heterogeneity.[56] If many intellectuals shored up their rhetoric with non-Hispanic concepts, it was a sign of maturity that they were reacting to the prevailing currents of European thought. Mexico's deepening relationship to the western world was providing the at-

[53] Javier Ocampo, *Las ideas de un día: el pueblo mexicano ante la consumación de su independencia*, pp. 109–111.

[54] Zea refers to José María Luis Mora as speaking of "positivism" in the 1830's (*The Latin American Mind*, p. 129).

[55] For a discussion of Comtean positivism in this respect, see Frank E. Manuel, *Shapes of Philosophical History*, p. 113; see also Michael A. Weinstein, *The Polarity of Mexican Thought: Instrumentalism and Finalism*, pp. 4–12.

[56] Moisés González Navarro, *Sociología e historia en México: Barreda, Sierra, Parra, Molina Enríquez, Gamio, Caso*, pp. 6–7.

mosphere necessary for the growth of ideas and the philosophical frameworks required for the numerous theories of national behavior and institutional development being advanced. It was another indication of Mexico's entry into the modern, international order.[57]

Typical of the intellectuals who took their cues from abroad was Francisco Pimentel, the economic essayist and scholar who saw the United States as the country par excellence of "political economy," because the government had limited its power and encouraged private enterprise. Contrasting the United States with Mexico, he censured the latter for its "anti-economic education" derived from its Hispanic origins. Nonetheless, Pimentel had read Michel Chevalier's *Cours d'économie politique* and concurred with this author that Latin America had imitated the governmental model of the United States though still lacking the necessary national characteristics to make it viable: the work ethic, business acumen, perseverance, and shrewdness. Pimentel in fact wrote to correct these "defects." Chevalier, it should be noted, belonged to the school of French travelers and intellectuals who had been influenced by the glowing aspects of Humboldt's essay on Mexico and whose own derivative writings probably influenced Napoleon III to intervene in Mexico. Since these writers emphasized the United States' encroachment on Mexico to justify the implications of French imperialism, Pimentel might have been led to conclude that one way to prevent American expansion in Mexico was to colonize the country with Europeans.[58]

Mexico was being buffeted in the nineteenth century by the western world. Its colonial accommodation with Spain, however straitened, had been shattered, and in one sense the country had no identity, torn as it was by internal forces divided among themselves, and threatened by encroachment from abroad. The United States looked covetously toward Mexico and dismembered its territory in the Mexican-American War. Some reactionaries spurred by the

---

[57] The fine arts, for example, struggled throughout the nineteenth century to attain a level of creativity that would make Mexico the equal to the rest of the world. See Ida Rodríguez Prampolini, *La crítica de arte en México en el siglo XIX*, I, 16–17.

[58] Francisco Pimentel, *La economía política aplicada a la propiedad teritorial en México*, pp. 13–25; Margarita Martínez Leal de Helguera, "Posibles antecedentes de la intervención francesa de 1862," *Historia Mexicana* 15 (July–September, 1965), 1–24; Pimentel, *La economía política*, p. 189.

dreams of Napoleon III saw Mexico as a playground for both old and new European values. But the loss of national territory to one foreign power and intervention by another, while deepening Mexico's sense of inferiority, served also to stimulate nationalism under both the conservatives and liberals, as well as to increase Mexico's awareness of the non-Hispanic order of which it had become a part.[59]

At the same time as Mexico clung to the old Spanish values, it searched for answers to its dilemma from outside powers that could strike it down at will. Neither liberal nor conservative could find the answer alone. Clearly by 1867, on the heels of a second major humiliation before foreign powers and in anticipation of a national rebirth, Mexico wanted to demonstrate that it was as civilized as other countries.[60] Within a few years one man found the way: Porfirio Díaz cut through the chaos and in effect created a subtle buffer state between western imperialism and national helplessness by bringing the Darwinian model and industrialization to Mexico.[61] Although his industrial state grew at the expense of social progress, he gained the needed respect abroad and so consolidated his hold on the country that it would burst forth in the creativity of the Revolution.

In political style there had emerged two Mexicos in the nineteenth century, each shaped by its principal leader: the romantic age of Santa Anna, impassioned and foolish, and the positivist world of Juárez and Díaz, disciplined and shrewd. Nevertheless, it was against this background of the forces of conservatism, liberalism, and foreign imperialism that Mexican nationalism began what Charles Hale calls

[59] For the relationship of Mexico to the French vision of empire, see Nancy N. Barker, "Monarchy in Mexico: Hare-brained Scheme or Well-considered Prospect?" *Journal of Modern History* 48 (March, 1976), 51–68. For the French intervention in Mexico as a reflection of the European Pan-Latinity movement, see John Leddy Phelan, "Pan-Latinism, French Intervention in Mexico (1861–1867), and the Genesis of the Idea of Latin America," in *Conciencia y autenticidad históricas*, pp. 280–298. For the role of national consciousness in the expulsion of the French, see Martín Quirarte, *Historiografía sobre el imperio de Maximiliano*, p. 45.

[60] See Clementina Díaz y de Ovando, *La escuela preparatoria: los afanes y los días, 1867–1910*, I, 14.

[61] For a discussion of how Mexico adopted an Anglo-Saxon mentality in order to confront the United States, see Leopoldo Zea, *El positivismo en México: nacimiento, apogeo y decadencia*, p. 319.

"the effort of differentiating Mexican culture, society, and values."[62] The paradox was that Mexico's widening relationship to the western world brought with it a cosmopolitanism that would reinforce cultural trends into the post-Revolutionary period.

While the thinkers were coping with foreign paradigms and internal chaos, the idea of the patria remained incipient and could not be constructed solely through nationalism. One of the effects of cosmopolitanism since the Enlightenment, however, had been to enlarge the Mexican's awareness of his history and culture. From abroad he would appropriate ideas to synthesize more meaningfully the contexts of his national problems. Pimentel in his elaboration of "political economy" based on French thought and comparison with the United States, and Barreda in his adaptation of French positivism, are cases in point.

Nineteenth-century Mexican historiography also reflects the cosmopolitan experience, as history based on contemporary European theory began to be written. Vicente Riva Palacio's multivolume *México a través de los siglos* (1888–1889) shows traces of Darwin, Spencer, and Bagehot, while being a milestone in interpretive history and laying part of the groundwork for the Mexicanist school of the twentieth century. For Riva Palacio, history was not predicated on the chronological narrative but on the "philosophical considerations" of "social evolution," "human progress," the "law of inheritance," "political geography," and the "relationship of environment and national character," ideas whose origins were found in European intellectual history from Montesquieu to Spencer. Through evolutionist concepts, the social formation of Mexico was elucidated, and the mestizo as the classic product was explained as the progenitor of the "national soul" of a pueblo that consisted of neither "the conquered nor the conquering."[63] It is noteworthy that Riva Palacio would inspire in Justo Sierra the logical completion of his historical organicism. Other thinkers embodied the cosmopolitan approach by applying romantic nationalism to an understanding of Mexico, arguing that the country had certain characteristics that determined its "nationality." Madame de Stäel, for instance, influenced some intel-

---

[62] Hale, *Mexican Liberalism*, p. 214.
[63] Vicente Riva Palacio et al., *México a través de los siglos*, II, 898, viii.

lectuals to idealize the "typical" in Mexican culture in order to further the recognition of "national originality."[64]

Confronted with the problems of nationhood after independence, Mexico bore its burden as best it could. Amid the forces of chaos, cosmopolitanism, and sense of inferiority, one factor that unified the political process was the growth of national identity. In effect, *lo mexicano* as the nationalistic instrument of the state was aborning and clustered around different experiences—history, literature, popular culture, journalism, social criticism, and even painting. The Mexican patria was beginning to be revealed in sentiment as well as in fact. Among the historians, Lucas Alamán stressed the urgency of studying Mexico's social evolution and contemporary problems. Elsewhere the same author delineated the by-now stock triptych of creole, Indian, and mestizo, and in one of the first expressions of intellectual history in Mexico, he noted the effect of ideas on the country since the eighteenth century. He probed pre-Díaz Mexico from the standpoint of its instability, thus demonstrating the attitudes of doubt and searching that were to permeate national self-analysis.[65]

If Mexico itself hovered on the abyss in much of the nineteenth century, the Mexican intellectual did not. He knew the situation and spoke accordingly. The historian Lorenzo de Zavala, advancing his liberal program as a solution to the country's colonial legacy, had a prescient grasp of "the Mexicans" and analyzed the distance existing between reality and governmental policy. He too was writing "to teach Mexico to know itself." Other historians like Carlos María Bustamante wrote on the Mexican character, and José María Luis Mora observed that the "dissimulation" of the Indian stemmed from the oppressive system under which he lived. Noting that one could not generalize about the Mexican ethos because it was still in a formative stage, Mora limited himself to a study of the public mood and argued with the typical liberal bias that the Mexican's morale, which had been lower under Spanish rule, had improved after inde-

---

[64] Jesús Reyes Heroles, "Estudio preliminar," in Mariano Otero, *Obras*, I, 14–15.

[65] See Lucas Alamán, *Disertaciones sobre la historia de la república mejicana*, I, 9; idem, *Historia de Méjico*, I, 19–34, V, 847–850.

pendence.[66] Thus these historians were bending to the new tasks of nationhood by positing a Mexican people and Mexican experience as fundamental to the growth of a national consciousness.

Indeed, there was no dearth of Mexicanist materials in the nineteenth century; *costumbrismo*, satire, scholarship, and social and political criticism contributed to the definition of Mexico. The prolonged state of warfare activated generations of writers preoccupied with removing the European canons of taste from the Mexican will to expression or with fixing the discrepancy between imported forms of behavior and the roots of native impulse.[67] Independence catalyzed the creole anxiety to identify a Mexican source of inspiration, and José Joaquín Fernández de Lizardi, transforming the softer generalizations of an earlier period into sublety and cynicism, exemplified the trend to tell it "a lo pelado" ("as it is"). The Mexican-American War produced the kind of crisis that stimulated analysis of the national problems. A key liberal ideologue of the 1840's, Mariano Otero, saw Mexico's woes in the framework of the Black Legend. Spain had bequeathed an elitist legacy to Mexico, the social, economic, clerical, and educational implications of which precluded effective nationhood. Countering widespread notions of the national character, Otero rejected the thesis that Mexico's difficulties were connected to racial defects or to the effects of climate. Similarly, the French intervention impelled Guillermo Prieto to employ popular imagery in censuring the interlopers.[68]

Invariably the groupings of intellectuals that came into being produced journals, newspapers, and literary and scientific societies that boosted interest in Mexicanism, while novelists like Luis G. Inclán, Emilio Rabasa, José Tomás de Cuéllar, Manuel Payno, and Ignacio Altamirano were leading fiction in a new Mexicanist direc-

[66] Lorenzo de Zavala, *Ensayo histórico de las revoluciones de México*, II, 320. For an example of the way Bustamante used a subjective framework to convey the Mexican sentiment during the wars of independence, see Carlos María Bustamante, *Cuadro histórico de la revolución mexicana*, II, 48–50. José María Luis Mora, *México y sus revoluciones*, I, 65–78.

[67] Guadalupe Monroy, "Las letras," in *La república restaurada: la vida social*, in *Historia Moderna de México*, by Daniel Cosío Villegas, III, 767.

[68] Agustín Yáñez, "Estudio preliminar," in J. Joaquín Fernández de Lizardi, *El pensador mexicano*, p. xix; Otero, "Consideraciones sobre la situación política y social de la República Mexicana en el año 1847," in *Obras*, I, 110–130; Malcolm D. McLean, *Vida y obra de Guillermo Prieto*, p. 60.

tion.[69] The savant and political activist Ignacio Ramírez combined scientific and literary pursuits with a predisposition for the problems of Indians and workers to become one of the institutional founders of modern Mexican culture. Writers regularly resorted to such stock *costumbrista* symbols as the *jarabe, china poblana, pulque,* and *mole* or satirized the dandy who aped foreign styles while snubbing his native culture. There were scattered examples of a nascent agrarian consciousness linked to education and a focus on the Mexican environment.[70] In 1864 art music was given organizational depth in Mexico within a nationalistic framework.[71] And if the study of Mexican antiquities was continued in the colonial tradition as well as through the impetus of the growing foreign interest in pre-Hispanic Mexico, there were also pleas for the redemption of the Indian, which constituted a precursory indigenism. On the other hand, in attempting to analyze the national ethos, Pimentel offered the classical solution —assimilation—to the Indian problem.[72]

If, in reading Altamirano's commentaries from the pages of *El Renacimiento,*[73] one senses the viability of Mexico's cultural future, it is wise to bear in mind that throughout the nineteenth century cosmopolitanism was a greater cultural force than nationalism, not only as the result of the continual interest of western nations in exploiting Mexico, but also as the manifestation of the Mexicans' tendency to look to Europe and the United States as models. Ironically, it was the polarization of foreign and native criteria that was to provide the creative tension of national identity.

[69] See Rafael Angel de la Peña, "Reseña histórica de la academia mexicana," in *Obras de Don Rafael Angel de la Peña,* ed. V. Agüeros, p. 402. Ignacio Altamirano played a leading role among liberal intellectuals in calling for Mexicanism in literature. For example, see his *La literatura nacional,* p. 170.

[70] See Malcolm D. McLean, *El contenido literario de El Siglo Diez y Nueve,* pp. 29–32; Jesús Díaz de León, *Disertación sobre la importancia del estudio de la agricultura en los establecimientos de instrucción pública.*

[71] Archivo General de la Nación, Ramo Instrucción Pública y Bellas Artes, Legajo 11, Expediente 240 (hereinafter abbreviated as AGN, RIP & BA, Leg., Exp.)

[72] See Julio Zárate, "La raza indígena," *El Siglo Diez y Nueve,* December 2, 1870; Francisco Pimentel, *Memoria sobre las causas que han originado la situación actual de la raza indígena de México y medios de remediarla,* pp. 238–239.

[73] Ignacio M. Altamirano, *Crónicas de la semana,* pp. 23, 99, 100, 102.

One intellectual who excelled in grasping the issues that confronted Mexico and in synthesizing the country's historical problems was the liberal journalist José María Vigil. His writing style was clear and swift, and his insight extended to Mexico's past as well as into its projected future. Vigil often examined the premises of nationhood in the context of the social character, and his thought was couched in a moralistic framework that allowed him to move at will in the myriad judgments facing a nation caught in the complexities of harmonizing traditions with the exigencies of a modernizing world. If one wishes to find a precursor to the *lo mexicano* movement, Vigil is an obvious choice. Through him, the search for national identity was passed on from Servando Teresa de Mier to Justo Sierra and the intellectuals who emerged with the Revolution, and many of the topics he wrote on would be expanded by his successors and would remain viable into the post-Revolutionary era.

Typically Vigil glossed European ideas and speculated on their adaptation to Mexico. Referring to the Scandinavian debate as to whether Old Norse constituted the classic language of that civilization rather than Greek and Latin and whether the sagas and the eddas should replace the works of Homer and Virgil as the national literature—a debate spawned by the Herderian-inspired movement in romantic nationalism and folklore—Vigil suggested that Mexico should base its education on "Mexicanism." His contention was that Mexico did not know its history and did not study what was close at hand. Mexico's pre-Hispanic culture should be preserved by the government, he argued, and the Spanish language should be considered equal to those of the advanced nations. Not wanting to negate the positive aspects of cosmopolitanism, he nonetheless insisted that a country must retain those native characteristics which made it unique. Vigil's implicit cultural nationalism would be linked to the role of education in developing Mexico and presupposed a self-knowledge that would transcend shallow patriotism. Pointing out that Mexicans knew more about other peoples than about themselves, he remarked that the national character was either praised or excessively criticized, whereas balanced observation was necessary to remedy the nation's ills. Thus his basic thesis was that Mexico needed education in self-awareness, but since the country's multiple

origins made problem-solving difficult, a variety of factors would have to be taken into account.[74]

Scattered throughout his writings, Vigil's conception of Mexican history revealed his preoccupation with national identity. Cautioning against a history written as simple chronicle and underscoring a critical approach, he urged that the study of Mexican history be impartial, flawed by neither Hispanic nor Indian bias. He suggested that Mexican history be viewed from the Conquest on, the Indian character analyzed, and European influences examined. The evolution of colonial government as well as the origins of independence should be traced, and the course of Mexican history should be followed into the contemporary period, where it might serve as a point of departure for the future. Ever pessimistic, Vigil noted that a "fatal destiny" seemed to hang over Mexico, making the clearest ideas turbid and paralyzing the best intentions. Vigil's pessimism was frequently focused on politics, which he usually attacked from his liberal stance. In coming to grips with what he considered to be a demoralized state of affairs in the country, he noted that because politics were a question of life and death, political contests degenerated into conspiracy and tyranny, which in turn led to inefficient administration. *Empleomanía* (job hustling), he thought, was one of the great vices of politics, yet he argued that this was not a causative agent but rather a product of the social system.[75] Other endemic failures he noted in the Mexican political system included legal infractions by government officials, *compadrazgo* (cronyism), the invocation of shibbo-

[74] José María Vigil, "Necesidad y conveniencia de estudiar la historia patria: I," *El Sistema Postal de la República Mexicana*, June 9, 1878. For a discussion of Vigil's articles in *El Sistema Postal*, see Juan Antonio Ortega y Medina, "Un olvidado ensayo histórico de don José María Vigil," *Estudios de Historia Moderna y Contemporánea de México* 3 (1970), 67–74. Vigil, "Necesidad y conveniencia de estudiar la historia patria: II," *El Sistema Postal*, June 15, 1878; idem, "Boletín del Monitor," *El Monitor Republicano*, June 27, 1879, and November 5, 1878.

[75] Vigil, "Necesidad . . . : III," *El Sistema Postal*, June 22, 1878; idem, "Boletín del Monitor," *El Monitor Republicano*, June 27, January 11, 1879, February 6, 1880, and May 5, 1879. Earlier Mora had made the same argument. For a discussion of this problem in the liberal context, see Abelardo Villegas, "El liberalismo mexicano," in *Estudios de historia de la filosofía en México*, p. 324.

leths, personalism as political style, policy emphasizing politics rather than administration, public indifference toward the political clique, and the lack of long-range planning.[76]

Society also came within Vigil's critical purview. While he saw crime and the ineffectual prosecution of it as one result of the country's many revolutions, he looked for the causes not in the national character, as was customary in a Darwinian age, but in the social structure. Nor did he ignore the external factors that shaped Mexican attitudes. Aware of the growing influence of the United States, he saw that country as a source of imitation for Mexico and warned against importing ideas with no practical application to Mexican problems. Calling imitation a national characteristic, he contended that the Mexican was easily swayed by a new and facile doctrine. Here Vigil embraced the conservative rationale that thinkers through Antonio Caso in the 1920's would employ to oppose the introduction of socialism in Mexico, arguing that socialism was predicated on advanced European society and that Mexico, with its basic development still to be achieved, could not support such a doctrine.[77]

Vigil wrote extensively on the conditions of the Indians, and his thought constitutes part of the nineteenth-century expression of indigenism. He approached the Indian through the liberal ideal: for the sake of progress, the Indian should be assimilated into the national community. He frequently saw the Indian in relation to the problem of land tenure and drew heavily on Mora to justify the Reform. While he could not offer an accurate analysis of the Indian, he did connect the Indian's marginal position in the social order to political and economic rather than racial circumstances, thus placing the Indian in a historical framework. Noting the inferior status of the Indian during the colonial period and that independence theoretically had erased racial stigma in Mexican society, Vigil entertained the liberal notion of a developing homogeneous culture. He therefore saw the Indian problem as basically educational and supported the Escuela Netzahualcóyotl and Sociedad Ruth, two organizations

---

[76] Vigil, "Boletín del Monitor," *El Monitor Republicano*, February 20, July 11, 1879, September 7, 1878, January 14, April 21, June 25, and August 18, 1880.

[77] Ibid., April 19, June 20, March 31, and August 9, 1879.

concerned with teaching the Indians.[78] Vigil challenged the alleged inferiority of the Indian, turning to Bartolomé de las Casas and Juan de Palafox for support, and called for the government to improve the Indian's lot. His criticism illustrates the symbolic continuity of the image of the Indian in the search for Mexican identity.

Another aspect of Vigil's critique dealt with the problem of inferiority, which he pursued in a sociohistorical context. He upbraided the Mexican for failing to recognize his social origins in the colonial period and employed a creole rationale to seek the causes of several social ills in the Conquest. The patria, Vigil maintained, was disdained in the present era because colonial sentiment had been unfavorable to it and because the Indian was denigrated—behavioral responses inherited from the psychological dislocation produced by the clash of cultures. Vigil explained that the Spanish rule had engendered an inferiority complex in the Mexican as a result of the conquistador's overweening superiority vis-à-vis the fatalism of the Indian. Bereft of a future, the Indian lacked faith in himself and carried his sense of insufficiency into the nineteenth century, to be diffused among the masses as an attitude of dependence. Other causes of inferiority, Vigil noted, lay in Mexico's relationship to the rapidly developing United States and in the negative characteristics attributed to the Mexicans on account of race and climate. But if Vigil considered the inferiority problem worthy of study, he could also dismiss it as the effect of transitory circumstances, noting with the liberal bias of his age that Mexico's self-esteem would improve when the country experienced serious immigration. However, he could also demonstrate his nationalistic conviction by arguing that if the Mexican was unaggressive, he was nevertheless in other ways the equal of the European.[79]

Vigil touched upon many themes in his endeavor to reach the roots of Mexican problems, and his analysis of the Mexican beset by a psychology evolved from the interaction of historical forces bore

[78] Ibid., June 12 and 13, June 10 and 11, 1879, October 15, 1878.

[79] Vigil, "Necesidad . . . : II," *El Sistema Postal*, June 15, 1878; "Necesidad . . . : IV," *El Sistema Postal*, June 29, 1878; "Boletín del Monitor," *El Monitor Republicano*, November 14, 1878; "Colonización," *El Siglo Diez y Nueve*, December 3, 1870.

witness to the deepening intellectuality of the search for identity. If he provided stock answers to the question of inferiority, he did conclude that the phenomenon pervaded Mexican society and colored the Mexican's self-image and his relationship to the outside world. Vigil had expanded upon Mier, but his legacy would not become apparent until post-Revolutionary intellectuals followed the same probing logic.

Vigil's Mexicanism went largely unheeded, for in the conflict between Mexican and European attitudes, the latter usually prevailed. The idea of Mexico as a nation still did not exist convincingly for all citizens, affirmers of the patria notwithstanding. Yet the Europeanization of Mexico could not prevent the growth of a native ideology that occasionally stimulated a barrage of invective against an alien presence. Typical were the attacks on writers who attempted to portray society in terms of French literature.[80] Nor were France and the United States the only countries that clouded the national self-respect; there was still the spectre of the Spanish past that for one critic, following the well-worn creole rhetoric, had deformed the Mexican character.[81] By the late nineteenth century, Mexico had become polarized in an intellectual drama of being. Was there, could there be a Mexico, or was there merely an indefinable entity that would acquire viable existence by assuming the form of the nations considered to be advanced by the western standards then in vogue? On the one hand, there was the Porfirian stalwart Francisco Bulnes, whose Darwinian analysis of Latin America reeked of pejorative inferences for tropical peoples and "races of corn"; on the other, there was the pathbreaking nativist José T. de Cuéllar, exalting Mexican popular culture over the European.[82]

National identity had acquired subtle ramifications as the conjunction of domestic and foreign forces changed public confidence in a sociopolitical order lacking an effective symbolism and compre-

---

[80] See Vicente Riva Palacio, *Los ceros: galería de contemporáneos por Cero*, pp. 154, 196; and Angel de Campo, "El Portero del Liceo Hidalgo. Los del porvenir: Micrós," *El Siglo Diez y Nueve*, November 3, 1894.

[81] Agustín Rivera, "Dialogue between A. R. and Florencito," in *Readings from Modern Mexican Authors*, ed. Frederick Starr, pp. 57–58.

[82] See Francisco Bulnes, *El porvenir de las naciones latinoamericanas ante las recientes conquistas de Europa en Norteamérica*, pp. 9–15, 41–47; and José T. de Cuéllar, *Ensalada de pollos y baile y cochino*, p. xvii.

hensive relationship to the masses. No longer solely a matter of the Spanish heritage or a topic of Enlightenment debate over the meaning of the New World, the problem of identity was now circumscribed by an evolving Mexicanist framework and reflected internal issues as well as the effects of ties to Europe and the United States. To be sure, language, religion, business, government, and the arts were stylized by European criteria of taste, and in many instances the cultural or social question of the moment merely revolved around the newer or older European fashion. But the nativist position kept working to the fore, partly in reaction to the negative context in which it often was placed, for Mexico was beginning to be sensitive to its marginal relationship to the West.

The nineteenth century in Mexico traditionally is conceived as a struggle between conservatism and liberalism, clericalism and secularism, scholasticism and the influence of the Enlightenment. In addition, there was a romantic exaltation of nationhood and the positivist emphasis on the instrumental nature of economic well-being. Not surprisingly, the logic behind this clash of values was argued from nationalistic as well as non-Mexican premises. Liberals wanted to substitute for religious sentiment a cold worship of knowledge such as could be found in the scientism of the age. Conservatives distrusted the rationalist investiture of leadership and policy making and favored a corporate, hierarchical society that deemphasized material progress at the popular level. Yet neither the conservatives with their organic protection of privilege nor the liberals with their abstract love of individualism were to win. The 1910 Revolution would alter both with its masses-oriented reform under the aegis of a modified patrimonial state.

Thus the idea of Mexico was about to reconcile Hapsburg immutability with the dynamic of change set in motion during the eighteenth cenutry. Born in the religious and cultural transferral of Europe to the New World, the colonial consciousness was built around the Spaniard and the Indian as polarized protagonists in a drama of human rights with symbolic as well as actual significance. Overall, the Indian was defamed, but he lingered on and gathered force, even though after independence secularization forced him to his social nadir as church and crown were replaced by the national government, the mission by the hacienda. Mexican identity contin-

ued to be permeated by an essentially creole vision, for although the conceptualization of the mestizo and the Indian had begun, it was not yet linked to the socioeconomic transformation of the pueblo.[83] The late nineteenth-century laissez-faire model could not provide the solution to Mexico's social problems, since its Anglo-Saxon rationale was untenable if fused with native communal traditions and the Hispanic corporate legacy. Thus the dominant modes of political expression were manifested essentially as elitist infighting, relegating the redemption of the masses to an occasional prophetic voice like that of Ponciano Arriaga or José María González or to a virtual underground of agrarian and labor reform.[84] While some intellectuals perceived this discrepancy, the pueblo as idea would become meaningful only in a revolution that would perpetuate a theory of responsibility to the cultures of the peasants and the urban workers and not to the elite groups of classical economics.

To summarize the growth of Mexicanism in the nineteenth century, a cultural reference may be useful. In 1873 José María Velasco painted his first "Valley of Mexico" canvas, a theme that would preoccupy him for more than a quarter of a century. The painting has nationalistic overtones. Water, the transparent light of the valley, "inditos," the Villa of Guadalupe, the eagle, and the cactus are symbols in a composition that, however, does not seem very Mexican. Indeed, it is all the Porfirian age would allow for Mexico. Yet the effect of the painting is to draw open a curtain on the country. In the post-Revolutionary period artists would crowd the aristocratic perspective of Velasco with such nativist exuberance that the beholder's vision would be arrested. Mexico's experience would be not unlike Germany's reaction in the eighteenth century to a French-oriented

---

[83] William D. Raat makes the point that by the late nineteenth century the differences between liberals and conservatives were blurred and both were indifferent to the welfare of the Indian. See "Ideas and Society in Don Porfirio's Mexico," *The Americas* 30 (July, 1973), 46–47.

[84] Ponciano Arriaga, speech given at the Constitutional Congress of 1856, in *Historia Documental de México*, ed. Ernesto de la Torre Villar, Moisés González Navarro, and Stanley R. Ross, II, 284–287. See *Del artesanado al socialismo, artículos de José María González*. See also the studies by John M. Hart, "Agrarian Precursors of the Mexican Revolution: The Development of an Ideology," *The Americas* 29 (October, 1972), 131–150, and "Nineteenth Century Urban Labor Precursors of the Mexican Revolution: The Development of an Ideology," *The Americas* 30 (January, 1974), 297–318.

universalism, or the North American break with the European Enlightenment—a romantic inversion away from the universal, a discovery of national being intimating that the world process could
emanate from within rather than from without. Part of the task was
to alter the exalted notion of Old World civilization that as late as
the 1890's was manifested in the surprise of one distinguished European thinker that there was an advanced intellectual life in Mexico.[85]

If positivism had ushered in a new and necessary historical synthesis for Mexico, its externally imposed premises were in the minds
of some a continuation of Thomism, and memorization was substi-
tuted for curiosity, doubt banished as non-productive.[86] The 1910
Revolution would provide the basic machine for the Mexican as he
sought to become the modifier of himself and his country and to expand his critical consciousness. He would then strive to achieve an
awareness of self and stake his identity on the re-creation of a society
denied him by historical fallacy. The question as to whether this
identity would be hypothesis, rhetoric, model, or failure became the
story of twentieth-century Mexico.

[85] Herbert Spencer to Ezequiel Chávez, February 10, 1895, Archivo Ezequiel Chávez (hereinafter abbreviated as AEC), Caja 8.
[86] See Genaro Fernández MacGregor, *El río de mi sangre: memorias*, p.
116.

2.

National Identity in a Positivist
Decade, 1900–1910

Mexico entered the twentieth century amid conflicting tensions. The Porfiriato as the iron rule of peace did not extend fully into the political, intellectual, and cultural spheres, and although positivism offered a supporting rationale for the Díaz regime, the hardcore positivists did not always associate themselves with the *científicos* who ran the country. Other currents of thought were at variance with Porfirism, which came under attack by old liberals, the metaphysical minded, anarcho-syndicalists, or simply people imbued with new ideas of psychology, sociology, and history.[1] Spiritualism and Tolstoyism were on the rise in Mexico and captured the soul of the most important political figure on the immediate horizon, Francisco I. Madero. The exaggerated estheticism of the literary movement known as modernism was perhaps a strange expression for positivist Mexico, but if modernism and positivism lived in harmony, it was because both tended to emphasize the universal over the national and concrete. Paradoxically, however, modernism became a reaction to the Porfiriato, pointing up its frivolity, its imitation of foreign culture, and its failure to promote the welfare of the nation.[2]

[1] See Moisés González Navarro et al., *El Porfiriato: la vida social*, in *Historia Moderna de México*, by Daniel Cosío Villegas, IV, 608; Leopoldo Zea, *El positivismo en México: nacimiento, apogeo y decadencia*, pp. 341–342; William D. Raat, "Ideas and Society in don Porfirio's Mexico," *The Americas* 30 (July 1973), 52. For a statement of how dissidents with Porfirism were preoccupied with some of the basic goals of the Revolution from 1900 on, see James D. Cockcroft, *Intellectual Precursors of the Mexican Revolution, 1900–1913*, pp. 4–6. Robert Quirk points out that the Catholics did not attack Díaz directly but were at odds with positivism (*The Mexican Revolution and the Catholic Church, 1910–1920*, p. 17).

[2] For an attempt to relate modernism to the Porfiriato, see José Emilio Pacheco, comp., *Antología del modernismo, 1884–1921*, I, xxx–1.

The decade 1900–1910 saw the intellectuals developing many of those trends which would characterize post-Revolutionary culture. Nationalism laced the writings of Justo Sierra and Andrés Molina Enríquez, the journal *Savia Moderna*, and the Ateneo de la Juventud. The term *lo mexicano* was now commonly used.[3] Significantly, a study of the ideas of the period reveals the continuity of themes between the nineteenth and twentieth centuries and throws light on the Revolution not as the wellspring of new thought but as an intensifier and modernizer of older traditions. Thus the preoccupation with *lo mexicano*, considered to have begun with Samuel Ramos, was in fact well advanced in the decade preceding the Revolution.

The Positivist as Mexicanist

Mexicanism is not usually associated with an era that was still dominated by positivism, yet under the powdered face and European lifestyle of the Porfiriato the country was responding to its native culture. A successful publisher of popular literature, Antonio Vanegas Arroyo, and his master illustrator, José Guadalupe Posada, were expressing an authentic Mexico in satire, song, and story. The *orquesta típica* was popular, as were puppet performances of national manners and customs, and traveling tent shows provided a comic entertainment precursory to Cantinflas. In painting, Félix Parra and Julio Ruelas were portraying native faces, and Ernesto Icaza was making genre paintings of rural life. José María Velasco was skillfully painting the landscape of the Valley of Mexico, and Dr. Atl (Gerardo Murillo) was beginning to preach nationalism in opposition to academicism.[4] In literature Micrós (Angel de Campo) was writing on native themes, and Porfirio Parra published his *Pacotillas: novela mexicana* (1900), which dealt with Mexican social psychology.[5]

[3] *Diario de Federico Gamboa, 1892–1939*, ed. José Emilio Pacheco, p. 163.

[4] This Mexicanism was the exception rather than the rule in this decade, however. Typical was the exhibition of Mexican artists in Europe in 1906 in which there was absolutely no ideology of the pueblo. See "Exposición nacional de los artistas pensionados en Europa,' *Arte Y Ciencia* 18 (January, 1907), 169–172.

[5] For discussion of *lo mexicano* in this novel, see Juan Hernández Luna, "El gran *Pacotillas*," *Historia Mexicana* 1 (April–June, 1952), 517–540.

The government was actively supporting the writing of Mexican history: Fernando Paso y Troncoso, since 1892, had been commissioned to conduct research in European libraries and archives. José María Vigil was being paid a monthly stipend to write a guide to Mexican literature, and Nicolás León was being funded for his bibliographical study of the eighteenth century. Ignacio B. del Castillo received remuneration for his publication in Mexican history under the direction of Genaro García.[6]

Ironically, this burgeoning nationalism had ramifications in the United States in a quiet cultural diplomacy seldom reported in the annals of power relationships. A representative figure in this interchange was the educator Ezequiel Chávez. Today he is all but lost to the professional pattern of Mexican history, yet his consistent behind-the-scenes work in higher education from 1900 into the 1920's contributed significantly to the humanistic orientation of institutional change in Mexico. A protegé of Justo Sierra, Chávez in this decade served as undersecretary of public instruction and fine arts and from 1903 on was engaged in reorganizing the National University. This task brought him into contact with the United States and gave him the opportunity to study a curriculum extending beyond the limitations of positivism. In 1908 the government sent him to the United States to publicize the Mexican centenary, and his mission was not without some impact on U.S.-Mexican cultural exchange. Stanford University thanked him for his gifts to their Mexican holdings, and the University of California offered him summer teaching and viewed him as a guiding spirit in organizing the Bancroft Library.[7] Chávez's activities shed light on the diversity of thought and experience in the traditionally stereotyped age of positivism.

Indeed, it was among the last positivist intellectuals—Justo Sierra, Porfirio Parra, Ezequiel Chávez, Julio Guerrero, Telésforo García, Agustín Aragón—that a strong Mexicanist preoccupation

---

[6] "Agreement," September 5, 1919, AGN, RIP & BA, Leg. 1, Exp. 33; "Agreement," June 1, 1906, Leg. 3, Exp. 177; "Agreement," June 1, 1907, Leg. 5, Exp. 224; and "Agreement," July 11, 1907, Leg. 3, Exp. 153.

[7] Leticia Chávez, *Recordando a mi padre*, II, 26–27; "Agreement," February 6, 1908, AGN, RIP & BA, Leg. 5, Exp. 258; David Starr Jordan to Chávez, September 16, 1909; Chávez to C. H. Rieber, December 28, 1908; H. Morse Stephens to Chávez, March 2, 1907; and Don E. Smith to Chávez, June 15, 1907, all in AEC, Caja 7.

emerged. Positivism as a mode of thought did not direct these thinkers toward their culture; rather, they were heirs to a century of intellectual nationalism and therefore could build on their predecessors who had scrutinized the tortuous course of Mexican history. Hence, insofar as they were concerned with Mexico, they were working in a current of national inquiry that underlay their theoretical positivist orientations. While Mexican positivism resembled an exercise in pedagogy and focused more on method than on subject, it nonetheless did not exclude Mexico as a topic for study.[8] Perusing the positivists' writings, one realizes that there was elbow-room for both positivism and nationalism.

This mutuality was demonstrated in Julio Guerrero's *La génesis del crimen en México* (1901), an exemplary work of the positivist age in Mexico.[9] Influenced by social Darwinism, French naturalism, and the new discipline of criminology, Guerrero combined social psychology with quantitative methods to study crime in the central plateau of Mexico. Yet the book is important not so much for its curious blend of Porfirian rationale and Catholic critique of materialism as for its forthright nationalism, which extolled nativist art and denounced the imitation of French models.[10] On the other hand, Guerrero allowed Porfirian attitudes to circumscribe his nationalism. His adherence to the elitist values of the age of steam forced him to exclude much of the Mexican experience that later would be embraced in a culture broadened by the Revolution and the new modes of perception imported from the West. Thus Guerrero's study offers a fine sense of the intellectual transition between the nineteenth and twentieth centuries, a summary of ideas in 1901 with hints of some of the themes of later intellectual history. His Christian ideal of love would be articulated by Antonio Caso, his esthetic of Anáhuac

---

[8] For a discussion of how a national consciousness was emerging from the positivist curriculum, see Moisés González Navarro, *Sociología e historia en México: Barreda, Sierra, Parra, Molina Enríquez, Gamio, Caso*, p. 15.

[9] The impact of Guerrero's book was sufficient for it to be formally discussed in a series of ten meetings of the Positivist Society, an organization that included many of Mexico City's leading intellectuals. The meetings devolved into a general debate on the national character. See Julio Guerrero, "Transiciones pasionales del ebrio mexicano," *La República* 1 (June 22, 1901), 1–7.

[10] Julio Guerrero, *La génesis del crimen en México: estudio de psiquiatría social*, pp. 5, 47–56.

given fuller treatment by Alfonso Reyes. His purpose of evaluating the negative aspects of social behavior would be elaborated by Daniel Cosío Villegas and Samuel Ramos, while his analysis of atavistic savagery as a national characteristic would be reexplored by Octavio Paz seventy years later.

A leading journal, *Revista Positiva*, witnesses further to the link between positivism and Mexicanism in the first decade of the twentieth century. No journal until the 1940's enjoyed such a continuous run—an indication of the length of time it took Mexico to reorganize its intellectual life after the Revolution. Although the journal's purpose was to spread Comte's "religion of humanity," especially in its Lafittean variation,[11] and its content was weighted toward the universal and scientific, together with eulogies to Barreda, Comte, Bridges, Lafitte, and Mill, there were also articles on Mexico.[12] The journal captured the period at the end of the Porfiriato and the beginning of the Revolution when history, sociology, and psychology had begun to complement each other. If its writers lacked political insight and overemphasized their positivist bias, the journal was nonetheless organizing and disseminating knowledge in Mexico.

Upon reading Agustín Aragón's annual editorials in *Revista Positiva*, one is aware that the term *positivism* was used somewhat loosely to denote serious thought and scholarship. Positivism represented an intellectual triumph over a century of reaction and ignorance, of the modern age over the theological age. On the other hand, the journal did not address itself to the more pressing social, political, and economic problems of Mexico, a task that was left for the anarcho-syndicalists, anti-reelectionists, and a few independents like Andrés Molina Enríquez. Although in its adherence to progress through order positivism was the intellectual corollary to Porfirism, it is simplistic to maintain that positivism was isolated from the Mexican circumstances. This notion of the complete separation between

---

[11] See William D. Raat, "Agustín Aragón and Mexico's Religion of Humanity," *Journal of Inter-American Studies and World Affairs* 11 (July, 1969), 442–443.

[12] Agustín Aragón, "Elogio de don José Antonio Alzate y Ramírez," *Revista Positiva* 4 (October, 1904), 564–572; Carlos Pereyra, "La sociología abstracta y su aplicación a algunos problemas fundamentales de México," *Revista Positiva* 3 (August, 1903), 351–386; Manuel G. Revilla, "Provincialismos de expresión en México," *Revista Positiva* 10 (January, 1910), 1–2, 53–66.

ideas and reality was to become part of the intellectual justification of the Revolution, part of the myth of Porfirian evil, which is a partial rather than a whole truth. The positivist concern with *lo mexicano* in large measure stemmed from its disciplinary structures of sociology, psychology, criminology, and history, which, because they had taken shape in European thought, had often been used to treat the subject of national character, especially from a racial viewpoint.[13] Reinforcing these trends was the nationalism of nineteenth-century Mexico and, at the turn of the century, of the rest of Latin America.[14] It should be noted that much of the positivist critique of the Mexican character was motivated by the desire to improve or even replace it by adopting Anglo-Saxon values.[15] Thus the problem of national identity was interrelated with European as well as hemispheric intellectual currents relevant to the forces of modernity in Mexico.

The Idea of Evolution

Mexican identity in the late nineteenth and early twentieth centuries was manifested in the concept of historical evolution common to the age. The newly organizing principle of *lo mexicano* needed a focal point round which its elements could cohere, and a logical one was the idea of Mexico as the evolution of different races and cultures. A characteristically Mexican experience could then be posited and extended temporally in a pattern of meaningful growth, while the country's social psychology could be derived from this historical process. The writer who provided the most compelling synthesis of historical evolution was Justo Sierra in *Evolución política del pueblo mexicano (1900–1902).*[16] The outstanding intellectual of his time,[17]

[13] This current of thought was popular in the late nineteenth and early twentieth centuries throughout Latin America. See Martin S. Stabb, *In Quest of Identity: Patterns in the Spanish-American Essay of Ideas, 1890–1960*, pp. 12–33; González Navarro, *Sociología e historia en México*, p. 30.

[14] See Antonio Rubio y Lhuck, "Necesidad de la fraternidad literaria hispano-americano," *Revista Positiva* 3 (July, 1903), 329–336.

[15] Zea, *El positivismo en México*, pp. 334–338.

[16] Sierra's work first appeared in *México: su evolución social*, vol. I, as "Historia política" (pp. 34–314), and in vol. II as "La era actual" (pp. 415–434).

[17] For a general study see Agustín Yáñez, *Don Justo Sierra: su vida, sus ideas y su obra.* For an intellectual treatment see Maty Finkelman Morgenstein,

Sierra stressed the idea that the Mexicans were the progeny of two races, born of the Conquest, with Spanish and indigenous origins. This evolution of a Mexican people, he contended, was the central historical theme and gave the country its "soul."[18]

A brief consideration of Sierra's book will shed light on the relationship between the concepts of evolution and *lo mexicano* in that period. Not totally original, the work was informed by the history of Vicente Riva Palacio (*México a través de los siglos*, 1884–1889) as well as by the Mexicanist humanism of José María Vigil. From Riva Palacio, Sierra drew his ideas of an interpretive, evolutionist history that saw the Conquest as the springboard of Mexican nationality; from Vigil he drew psychological insight into the Mexican character. However, it is for his improvement upon all nineteenth-century historians that Sierra must be credited. His work crystallized a new strain in Mexican historiography in its critical appreciation of events, and if Sierra continued the technique of Riva Palacio, he did so by intensifying it, thus grasping and advancing the main thrust of intellectual nationalism. His happier style and sharper sense of the ironic integration of history quickly gave his book a place of unquestioned eminence. With Sierra, writing began to turn inward and a new philosophical inquiry into Mexican culture was born; its followers were to be, among others, Martín Luis Guzmán, Manuel Gamio, Antonio Caso, Samuel Ramos, Leopoldo Zea, Octavio Paz, and Carlos Fuentes.

Sierra's work is distinguished from nineteenth-century historical literature by its expression of transcendence in Mexican evolution, its projection of the diachronic determinants of a national being. Thus in his analysis of the growth of Mexican society, Sierra pointed to the formation of a national character in the colonial period, inferring the future leavening role of the mestizo from his unstable social position. Sierra joined the political and *costumbrista* aspects of previous historical scholarship and emphasized the Mexican in his native circum-

---

"El pensamiento de Justo Sierra y el sentido de sus aportaciones historiográficas" (Licentiate thesis, Universidad Nacional Autónoma de México, 1966); and Richard Whitney Weatherhead, "Justo Sierra: A Portrait of a Porfirian Intellectual" (Ph.D. diss., Columbia University, 1966).

18 Justo Sierra, *La evolución política del pueblo mexicano*, in *Obras completas*, XII, 56.

stances, recognizing, as Carlos Pereyra put it, the "deep and violent rumble of the popular soul." He outlined the development of modern Mexico by balancing a political account with anthropology, psychological insight, and literary humanism. Relating Sierra's work to the European essay, Pereyra called it a "creation," not only for its evocation of people and events but because for the first time it traced the genesis of nationality and elucidated the formative elements in Mexican history.[19] This conceptualization of a Mexican experience as an evolutionary process would underlie the preoccupation with national identity in the twentieth century and characterize a substantial movement in the history of ideas. One can maintain that the century's closing, the commemorative nature of Sierra's work, and the author's ideas of Spencerian evolution controlled the structure and style of the book, but this would only be to detract from Sierra himself.

Another treatment of the evolution of Mexican history was offered by Andrés Molina Enríquez in *Los grandes problemas nacionales* (1908). Dreary style, tedious asides, and racial convolutions make the book arduous reading, but it is unmistakably one of the most complete accounts of Mexico ever written, synthesizing a wealth of data from cooking to character analysis, from irrigation to immigration.[20] Written on the eve of the Revolution, its implicit nationalism made it a prophetic testament, and like Guerrero's *La génesis del crimen en México*, it was an early study in what may be called the sociology of *lo mexicano*. The key terms in Molina's theory were *evolution* and *selection*, with which he paired off two contending peoples in Mexico, the brown and the white. The whites were superior to Indians by virtue of their greater "efficiency of action," the conse-

[19] Ibid., 127; Carlos Pereyra, "Una obra maestra de la literatura patria," *Revista Positiva* 3 (November, 1903), 480, 472–473.

[20] For the concept of race in Molina Enríquez, see Juan Comas, "Razas, mestizaje y clases sociales en la obra de Andrés Molina Enríquez: 1909," *Cuadernos Americanos* 72 (March–April, 1966), 122–141; González Navarro, *Sociología e historia en México*, pp. 40–52. For the influence of nineteenth-century Mexican thought on Molina Enríquez, see Luis Villoro, *Los grandes momentos del indigenismo en México*, p. 169. Luis Cabrera bitterly remarked that the Mexican reader might neglect Molina's work, believing that Mexico had no philosophers and sociologists who studied the country's problems (cited in Silvano Barba González, *La lucha por la tierra*, III: *Ponciano Arriaga, Andrés Molina Enríquez, Luis Cabrera, Pastor Rouaix*, p. 115).

quence of a more "advanced evolution"; the Indians were superior to the whites by virtue of their greater "efficiency of resistance," the result of a more "advanced selection." Molina thought the capacity for resistance was superior to that for action because the latter wore down more easily. The Spaniards had exhausted their energies, as the weakness of Spain and of the creoles in Latin American demonstrated. Meanwhile, he explained, the powers of the Indians were developing in the mestizos.

Molina's social analysis reflected evolutionist use of time: the present, a fluid state, was projected simultaneously to the past and the future, forming a structure malleable to the data and ideas of the manipulator. This philosophical futurism became for Molina an embryonic version of Vasconcelos's "cosmic people" and pointed to the intellectual's dissatisfaction with the status quo and the influence of the past in shaping an ideal present. Molina saw the European and the North American as inferior to the Mexican. Viewing United States history within an Anglo-Saxon frame of reference, Molina compared that country's evolution with Mexico's, noting its environment, which favored prosperous development, and its lack of serious problems of acculturation. Yet Molina countered United States superiority by arguing that in spite of his substandard living conditions, the Mexican worker was more capable than either the North American or the European. The mestizo and the Indian were superior in fighting ability to the creole and the foreigner, whereas the western immigrant to Mexico could not survive without the trappings of his own culture. Molina saw deviations in the Mexican historical process but nothing that could not be corrected. The Indian resented his evolutionary lag, and although the mestizo was circumstantially caught between the Indian and the creole, he would eventually absorb the two lesser groups and create the "true national population."[21]

Molina's exaltation of the Mexican laborer as well as his consciousness of *mestizaje* and the role it would play in determining the evolution of Mexican society indicated a shift away from the abstract, creole national identity of the past century to one based on awareness of concrete Mexican qualities—the elements of the pueblo that would characterize the idea of nationhood in post-Revolutionary

[21] Andrés Molina Enríquez, *Los grandes problemas nacionales*, pp. 253–261.

Mexico. The racial cast of Molina's thought, which would typify national identity for the next several decades, illustrated a Mexico confronting itself by reinforcing its classical social evolution since the Conquest.

This growth of Mexicanist criteria enabled thinkers to recast their country's history in both chronology and substance. Since evolution was a theory that essentially explained the interrelatedness of phenomena, it could be readily used by the intellectual grappling with a scheme of identity. Moreover, the notion of gradual accruement of Mexican power mirrored western man's preoccupation with progress and moral purpose. Evolution worked to "better" society, building continually through organic improvement.[22] Such rationalization was attractive because it inspired the integration of history and created the sense that the concatenation was a process unfolding in an ever-higher synthesis of national meaning. In the main, the theory was valid, for slowly and painfully the Mexican was superimposing a newer identity upon a former one, working out a destiny upon the passage of time and the accumulation of experience.

The Idea of Nationality

As a monolithic paradigm, however, the concept of evolution did not give the intellectual the rounded picture he wanted of his country. If he could postulate Mexican history as organic development, he also needed to halt this process and view evolvement as well as evolving, for then he could verify the design of his nativist teleology. Thus chronology must congeal into actuality, chaos resolve into form, and raw creation issue into a finished product. For a century the Mexican intellectual had struggled with the concept of nationality, and now his expanding knowledge of himself and his country was to make him adept at conveying the behavior and structure of his society.

Molina Enríquez persuasively discussed nationality in this decade, underscoring the idea of evolution and letting his racial bias

[22] For discussion of the concepts of evolution, history, and progress, see R. G. Collingwood's *The Idea of Nature*, p. 134, and *The Idea of History*, pp. 128–129; and Richard Hofstadter's *Social Darwinism in American Thought*, pp. 3–6.

determine his analysis of the mestizo. Tracing the course of post-independence political development, Molina saw the mestizos as a liberal and revolutionary group that opposed the "conservative creoles" and the "new creoles" who were landowners or capitalists dependent on international finance. A conflict of mind as well as of interests ensued between the two groups. The mestizos were instrumental in achieving the Reform and struggled to power with Juárez. The "new creoles," however, remained the privileged class, their capital linked to England and the United States. The "conservative creoles" controlled the land. Díaz supported both. But in their disadvantaged social position, Molina argued, the mestizos fought back, gaining as ally the indigenous class, formerly the most oppressed by the creoles. Finding themselves in control of the Indians, Molina stated, the liberal bourgeois mestizos became conscious of a new role: that of creating a nationality, a patria. Neither the Indians, divided and backward, nor the creoles, with their exclusive interests, could accomplish this. But the mestizos, by dissolving the creole classes and absorbing all social groups, could create the "true nationality," "strong and powerful," with "one life" and "one soul."[23]

Like all racial analyses of nationality, Molina's suffered the simplistic determinism inherent in such an approach, and his treatment of the mestizo and creole in the nineteenth century was sadly distorted. But it was Molina's Mexicanist definition of society rather than his methodology that made his book of paramount value to the search for identity. His idea of a national unity, composed of such lesser "unities" as living conditions, customs, language, and shared goals was basic to a cohesive polity, and when he wrote that the land should be divided so all citizens could have equal opportunities, he was of course stating the problem of agrarian reform in terms of the coming Revolution.[24] If Molina framed nationality as an ideal to be fulfilled, others doubted the inevitability of such an assumption. While Molina optimistically posited the inviolability of a future Mexico, there were those who wondered if historical circumstances warranted a sanguine acceptance of nationhood. Yet the preoccupation with nationality was another exercise in national self-discovery

---

[23] For a resumé of these ideas, see Villoro, *Los grandes momentos del indigenismo en México*, pp. 171–176.
[24] Molina Enríquez, *Los grandes problemas nacionales*, pp. 277–300.

that brought the intellectual to an awareness and judgment of his culture, and in viewing the more abstract process of his historical formation, the Mexican penetrated his being until he met himself face to face and felt uneasy in his understanding.

Ethos and Society

The formalistic themes of evolution and nationality were not entirely convincing to the intellectual in quest of Mexicanism; they were neat explanations that summarized knowledge but did not necessarily allow him to develop a national typology in keeping with his European tradition. Over against the broad themes of an intensified search for identity during the years 1900 to 1910, the Mexican began to seek the minute and the concrete in his society. Nationality was to be viewed in its constituent parts, and the intellectual's role as social critic would allow him to point up behavioral defects for the purpose of moral and social improvement. Hence a range of subjects dealing with such concepts as the "national character," the "national soul," and the "national consciousness" had become pervasive in Mexican thought. Justo Sierra, for example, saw that in the midst of the cosmopolitanism in which Latin Americans lived, a native personality was emerging, and he felt that it was necessary to create a "national soul." Psychology had worked its way into the curriculum of the National Preparatory School, and character study was common in the works of writers in this period. Typical were the attempts by Porfirio Parra to express the theoretical nature of character, while Andrés Molina Enríquez noted that each country had a "singular character" and that in Mexico each sector of the population had its own social psychology.[25]

The year 1900 saw the essay by Ezequiel Chávez entitled "Essay on the Distinctive Traits of Sensibility as a Factor in the Mexican Character" delivered in the Concurso Científico Nacional. Chávez, who had helped introduce psychology into the National Preparatory School curriculum, was influenced in this essay by Rafael Altamira

[25] Sierra, *Discursos*, in *Obras completas*, V, 276; Porfirio Parra, "División del carácter," *Revista Positiva* 5 (December, 1905), 550–553; idem, "Etología o ciencia del carácter," *Revista Positiva* 5 (December, 1905), 546–549; Molina Enríquez, *Los grandes problemas nacionales*, p. 320.

y Crevea's *Psicología del pueblo español* (1899) and probably by the writings of Francisco Bulnes and José María Vigil. In view of the materials that treated the approximate themes of *lo mexicano* from the eighteenth century on, it would be incorrect to call Chávez's essay the first to articulate the problem of the Mexican character, but it examined it in a more comprehensive psychohistorical framework. Although Chávez failed in his positivist attempt to speak factually within the discipline of empirical psychology, his speculative essay underscored the necessity of harmonizing institutions and laws with the peculiarities of the country. Chávez suggested that Mexico was dysfunctional in this respect, in part due to the imitative nature of governmental policy, a judgment that impelled him to consider the historical roots of the Mexican ethos and to urge the organization of a psychology institute to investigate the pressure points in social planning.[26]

Chávez's plea for the study of the Mexican character was answered by Julio Guerrero, who, borrowing an Enlightenment environmentalist approach refashioned by turn-of-the-century social analysis, treated the psychology of vices as a result of climatic and historical determinism. In Guerrero's view, the climate was conducive to ennui, but as soon as danger or want threatened or pride was wounded, the Mexican "exploded" and fought heroically. To the depressive effects of the atmosphere Guerrero also attributed the culture of verbal insult. He hypothesized that when the tension in the atmosphere was dissipated, a person's behavior became subdued, which, however, induced the melancholia commonly expressed in elegiac poetry and in songs played in a minor key. In a passage anticipatory of Octavio Paz's character analysis in *El laberinto de la soledad* (1950), Guerrero remarked that alcohol could transform the joking but stoical Mexican into a malevolent being hurling insult and confronting death with knife and pistol.[27]

The Mexican passion for gambling was integral to Guerrero's analysis of the national character. He interpreted it as a device to

---

[26] For a study of Chávez's Mexican psychology, see Julio Pizano Aguilar, "Ezequiel A. Chávez y su contribución a la psicología del pueblo mexicano" (master's thesis, Universidad Nacional Autónoma de México, 1965). See also Ezequiel A. Chávez, "Ensayo sobre los rasgos distintivos de la sensibilidad como factor del carácter mexicano," *Revista Positiva* 1 (March, 1901), 83, 97.

[27] Guerrero, *La génesis del crimen*, pp. 17–24.

distribute wealth, as a cabalistic survival, and as another example of the effect of climate on behavior. The culture of gambling, he explained, grew out of the belief that life was irrational and depended on "anomalous and exaggerated" variables. From this assumption he linked superstitution and the idea of chance to liturgical practice as a means to influence the future and attacked Aztec prognostication as well as the Guadalupe cult. Guerrero's theory of national character, however, was not monistic but was based on the historical causes of behavior. He emphasized that class structure was not determined by social psychology and sought to dispel the myth of Mexican laziness by arguing in the vein of Vigil that its origins were to be found in nineteenth-century militarism, which uprooted the people and created occupational instability.[28]

Although not explicitly stated in his study, Guerrero's theories of social psychology were linked to his role as critic, if not reformer, of the existing political system. For example, he examined the phenomenon of presidential succession in light of the psychopolitical effects of the rumors of Díaz's poor health and related the climatic determinants of behavior to federal legislation. His position in the Díaz regime was ambivalent in the final analysis, yet he went so far as to suggest that the government should distribute his book to top-level officials.[29]

Guerrero's point of departure for his Mexicanist critique was his idea that the country's social organization and environment were unique among nations. Thus "European" knowledge was ineffectual in developing canons of art or establishing guidelines for industry. Mexico needed its "own psychology," and industrialization should proceed according to "policy" and "methods" that were "national." Hence Mexico was enjoined "to know itself," to study its "mode of being," unfettered by illusion, on the assumption that self-knowledge would reinforce the country against "foreign conquest."[30] Because Guerrero never directly challenged the social and political order, he

[28] Ibid., pp. 157, 130–140.

[29] Julio Guerrero, "El fin del cesarismo," *La República* 1 (June 7, 1901), 5–13; idem, "La humedad atmosférica: los delitos de ira: crónica de la sociedad positivista," *La República* 1 (June 7, 1901), 19–25; Guerrero to Porfirio Díaz, June 30, 1906, AGN, RIP & BA, Leg. 3, Exp. 125.

[30] Julio Guerrero, "Trascendencia política de los estudios nacionales," *La República* 1 (June 22, 1901), 15–29.

has entered history as a conservative, yet his efforts to stimulate a social consciousness and a critical approach to Mexican problems places him in the chain of thinkers from Mier to Ramos.

Other writers, aspiring to clear the way for an enhanced Mexican identity, played with the concept of national character and the politics of national taste. Elaborating European romantic notions of the collective soul, the physician-educator Alfonso Pruneda argued that the "Mexican soul" was derived from race and environment.[31] Echoing nineteenth-century Mexico's sentiment for a national literature, Agustín Aragón, the high priest of positivism in the last decade of the Porfiriato, said that Mexicans should prefer their native works, since they "present us as we are and not as we would like to be." Aragón approved of the novel *Pacotillas* by his teacher Parra, because it had the stamp of the "Mexican character." In a review of Sierra's *Juárez: su obra y su tiempo*, Aragón commented that Mexican literature should treat native life, which he associated with *mestizaje*. Following this criterion, Aragón thought, contemporary Mexican culture could sustain a harmonious relationship with its origins.[32] The preoccupation with the national character, heir to more than a century of racial determinism, was by this time infused with the trinitarian mythology of Indian, creole, and mestizo.

The Indian had long been a subject in Mexican letters. From the colonial chroniclers to the romantic *costumbristas* of the nineteenth century, the Indian was viewed as the enigmatic presence of Mexico, and there was endless dispute regarding his role in the social order. For the indigenists he became the key to understanding Mexico, and around him a significant strain of ideology developed; for the Hispanists, he represented the raw material of nationhood to be shaped in a Euro-Christian mold by the Spaniards. During the period 1900–1910, his image was in limbo; he was neither the sympathetic but distant figure of most of the earlier humanistic writers, nor was he yet the object of pragmatic social reform he would become during the institutional phase of the Revolution. But significantly, he was viewed in this period in a preeminently social and

[31] Alfonso Pruneda, "Discurso," *Revista Positiva* 5 (September, 1905), 417.

[32] Agustín Aragón, "*Pacotillas*: novela mexicana por el Doctor Porfirio Parra," *Revista Positiva* 1 (January, 1901), 25; idem, "Juárez: su obra y su tiempo," *Revista Positiva* 6 (March, 1906), 190.

nationalistic context. Clearly, he must be made to contribute to the patria; he was on the eve of his "redemption."

Rethinking an existential analysis rooted in the colonial period, Ezequiel Chávez considered the Indian stoic, tradition-oriented, and disdainful of everything—progress, life, death, work as well as rest, hope as well as despair. According to Chávez, the Indian had a quiet, internalized behavior and, though not impulsive, nevertheless could express himself explosively. Since the Indian was temperamentally indifferent, he was excited only through pressure over a long period of time. He experimented only if a strong need arose, and it was difficult for him to conceive of the patria mexicana. But he did have a vital relationship to his land, and while he would not spontaneously offer allegiance to abstract national ideals, he would defend his mountain or plot of land. Chávez explained that the Indian's telluric traditions and an oppressive social structure made the Indian distrustful of innovations and forced him into a marginal existence. Despairing when he found himself in an alien culture and knowing that it was hopeless to overturn the system that stifled him, he sought escape in alcohol. But drunkenness was transitory and the burden of life constant, Chávez wrote, so the Indian either chose suicide or remained indifferent.[33]

While Chávez displayed an intuitive ability to penetrate the Indian's social behavior, Andrés Molina Enríquez focused more formally on the Indian's character as it related to history and nationality. Thus the origins of the Indian's famous passivity lay not in the social structure but in the fact that, except for the Aztec incursion, the Indian had not had a martial evolution. Molina pointed out that the Indian's resilience in the face of adverse circumstances was a significant element in the growth of Mexican nationality. Here Molina differed from Chávez, arguing that while the Indian was taciturn because formerly he had been enslaved, he nevertheless could assume a patriotic role in spite of his disinclination toward revolution.[34] Similarly, Esteban Maqueo Castellanos, a regionalist and essayist, considered that the Indian had been rendered docile by his spiritually destructive past. However, Maqueo temporized and granted that the Indian demonstrated an intellectual capacity.

[33] Chávez, "Ensayo sobre los rasgos distintivos," pp. 85–88, 93–94.
[34] Molina Enríquez, *Los grandes problemas nacionales*, p. 321.

If insufficient diet and housing diminished his strength in the competitive struggle, it was equally obvious that he was muscular, could absorb fatigue, and was endowed with a sensitive nervous system.[35]

Belying the western context of progress, the views held by these writers on the Indian suggested that he was a variable factor in a society whose cultural parts had not yet coalesced into a national community. The interpretations of the Indian illustrate the lack of consensus regarding that figure, who was seen against his historical background, yet judged from the standpoint of contemporary criteria. Thus, conceptually, the Indian was being transformed into a role that would be disproportionate in the shaping of a myth of nationalism.

If the dominant image of the Indian was that of inert substance in the formation of the Mexican, the creole was held to be the force that wrought the change in social evolution. The creole is usually associated in Mexican thought with European civilization and native conservatism, although this conclusion is devoid of historical qualification. Yet by 1900 racial and social stereotypes had become so pervasive that any discussion of the creole character was fraught with negative connotations; indeed, the creole was portrayed as un-Mexican.

In this period Molina Enríquez treated the creole extensively, describing his capacity for immediate action and classifying his behavior as audacious and vain. The creole, Molina thought, was bold because his Spanish progenitors were, frivolous because he belonged to the aristocracy. Among the "new" or "liberal" creoles was the non-Spanish immigrant to Mexico in the nineteenth century, whom Molina characterized as diligent, sober-minded, calculating, greedy, learned, and sociable. In analyzing his political potential, Molina considered the creole's notion of patria to be weak.[36] Although a superficial denigration colored Molina's idea of the creole, he could not conceal a certain admiration for him, especially his dynamism which Molina thought lacking in the Indian. Molina's attitudes toward the Indian and the creole were typical manifesta-

[35] Esteban Maqueo Castellanos, *Algunos problemas nacionales*, p. 83.

[36] Molina Enríquez, *Los grandes problemas nacionales*, pp. 67, 287–296, 320–321.

tions of the conflict between tradition and modernity, between the New World and the Old, harking back to the problems of evolution and nationality. The Indian could not serve as a model for progress, nor, his sophisticated leadership notwithstanding, could the creole be emulated for his social finesse. It was as if the creole were untrustworthy as a Mexican. Here, then, was the thrust of the racial commentary: the premise that the Mexican was neither Indian nor creole, neither pre-Hispanic nor European in his outlook, but someone around whom semantically and psychologically a cohesive nationality, a Mexican *patria*, could be constructed.

The sociocultural type who has come to dominate the mainstream of Mexican history is the mestizo; indeed, much scholarly glorification of Mexico in the twentieth century concerns mestizo Mexico with a strong Indian element and a less significant creole or European one. Since *mestizaje* has been regarded a key factor in historical change in the national period, the image of the mestizo is fundamental to national identity and constitutes an essential chapter in intellectual history. By the first decade of the twentieth century, the Mexican held notions of the mestizo that were neither flattering nor degrading.

Searching for the mestizo's "traits of sensibility," Chávez saw him as a child of ephemerality and chance who was destructive and disobedient rather than cooperative. Rootless, the mestizo took the easy way out and did not live for the comforts of life. He entered easily into love relationships and engendered families that were soon disunited. He spent more than his means, and because he was temperamentally unstable, he was incapable of grasping the future and was basically improvident. Chávez described the mestizo's mentality as intuitive and imaginative rather than intellectual and concluded that his character was evasive, externalized, expansive, and impulsive.[37]

While Chávez delineated character, Molina Enríquez looked to historical factors, arguing that the mestizo was energetic because he embodied the vitality of both Spaniard and Indian. Molina noted that although the inception of *mestizaje* was associated with an in-

[37] Chávez, "Ensayo sobre los rasgos distintivos," pp. 88–89, 95.

ferior class status, the mestizo eventually climbed into preeminence and assumed the presumptuous role of the creole.[38] For Chávez and Molina, the mestizo was not the dominant element in the national ethos that he would become in later thought; however, he was obviously emerging as an intermediate figure between the Indian and the creole and was endowed with special Mexican attributes. In this early period of *lo mexicano* analysis, if concepts of the national character did not crowd the intellectual panorama, they were nevertheless developing with maturity and flexibility and indicated a more incisive approach to social criticism.

Societal images were formed of female as well as male aspects of the national character. Not surprisingly, in the period preceding the Revolution, woman was portrayed in such traditional roles as sex object and mother, but the contention that she functioned as a bulwark against Yankee influence was an indication of an undercurrent of change in attitudes toward the female within the male-oriented power structure. The Mexican woman netted as much praise as criticism, in part due to the romantic attitude with which the intellectuals approached her. Typical was the treatment by Julio Guerrero, who based his discussion of wife and mistress on an implicit double standard. The wife was for duty, the mistress for fun. The wife gave dignity to home and society, the mistress perfected her charms. In his efforts to analyze the sociology of sex, Guerrero noted that the social stigma of the mistress originated in an older, severer Catholicism, which, however, had grown permissive.[39] Horacio Barreda's saccharine ideal of womanhood contained nationalistic overtones.[40] Barreda stated that the Mexican woman was not so strong as the Anglo-Saxon but possessed an exquisite sensibility. She was timid and irresolute rather than aggressive, although she had a heroic abnegation that endured suffering. She had a natural sagacity, taking stock of things precisely and rapidly. Her "high moral being," "noble inclinations," and "maternal instinct" were qualities threat-

[38] Molina Enríquez, *Los grandes problemas nacionales*, pp. 22–24, 320, 322.

[39] Guerrero, *La génesis del crimen*, pp. 336–343.

[40] For a discussion of the idealized image of women in Latin American society, see Ann M. Pescatello, *Power and Pawn: The Female in Iberian Families, Societies, and Cultures*, p. 198.

ened by the invasion of North American materialism, Barreda maintained, and he denounced Mexican feminists who urged the Americanization of the Mexican woman.[41]

In these writings the evocation of a Mexican experience was emerging as a controlling principle to explain national identity. Once concepts of knowledge relating to Mexico were formulated, however imprecise they might be, and a general framework of history outlined in terms of evolution and nationality, the intellectual could approach his materials with a sharper perspective. Although the Mexican ethos was still imperfectly expressed, its contours were being shaped and would give us the familiar picture of a country struggling to achieve entry into a wider world that would impinge upon its developing nationalism.

Criticism of Foreign Influence

In the course of its nationhood, Mexico has had to witness a contest between its native values and the guidelines imposed from abroad. It is the colonial thesis of its history that Mexico remains dependent upon foreign life at the intellectual as well as at the popular levels. Whether the foreign party involved is Spain, France, or the United States, the inference is the same: the Mexican expression is suppressed or destroyed. The evidence supports some dark pages of Mexico's history, while the country's efforts to overcome the foreign yoke illuminate some of the brighter pages. The concern of intellectuals and political leaders to diminish foreign influence has occasioned an official soul-searching whose warnings are aimed at reinforcing mass appeal. Through the ideas of self-awareness, evolution, nationality, and ethos, the Mexican intellectual could hope to construe his country's identity, yet this would be possible only while admitting to the dialectic of nationalism and cosmopolitanism. The road toward national unity could not be traveled through purpose alone; it entailed compromise, circuitousness, violence, and a willingness to accept something less than perfection. Mexican history could be examined from its native circumstances or from its dependence upon foreign powers. While the truth rests on both internal and ex-

[41] Horacio Barreda, "Estudio sobre 'el femenismo'. VI: Del 'femenismo' en México," *Revista Positiva* 9 (June, 1909), 274–277.

ternal factors, the notion of the pernicious effect of foreign influence on Mexico has been a major theme in the search for national identity. The foreign model provided Mexico with a developmental dilemma: entry into the modern world depended on a rationale and an infrastructure derived from advanced western technology, and this created a conflict between progress and tradition. Ezequiel Chávez saw the problem in terms of the sociopsychological origins of nations and argued that educational and political institutions could not be transplanted in a country where they were not responsive to the native mentality. It was not enough, he explained, for law to satisfy the intelligence abstractly; it should relate concretely to the local circumstances in which it was written. Chávez went on to say that Mexicans ignored their historical uniqueness and harbored the illusion that institutions beneficial to other peoples were, without modification, good for Mexico.[42]

With a stronger nationalistic exhortation, Andrés Molina Enríquez reinforced Chávez's ideas, extending them into other sectors of society. It was necessary, Molina explained, for workers to outstrip the immigrants, for consumers to accept the native product, for manufacturers to stop copying techniques from abroad, for scholars to study their country's problems, and for artists to be inspired by native sources. Molina noted that Mexico's writers had done themselves a disservice by imitating foreign models. Scientists often did not write in Spanish, he complained, and Mexicans were thinking in English.[43]

Much of the criticism of foreign influence was directed toward the North Americanization of Mexico. Molina found the North American residents in Mexico brusque and willful and considered that their lack of scruples was disguised as practicality. The North American had nothing good to teach Mexico, Molina thought, pointing out that if a Mexican businessman was discourteous, and if doctors had given up the humanitarian house call for the professional appointment, it was owing to North American influence. He reinforced his attack with the notion that the values of a Spanish gentleman were worth more than those of a North American. This line of reasoning led him to see the collusion of foreigners and creoles as a

[42] Chávez, "Ensayo sobre los rasgos distintivos," pp. 81, 84.
[43] Molina Enríquez, *Los grandes problemas nacionales*, pp. 313, 327.

threat to nationality. Arguing that native customs symbolized national life, he thought their conscious dismissal in favor of other values
violated the individuality of the Mexican people. The solution, according to Molina, lay with the mestizo, who had evolved from the
union of Indians and Spaniards in centuries of "common life" and
represented a successful adaptation to the "national soul."[44]

The Porfirian Peace is Shaken

While the intellectual was loosing his barbs against foreign influence in Mexico, he was also pointing up the internal ills of his
country. Ever since Daniel Cosío Villegas gave direction to the idea
that the origins of contemporary Mexico were to be found in the
Porfiriato (1876–1911), scholars have scoured the period for hints of
the subsequent reaction to the Díaz rule, interpolating an experience
anticipatory to *mexicanidad*. Gradually the concept of a "pre-Revo-
lution" emerged, which established a relationship of "precursory"
data to the course of history after 1910. It is in this context that
Emilio Vázquez, who attacked unlimited reelection in 1892, is viewed
as a precursor to the Revolution,[45] while Wistano Luis Orozco, who
in 1895 pointed to the misery of the marginal classes, is looked upon
as the first to inveigh against the social foundations of Porfirism.[46]
During the years 1900–1910 the attack on Porfirian institutions increased through a series of events linked to the beginnings of the
Revolution: anti-Díaz political groupings, labor unrest, agrarian
discontent, and middle-class intellectual disenchantment.[47] Much of
the criticism warned against a potentially explosive situation caused
by the gap between governmental policy and the needs of the
people. Thus a Mexicanism was conveyed at this time that later
would be synthesized into the Revolutionary mystique.[48]

---

[44] Ibid., pp. 310–311, 303.

[45] See Daniel Cosío Villegas, *El Porfiriato: vida política interior*, pt. 2, in
Historia Moderna de México, IX, 644.

[46] See the discussion by Arnaldo Córdova, *La ideología de la Revolución
mexicana: la formación del nuevo régimen*, p. 122.

[47] Ibid., pp. 87–107.

[48] Typical was the case of Félix F. Palavicini, who as a young man formed
a revolutionary consciousness as agrarian dissenter and school teacher. See his
Mi vida revolucionaria, pp. 13–15.

As dissatisfaction with the Porfirian peace mounted, political criticism became an important medium for channeling frustrated energies. It was the moralistic critique by a patrician sympathetic to the pueblo that would help, more than any other single work, to awaken Mexico from its Porfirian lethargy. In focusing on the issue of presidential succession, the Díaz-Creelman interview (1908) had thrown open the problem of Mexico, and in *La sucesión presidencial en 1910*, the anti-reelectionist Francisco I. Madero analyzed the national situation as a contrast between the servility of the people and the egoism of the state. A wealthy, privileged class supported by the government, he wrote, wallowed in luxury and enjoyed a liberty for its lifestyle as well as a relative impunity against attack. Mexico was "asleep from the noise of the steam whistles and the power of industry, dazzled by the uses of electricity, and, busy with economic development, it trusted its Caudillo and ignored the public problem."[49] Madero invoked the idea of the patria and opposed a Mexico of underdogs to the arrogant surrogates of the Porfiriato. To "dignify the Mexican" was the primary task confronting the nation.

Madero's rhetoric expressed an emergent populism, and other writers sought more intellectual explanations for his principles. Under the pseudonym of Blas Urrea, Luis Cabrera, who contributed to the unmasking of the Díaz regime in a series of exposés, found the chief culprits of the anti-patria to be Díaz's economic advisors, the *científicos*. In one of his articles he stated that through their interpretation of sociology, the *científicos* had begun to preach a dangerous cosmopolitanism contrary to the idea of patria. Sociology had influenced them to believe that national frontiers were erected by egotism as barriers to progress. The "races of wheat" were considered more capable than the "races of corn" and were therefore chosen to conquer the world. The Anglo-Saxons were superior to the Indians, who had no capacity for progressive evolution. It was this sort of intellectual distortion that Cabrera condemned when he exclaimed, "Damn the knowledge that makes the idea of patria disappear!"[50]

By 1910 Mexican political commentary had developed a formula for assessing events and articulating responses: using a dichotomy

[49] Francisco I. Madero, *La sucesión presidencial*, p. 144.
[50] Luis Cabrera, *Obras políticas del Lic. Blas Urrea*, pp. 2–3.

of the pueblo and the elite, which conveyed a sense of impending conflict through the selection of appropriate symbols. When the Independence Centenary was celebrated in Mexico City in September, 1910, Cabrera captured it critically in an article on the "two patriotisms." The celebration underscored the social division between the aristocrats, bureaucrats, and businessmen, who turned out for the foreign visitors, and the pueblo, which was excluded from the festivities, their traditional serenading after the *grito* on the fifteenth prohibited. Cabrera sharply distinguished "these" who suffer and work from "those" who profit and dominate.[51] Shrewd Porfirio himself seemed to sense the imminent confrontation in Mexico. The novelist Martín Luis Guzmán related an anecdote concerning a student group who requested permission from the government to parade and give speeches in commemoration of independence. When Don Porfirio received the group, he granted the request with the admonition to be careful because there were "sleeping atavisms" in the country that, once awakened, would be impossible to contain. Guzmán mused that the atavisms were the anxieties of a nation wanting to find itself.[52]

Mexicanidad often conveyed apocalyptic energies awaiting release in the rending of the old order. "The whole patria is a volcano on the point of spewing forth the choleric fire of its insides." So wrote the utopian revolutionary Ricardo Flores Magón on September 3, 1910. On the eve of the Revolution, he predicted that the upheaval would occur at any moment, that after thirty-four years of shame the Mexican pueblo would rise and break the yoke that oppressed the people. "The revolution, uncontainable and all-subduing, will not be long in coming."[53] The firebrand rhetoric of Flores Magón lent force to the warning of what was to come—the earthiness, the ideal, the outburst, the violence, the sudden revelation of *lo mexicano*. The pre-Revolutionary themes that suggested reform had a special significance for the dissemination of Mexicanist myth. The concept of social disequilibrium, the relationship between ethics and progress, and the Darwinian assumptions of development

[51] Ibid., pp. 333–334.
[52] Martín Luis Guzmán, *Academia*, pp. 36–37.
[53] Ricardo Flores Magón, *La Revolución mexicana*, p. 16; idem, "La Revolución," in *Antología*, ed. Gonzalo Aguirre Beltrán, pp. 25–28.

would later feed a neurotic nationalism whose structure integrated a nativist morality by juxtaposing the redemptive force of the Revolution to the putative regressiveness of the Porfiriato.

Justo Sierra and Self-conscious Mexicanism

The thinker who most consistently and eloquently addressed the problems of national identity during the pre-Revolutionary period was Justo Sierra. One of his works opened the decade, and another may be said to have closed it. In his speech at the reopening of the National University in 1910, it was almost as if he sensed the coming Revolution that would convert his plea for the Mexicanization of knowledge into reality. A master document for the study of twentieth-century Mexico, the speech illustrates the intellectual atmosphere during the transition from the old regime to the new, placing an emphasis on national culture and Mexican studies. In his discourse Sierra shifted from the concepts of strength in German and American thought to the ideas of Bergson and William James, thus exchanging the Porfirian awe of Anglo-Saxon power for the new Revolutionary humanism. Growing out of his program of education, the speech culminated Sierra's life as a thinker and an educator. Sierra had gradually been rejecting positivism and its ready-made approach to life and was turning toward history and metaphysics.[54] Ever abreast of intellectual currents, he was moving from the abstract and universal to the local and concrete until, as Edmundo O'Gorman stated in 1949, he was "one step away from historicism, the heart of our contemporary philosophy."[55] Becoming skeptical of what he obviously saw in the Porfiriato, he made a stand for a science of the provincial and the cultural in which knowledge would be transmuted into social responsibility.

Sierra eschewed the purely intellectualizing role of the university for a moral relationship with society. He warned against a "scholarly caste" removed from its "mundane responsibility," in-

---

[54] González Navarro places Sierra midway between the Spencerian positivists and antipositivist humanists (*Sociología e historia en México*, pp. 11–15).

[55] Edmundo O'Gorman, "Justo Sierra y los orígenes de la Universidad de México, 1910," *Filosofía y Letras* 17 (April–June, 1949), 247.

different to a turbulent reality surrounding it. Instead, Sierra wanted the scholar to "nationalize study" and "Mexicanize knowledge." "Train the telescope on our sky," he said, the microscope on Mexico's flora, fauna, water, and blood. Physical sciences as well as the social sciences were included in Sierra's scholarly scheme, but history underlay his vision. Sierra's mind swept over the indigenous peoples and culture of his land; he wondered about origins, unity, diversity, language, religion, and architecture. "What a profusion of topics for our intellectuals," he mused. The task of the National University was to demonstrate that Mexican selfhood was rooted in the country's natural environment and history, and that while it shared elements with other New World countries, it also had its own unique experience. But if Sierra pleaded for the Mexicanization of knowledge, he also admonished that the latest research methods should be used.[56] Sierra's *mexicanidad* was a reflection of the intellectual revolution in Mexico, the break with positivism, which occurred prior to and independent of the political upheaval, although both were manifestations of the same sense of dysfunction pervading the country and later would share common ideological elements.

Thus at the end of the decade the transition occurring in the political arena had its counterpart in intellectual and institutional change. The year 1910 was balanced between the cosmopolitan Hispanism of the poet Amado Nervo's generation and the sharper nationalistic and professional rationale of the new School of Superior Studies.[57] The Revolution, with its tighter social and esthetic appeal to Mexican identity, would increasingly underscore the latter and reshape all cultural influences, national as well as foreign, into a more compatible synthesis.

[56] Justo Sierra, "Discurso pronunciado en la inauguración de la Universidad Nacional de México el año de 1910," *Prosas*, pp. 163–190.

[57] See Nervo's reports (1910) from Spain to the Mexican government (AGN, RIP & BA, Leg. 7, Exp. 337). The School of Superior Studies, organized in 1910 by Ezequiel Chávez under the direction of Justo Sierra, was the seat of humanities in the new university. Chávez gave an inaugural speech at its opening similar in content and rhetoric to the one given by Sierra for the University. See Ezequiel Chávez, "Discurso," in *Documentos y discursos alusivos a la solemne inauguración de la Escuela Nacional de Altos Estudios*, pp. 3–12.

3.
The Revolution and National Identity, 1910–1920

THE designation of the 1910 Revolution as the beginning of Mexico's contemporary history has been interpreted by some intellectuals as signifying a protean mythos of nationhood. The novelist Carlos Fuentes, for example, holds that Mexico discovered itself in the Revolution. The philosopher Leopoldo Zea argues that all topics related to the knowledge of Mexico sustain the Revolution as their historical basis. The historian Guillermo Palacios finds in the Revolution the common denominator of twentieth-century Mexican life, while according to the sociologist Gabriel Careaga, the scholar who seeks to explain his society invariably turns to the Revolution for his point of departure.[1] These statements pose the problem of the relationship between the Revolution and national identity in the years 1910–1920. What were the origins of these all-embracing premises made so long after the initial revolutionary activity? What effect did the confusing series of events somewhat inaccurately collected under the rubric "Revolution" have on an already developed Mexican symbolism? Before the Mexican trends of the period can be elucidated, some considerations regarding the various approaches to the Revolution are necessary in order to understand the selective basis of interpretation crucial to the study of ideas.

The Search for Concepts

The only event, Mexican thinkers have reasoned, that equals the Revolution in transcendental meaning is the Conquest, to the ex-

[1] Carlos Fuentes, *Tiempo mexicano*, p. 83; Leopoldo Zea, *Conciencia y posibilidad del mexicano*, p. 24; Guillermo Palacios, "La idea oficial de la Revo-

tent that it prefigured a new civilization. But the relationship between the Revolution and the Conquest offers more than a parallel useful for a philosophy of history, for the Revolution attempted to restructure the society created by the Conquest and only negligibly improved for the masses during a century of national experience. Hence the Revolution tried to provoke from the people a positive reaction to their history, and the earlier preoccupation with Mexican identity was now transformed into the new watchwords of political nationalism.[2]

It is simplistic to view the Revolution monolithically, for there were revolutions within the Revolution, neither simultaneous nor equal in achievement.[3] While it is impractical not to conceive of the Revolution organically, it is also useful to assume a nominalistic approach to the phenomenon and to chart its successes and failures in that light. For this reason one scholar suggested that the Revolution should be separated into its component elements and analyzed through its "images."[4]

If there were multiple revolutions, there were also various levels of thought about the Revolution, ranging from incomprehension to abstract perception. The composite notions of the Revolution grew slowly and acquired different meanings and contexts. The effect of the Revolution has to be noted at the village and the regional levels, where usually it is a matter of implementation, as well as at the national level, where it tends to be theoretical.[5] That the Revolution could be devoid of measurable impact is illustrated in the remark of

lución mexicana" (master's thesis, El Colegio de México, 1969), pp. I, iii; Gabriel Careaga, *Los intelectuales y la política en México*, p. 55.

[2] For the classical expression of these ideas, see Octavio Paz, *The Labyrinth of Solitude: Life and Thought in Mexico*, trans. Lysander Kemp, especially pp. 100, 135–136.

[3] For the idea of multiple revolutions and the problem of their interpretation, see Peter Calvert, "The Mexican Revolution: Theory or Fact?" *Journal of Latin American Studies* 1 (1969), 53; and Jean Meyer, "Periodización e Ideología," in *Contemporary Mexico: Papers of the IV International Congress of Mexican History*, ed. James W. Wilkie, Michael C. Meyer, and Edna Monzón de Wilkie, pp. 717–718.

[4] See Stanley R. Ross, "Imágenes de la Revolución mexicana," *Latinoamérica* 1 (1968) 46.

[5] In this respect, see Luis González, *Pueblo en vilo*.

Luz Jiménez of Milpa Alta that she did not know what the *zapatistas* had against Díaz.[6] For many campesinos political rhetoric was not necessary. They fought instinctively to redress the grievances of their patria chica, and to them the Revolution referred to troop strength, fire power, and battle strategy.[7] The consciousness spanning the upheaval extended from Juan Pérez Jolote, the semi-fictionalized Chamula dragged existentially into the Revolution,[8] to Francisco I. Madero, the *norteño* who glossed the Baghavad Gita and wrought political, if not spiritual, change for the country.

Throughout much of the post-Revolutionary period myths have accounted for historical substance in the decade 1910–1920. One reads of the chaos, the groping this way and that, the blindly flowing social energy, the lack of purpose, the telluric momentum of the pueblo raking the land in scythe-like fury—when this may indicate only a paucity of monographic analysis. Or one reads that the Revolution grew without ideas, although in the space of seven years it progressed from bandit reports to the Constitution of 1917, a document that completed a process of secularization begun in the eighteenth century and that was a radical mandate for its age, notwithstanding its basis in the Constitution of 1857. Obviously there were ideas before the Querétaro Congress (1916–1917), however insignificant they may have been to a Demetrio Macías (the protagonist in Mariano Azuela's novel, *Los de abajo*) or however will-of-the-wispish to the hard-riding Villa. More accurately, there were attitudes: socially, those of an expanding mestizo group wresting for upward mobility; economically, those of a people suffering injustices in the countryside or in the factories; intellectually, those of a youthful middle class fearful for security amid Porfirian elitism; politically, of those conscious of the stultification of the Díaz regime.

How does the much-studied political crystallization of these attitudes testify to the unitarian structure of national reform in the making? Simply that in the period 1910–1917 there was an obvious shift in the Mexican's idea of himself and his nation, initiating a slow,

[6] Fernando Horcasitas, *De Porfirio Díaz a Zapata: memoria náhuatl de Milpa Alta*, p. 103.
[7] Arturo Warman, . . . *Y venimos a contradecir: los campesinos de Morelos y el estado nacional*, pp. 104–105.
[8] Ricardo Pozas A., *Juan Pérez Jolote: biografía de un tzotzil*, pp. 34–50.

and sometimes unrevolutionary, change in goals and institutions. Thus agrarian reform, articulated intellectually by Andrés Molina Enríquez and Luis Cabrera, among others, given national implications by the Plan of San Luis Potosí and the Manifesto of the Mexican Liberal Party, programmed at the popular level by Zapata, evolved through the National Agrarian Commission, the Ministry of Agriculture, the various proclamations against Madero and Huerta, the Torreón Pact, the Aguascalientes Convention, the January 6, 1915, decree, and Article 27 of the Constitution. Similarly labor reform, whose origins lay in the pre-Revolutionary period, was absorbed into the Revolution by the Flores Magonistas, the Casa de Obrero Mundial, the Confederación de Círculos Obreros Católicos, legislation, and *carrancista* expediency, and was mandated by Article 123.[9] And education, also reformed during the late Porfiriato, went through the process of Revolutionary codification and was made legal theory by Article 3. Whether these reforms were mere echoes of such western trends as socialism and progressivism, or whether they actually improved the life of those they intended to benefit are questions belonging to a different inquiry.[10] In terms of the deepening adjustment to the tensions produced by Mexico's industrialization during the Porfiriato and the demoralizing conditions of the masses, these basic examples suggest a dynamic interplay of ideas that enlarged the national consciousness.

In contrast with the rawness of the Revolution, then, a developing logic of ideas and political concourse was destined to catalyze the process of national identity. Hence scholars linked *lo mexicano* and the Revolution so that they were virtually synonymous in meaning,[11] signifying the moralistic exaltation of a Mexico to be refash-

---

[9] For an overview of agrarian and labor reform in this period, see Berta Ulloa, "La lucha armada (1911–1920)," in *Historia General de México*, IV, 4–42.

[10] For an example of the revisionist interpretation of the Revolution—that Mexico underwent no radical socioeconomic change—see Ramón Eduardo Ruiz, *Labor and the Ambivalent Revolutionaries: Mexico, 1911–1923*, p. 2. For the historiography of the Revolution, see David C. Bailey, "Revisionism and the Recent Historiography of the Mexican Revolution," *Hispanic American Historical Review* 58 (February, 1978), 62–79.

[11] See, for example, Daniel Cosío Villegas, "La crisis de México," in *Ensayos y notas*, I, 115; Hugo Díaz Thomé, "El mexicano y su historia," *Historia Mexicana* 2 (October–December, 1952), 256; Eugenia W. de Meyer, "Del ser

ioned in a reformist mold in order to keep reaction on its guard. As Frank Tannenbaum, one of the early scholars who saw Mexicanism as an edifying process, put it, "The Revolution—the real Revolution —has been moral and spiritual. All other changes that have occurred in Mexico since 1910 . . . are relatively less important. . . ."[12] Slowly a regenerative symbolism would permeate the programs of social and economic reform and precipitate a cultural nationalism,[13] which would convey the search for nationhood and selfhood. Mexican identity in the decade 1910–1920 reflected the Revolution's discrete beginnings which, if apparently unconnected, at least shared an emergent unity and purpose associated with nationalism. No one intellectual or political leader totally comprehended the Revolution in this formative stage, and to control the dispersive events was the task facing provincial chieftain and urban ideologue alike. Thus the decade acquired the distinction of providing a group encounter among the Mexicans, pulling them together as well as apart, but generating the sense of a new era in which the intellectual could wipe the slate and begin to establish credibility for Mexican values.[14]

Violence and Vision

The quest for a Mexican identity in this decade was determined in large measure by the paradox of the Revolution as ideal and upheaval. Yet rather than the intellectual, it was the guerrilla, marking

mexicano y de la historiografía de la Revolución," in *Conciencia y autenticidad históricas*, p. 219; Michael C. Meyer, "Perspectives on Revolutionary Historiography," *New Mexico Historical Review* 18 (1969), 169; José Muñoz Cota, "El mirador de la Revolución: Revolución y mexicanidad," *El Nacional*, June 13, 1962; Ross, "Imágenes de la Revolución mexicana," p. 48; Frank Tannenbaum, "Spontaneity and Adaptation in the Mexican Revolution," *Journal of World History* 9 (1965), 88; Emilio Uranga, "El significado de la Revolución mexicana," *Novedades*, November 19, 1950; Leopoldo Zea, *La filosofía en México*, I, 38.

[12] Frank Tannenbaum, "Some Reflections on the Revolution," in *Is the Mexican Revolution Dead?* ed. Stanley R. Ross, p. 199.

[13] For a treatment of the social and cultural aspects of the Revolution and nationalism, see Frederick C. Turner, *The Dynamic of Mexican Nationalism*, pp. 101–155, 254–306.

[14] Miguel Jorrín and John D. Martz consider that the entire national system in Mexico is predicated on a nationalism of the higher values of the spirit (*Latin American Political Thought and Ideology*, p. 226).

time in his desert redoubt or mountain pass, who conveyed the Revolutionary message in telegraphic intrigue and ambuscade. Slowly a nationalistic iconography was developing that expressed the outrage among the groups most repressed during the Porfiriato; hence ideas were noteworthy for their relationship to the pueblo. With a few exceptions, sophisticated thought was in limbo because Revolutionary-oriented intellectuals had not yet fully replaced those who represented the older Porfirian traditions. It was not the urbane men-of-letters like Federico Gamboa or Alfonso Cravioto who were changing the course of Mexican identity, but the provincials like Otilio Montaño, Francisco Mújica, and Pastor Rouaix who were expressing the attitudes of those who, living under the heel of nonadvancement, had the most immediate grievances against the reigning socioeconomic order. From such men the official post-Revolutionary thinkers would derive their bread-and-butter myth of the awakening masses based on a nativism that was often more military than civilian in the early years. The emergence of the pueblo now became the most important determinant of national identity. Thus the Plan of Ayala was more politically significant than the Plan of Guadalupe; the provincial, not the centralist, energies at the Querétaro Congress provided the greater Revolutionary impact; Goítias' painting was more symbolic of Mexican art than Ruelas'; Azuela's writing was more enduring than Gamboa's.

The concept of violence, therefore, was linked to that of the struggling masses, and by extension their projected social redemption was articulated in vague compacts purporting to advance political democracy. The Díaz regime served as a foil for Revolutionary rhetoric, which in turn sanctified the violence unleashed supposedly against the Porfirian entrenchment. Thus the Mexican intellectual viewed the violence brought about by the Revolution as a phase in the growth of national self-awareness.[15] "The Revolution was inevitable," the orator Jesús Urueta wrote, "a necessary and legitimate fact of our political life . . . that produced in a few months a hecatombe and even greater glory."[16] "The Revolution is the Revolu-

[15] See Daniel Cosío Villegas, "La escuela del servilismo," *La Antorcha* 1 (June 13, 1925), 19.

[16] Jesús Urueta, "Discurso de apertura en la convención del partido constitucional progresista," in *Obras completas*, p. 374.

tion" was the remark popularized to give finality to the convulsions that shook Mexico. Echoing Cabrera's "these" and "those," the Constitutionalist general Francisco L. Urquizo noted that there was no middle ground during the Revolution. One either laughed or cried; one was absolutely good or extremely bad; old patterns of morality crumbled and new virtues appeared.[17] It was a time when the *chingar* complex—the brutal put-down both verbal and physical—became the cultural response of marginal people living under a system that had perpetuated gross inequalities.

Thus violence was frequently placed in a context of the dionysian destruction of order and hierarchy and seen as an expression of desire and excess. For various political reasons some thought that Mexico was on a "vacation of crime";[18] the revolutionary who was a thief was *simpático*.[19] Historical scholarship has substantiated the image of violence as the force that radically rearranged Mexican life. The language and the look of the people changed, while groups and interests seemed to emerge out of nothing.[20] Indians became mestizos overnight.[21] People traveled, news was exchanged, and some communities in the midst of violence fleetingly found an ancient utopia.[22] The geopolitical map of Mexico was redrawn, with regions formerly peripheral to the core traditions of Mexico now thrust into a position of dominance.[23] The violence spawned by the Revolution assumed a lyrical quality in Mexican identity, conveying a sense of freedom and a renewal of traditional life that lessened the imitation of European culture. Much of the Revolutionary program would be linked to images of the initial violence—the Constitution, the novel, the mural, the *corrido* (ballad), and the *ejido* (communal land-holding).

[17] Francisco L. Urquizo, *Recuerdo que: visiones aisladas de la Revolución*, pp. 188–189.
[18] Luis Cabrera, "La Revolución dentro del gobierno," in *Obras políticas del Lic. Blas Urrea*, p. 271.
[19] Querido Moheno, *Sobre el ara sangrienta*, p. 3.
[20] Daniel Cosío Villegas, "Del Porfiriato a la Revolución," *Novedades*, November 2, 1952.
[21] Manuel González Ramírez, *La Revolución social de México, I: Las ideas —la violencia*, p. 250.
[22] See John Womack, Jr., *Zapata and the Mexican Revolution*, pp. 224–255.
[23] Héctor Aguilar Camín, *La frontera nómada: Sonora y la Revolución mexicana*, pp. 9–10.

But the violent fiesta, as intellectuals would conceive it, had no name: it had sprung new to purge centuries of tortured Mexican self-esteem and was incarnated almost surrealistically in Villa and Zapata. Neither a religious event nor as yet a cohesively political one, its meaning had to be invented through a historical justification of nationalism.

The idea of violence became interwoven with the vision of constructive change. If Madero was the agent in the political transition from one regime to the next, he was also a prophet of the new reaction to Mexican history, envisioning nationhood in a future context: "A new era has begun for our fatherland. We have reconquered our rights as citizens, and the Mexican is no longer the pariah who sadly carries the chains of tyranny. He is the proud citizen who exercises his political rights. This new era will be fecund for our fatherland, in art, learning, and industry." Such a transformation, Madero thought, committed the Mexican to greater purpose, and he urged self-reliance: Mexico was going to "govern itself alone. . . . I want every citizen to realize the immense responsibility of the fatherland. . . . In order to reconstruct the country, to get it on the road to progress, everyone should rely on himself . . . on his individual and collective efforts." [24] In effect, Madero was warning the Mexicans of the lethargy and paternalism in their history; thus it was a departure from Porfirism to encourage the individual to become socially and politically involved. This shift of attitude was to temper the older nineteenth-century liberalism while reinforcing the basis of selfhood. "We are worth more today than yesterday" was the way Jesús Urueta phrased it, and the poet Ramón López Velarde said that although "we are not living in a republic of angels, we are, thanks to Madero, living like men." [25] As the Revolution advanced, the intellectuals became fired by the possibility of contributing to the national well-being. According to a later commentator on the decade, it was a

[24] Francisco I. Madero, speech published in *Nueva Era*, November 1, 1911; idem, "Discursos pronunciados por el Sr. Madero en la ciudad de Puebla," in *Documentos históricos de la Revolución mexicana*, ed. Isidro Fabela, V, 431–432.

[25] Jesús Urueta, "Carne de cañon; carne de libertad," in *Obras completas*, p. 359; Ramón López Velarde, "Carta a Eduardo J. Correa," in *Prosa política*, p. 324.

"whole new vision of Mexican society" amounting to religious faith.[26] The notion of a new era and a new Mexican was to be constructed out of an intellectual revolution. Influenced by the European neoromantic reaction to positivism, Mexican thinkers were preoccupied at the beginning of the Revolution with concepts of morality, will, intuition, creative freedom, charity, and spiritual transcendence. Ideas expressed as "the exaltation of man" and "the opening of unlimited horizons"[27] reflected partial answers to the tasks posed by Madero. The philosopher Antonio Caso spearheaded the attack on positivism with his critical melange derived from Kant, Bergson, and nineteenth-century French spiritualism, but it was José Vasconcelos, another philosopher, who applied more concretely the new romantic thought to Mexico. As described by Vasconcelos, the struggle was between *maderismo* ("heroism and almost saintliness") and *porfirismo* ("contumacy and evil"). He said that the "values of consciousness constitute a superior reality, which can and must dominate the chaos of events. He who decrees the spiritual over the worldly will see his destiny take a leap. We took that leap for the destiny of Mexico. For that we engaged in revolution, to impose spirit over reality by force of the people."[28] The polarity of violence and vision compelled the thinker to predicate the search for Mexican identity on the challenges posed by the Revolution; hence the rapidly growing nationalistic literature exuded fascination with a Mexico that was alluring yet forbidding in its hitherto concealed opportunities for nation making.

Know the "Soul of the Pueblo"

The quest for national identity defined the contemporary experience as crisis, transition, exploration, and self-discovery. As the country reacted to values presumed to repress rather than liberate the Mexican, intellectuals were led inwardly to the pueblo, relating

[26] Cosío Villegas, "Justificación de la tirada," in *Ensayos y notas*, I, 14–15.

[27] Vicente Lombardo Toledano, "El sentido humanista de la Revolución mexicana," in *Conferencias del Ateneo de la Juventud*, ed. Juan Hernández Luna, p. 179.

[28] José Vasconcelos, *Ulises criollo*, p. 414.

its culture to the awareness of daily life brought forth by the col-
lapse of one regime and the birth of the next. Populism now colored
intellectual life and emerged in the 1911 Madero–Pino Suárez elec-
tion when students were mobilized to politicize the pueblo.

So much has been written about the disruptive effects of the
Revolution that one has the impression of cultural stagnation during
the course of violence. However, there was a healthy, if disconnect-
ed, institutional growth such as Sierra and Chávez called for in 1910.
In education it is obvious that instruction increasingly reflected
the new Mexican humanism that would characterize the post-
Revolutionary generations. In 1912 the faculty of the National Preparatory School included Antonio Caso, professor of logic; Rubén
Campos, professor of national language; Pedro Henríquez Ureña,
professor of general literature. In 1912–1913 the faculty of the School
of Superior Studies had Alfonso Reyes teaching Spanish literature;
Pedro Henríquez Ureña, Anglo-American literature; and Antonio
Caso, esthetics and general philosophy.[29] Since the majority of Mexico's important intellectuals would pass through one or both these
schools, it is significant that the curriculum that would reinforce the
trends conducive to an enhanced national consciousness was developing early in the Revolution.

By 1912 the Ateneo de la Juventud had become the Ateneo de
México, but the rarified literary atmosphere of the organization assumed a more mundane air as its members organized a university
extension service that became the Popular University of Mexico and
functioned until 1922. The Academy of Industrial Arts was founded
by the architects Samuel Chávez, Carlos Lazo, and Federico Maris-
cal and opened a night school in workers' districts.[30] Andrés Molina
Enríquez proposed the governmental organization of popular arts
and crafts.[31] The amphitheater of the National Preparatory School,
the Arbeu Theater, and other buildings and patios served to orient

[29] "Faculty List," August 31, 1912, AGN, RIP & BA, Leg. 11, Exp. 225;
and "Faculty List," May 30, 1913, AEC, Caja 12.
[30] See Alberto J. Pani, *Apuntes autobiográficos*, I, 111–112, 121–139;
John S. Innes, "The Universidad Popular Mexicana," *The Americas* 30 (July,
1973), 110–122; and "Report," March 27, 1917, AGN, RIP & BA, Leg. 2, Exp.
30.
[31] Andrés Molina Enríquez, "Proposal," May 27, 1915, AGN, RIP & BA,
Leg. 20, Exp. 10.

culture along populist lines.[32] The Popular Orfeon of the Díaz era was enlarged, and its activities illustrate the attempt of the government to identify with the masses through choral music.[33] The open-air schools of painting as the pedagogical counterpart of the mural movement successfully demonstrated the populist dimension of the Revolution. Clearly the institutional basis of the cultural renaissance of the 1920's was being laid during the violent phase of the Revolution. To the extent that the Mexican's complex past, as well as his chaotic present and his perplexing social character, was illuminated, the Revolution had begun to expand the trends of the preceding decade by instilling in the Mexican the need to know his country.

Esthetics and the fine arts were now to be integrated into basic educational criteria.[34] Officially art was to be democratized and no longer taught by strict European rules.[35] In the National Preparatory School, curriculum reform called for an expanded program in the sciences as well as in the humanities. The study of Mexican history was emphasized in view of the lack of methodology in that discipline.[36] A national academy of history was funded whose membership would include Mexican as well as foreign scholars.[37] Always the purpose of educational reform was either to stimulate a popular identity or to intensify the focus on Mexico.[38] In medical research, for example, plans were made for a "Mexican pharmacology." As Sierra had urged, native plants, herbs, and drugs were analyzed, and even historical sources were tapped to provide scientific continuity to the project.[39]

[32] "Datos para el Mensaje Presidencial del 15 de septiembre de 1912," AGN, RIP & BA, Leg. 1, Exp. 4.

[33] "Report of the Orfeon Popular," February 28, 1914, AGN, RIP & BA, Leg. 13, Exp. 310.

[34] "Report," National Preparatory School, December 17, 1913, AEC, Caja 9.

[35] "Agreement," October 27, 1914, AGN, RIP & BA, Leg. 10, Exp. 5; "Plan of Reorganization," May 13, 1916, AGN, RIP & BA, Leg. 4, Exp. 200.

[36] "Report of University Council on Curriculum Proposal of National Preparatory School," December 22, 1913; and "Report," National Preparatory School, December 17, 1913, both in AEC, Caja 9.

[37] "Decree," June 11, 1914, AGN, RIP & BA, Leg. 49, Exp. 1; "Minutes," June 25, 1914, Exp. 5.

[38] Ezequiel Chávez to Rector of National University, March 31, 1914, AEC, Caja 6.

[39] "Report," National Medical Institute, 1910–1911, AGN, RIP & BA, Leg. 9, Exp. 171.

Summarizing these changes, Pedro Henríquez Ureña noted that positivism was definitely on the wane in Mexico and outlined the new educational theory. Comparing Mexican to United States and European educational institutions, he argued that in the latter change was constant because it had a legal basis, whereas in Mexico it depended upon the political system. Thus progress, he concluded, was more difficult and was achieved not by evolution but by revolution. In a line of reasoning similar to that later pursued by Samuel Ramos, he maintained that Barreda's plan was important for its age, but that in emphasizing science over the humanities, it broke with "the best of Mexico's intellectual traditions." Eventually only pedantry resulted from such reform, but this had been recently rectified by the restoration of philosophy to education, not the positivistic variety, but one that dealt with the great problems—knowledge, existence, and life values.[40] Here, of course, was the framework for the new era of Mexican self-analysis.

Not infrequently this change produced a sense of groping as well as fulfillment. Discussing the transformation of Mexican institutions wrought by the Revolutionary reforms, Agustín Aragón realized that it was necessary to create a "national consciousness" and called for a knowledge of the "national individuality" to reinforce civic consciousness.[41] When the Revolution took a turn for the worse after Madero's assassination in 1913, it brought despair to some intellectuals at the same time that it deepened their moral preoccupation with their country. Whether writing from distrust of the Revolution or from sympathy, Aragón stated that an understanding of the "grievous crises" of Mexico could come only from a study of quotidian life. In order to know the "biological, social, and moral atmosphere of Mexico," he grandiosely suggested that one begin not with political sources but with an examination of the "soul of the pueblo."[42]

It was not fading positivists like Aragón, however, who were to give new direction to Mexican thought in this decade. Intellectual leadership was to emerge from the middle-class youth dissatisfied

[40] Ureña to Julio Jiménez Rueda, January 30, 1914, AEC, Caja 9.
[41] Agustín Aragón, "Notas políticas," *Revista Positiva* 11 (December, 1911), 643.
[42] Agustín Aragón, "México," *Revista Positiva* 14 (May, 1914), 247.

with Porfirian norms, from romantic dissidents preoccupied with Mexico's cultural roots, and above all from those imbued with the fervor of Revolutionary humanism. Such categories describe Antonio Caso, who in the difficult period between 1912 and 1915 turned away from abstract philosophy to enter the improvised and often ill-starred course of political involvement. Caso was a prime example of how the Revolution forced the intellectuals to a soul-searching analysis of their history, which culminated in their attempt to give meaning to the confusion surrounding Mexico's national existence. Caso had accepted the stock condemnation of positivism and was hardly contributing to the scholarly investigation of ideas at this time. Yet his writings are noteworthy because they illustrate how the political and intellectual revolutions, initially unconnected, were beginning to fuse.

In two articles, whose themes were to be evoked by the generation of Samuel Ramos and beyond, Caso initiated a Mexicanist inquiry that summarized previous knowledge in light of the Revolution. Accepting democracy as a growing trend in western civilization, Caso focused on the gap between theory and its implementation, building his critique on "Bovarism," the concept of the disparity between the ideal and reality, which he based on the elaboration of Flaubert's characters by Jules de Gaultier. Trying to elucidate the reasons for Mexico's political turmoils, Caso argued that the country bore the repercussions of a too hastily imposed federal system and that the weight of its colonial past was feebly countered by the idealism of the 1857 Constitution whose precepts were scarcely followed in the pursuit of democracy. It was necessary, Caso said, to adapt the constitution to the historical circumstances and even to the moral environment; because this had not been the case, Mexican democracy was "tragically imperfect." The colonial heritage, manifested in the formidable problems of education, justice, suffrage, and the economy, conspired against a workable democracy, and although from time to time "apostles" appeared to redeem the nation, once in power they exhibited the very defects in political behavior they had formerly criticized.[43]

Caso's Mexicanist diagnosis was structured on several of the

[43] Antonio Caso, "El bovarismo de la ley," in *Obras completas*, II, 181–186.

prevailing notions of the Hispanic character, which led him to anti-Arielist conclusions. Spain, he said, had bequeathed attitudinal underpinnings of Bovarism to Latin America in a creole lethargy and quixotism, one marked by caution and tradition and the other by enthusiasm and idealism. Caso also viewed unfavorably the fact that the culture and temperament of the Hispanic peoples were also shaped by French influence. Caso outlined three eras for the national period in Mexican history: the early or Jacobin period, when the distance between the ideal and the real was enormous; the Porfirian period, whose positivist rationale developed one sector of the nation at the expense of the others; and the 1910 Revolution, which had become the justifiable reaction to the assassination of Madero. Identifying with the Constitutionalist cause, Caso looked to a political synthesis that would obviate the mistakes of past regimes and urged the convocation of a Constitutional Congress. Interestingly, he provided a cue to one of the later themes of his pupil Daniel Cosío Villegas by pointing out that the use of high-sounding words had damaged governmental credibility.[44]

If Caso sought the roots of Mexico's contemporary predicament by delving into its colonial heritage vis-à-vis republican idealism, Manuel Gamio apotheosized the age by basing his nationalistic theories on the new social and intellectual interest in the pueblo. Educated in the positivist tradition and a student of Franz Boas at Columbia University, Gamio was young enough to feel the romantic thrust of the Revolution and became one of its enthusiasts and finest technocrats. Like José Vasconcelos, he fused education, politics, and thought, action and the ideal, the universal and *lo mexicano*. His book, *Forjando patria*, which foreshadowed his work at Teotihuacán and launched social anthropology in Mexico and which reflects both his positivist training and his Revolutionary commitment, is indispensable for the study of the year 1916 in Mexico, when the Constitutional Congress was being convened.[45] Much of the subsequent national experience is anticipated in the miscellaneous chapters of

[44] Caso, "Jacobismo y positivismo," in *Obras completas*, II, 190–198.

[45] For a review of Gamio's life and work, see Juan Comas, "La vida y la obra de Manuel Gamio," in *Estudios antropológicos publicados en homenaje al doctor Manuel Gamio*, pp. 1–26; for a discussion of Gamio's "integral education" and his social experiments at Teotihuacán, see Ramón Eduardo Ruiz, *Mexico: The Challenge of Poverty and Illiteracy*, pp. 43–44.

Gamio's book. For instance, he dealt with the role of woman in Mexican society. Exemplifying the Revolution's exaltation of the woman, Gamio described her capacity to harmonize divergent experiences—the earthy and the spiritual, the natural and the artificial. Possessing "innate psychological judgment," the Mexican woman knew the weakness and strength of an issue, and Gamio concluded that she was the woman par excellence.[46]

Gamio elaborated a program aimed at incorporating the Indian into national life, thus illustrating the Revolutionary emphasis on the role of the Indian in constructing the patria. Yet his book synthesized many of the identity issues whose roots lay in the colonial period. Raising once more the question of whether the Indian could become westernized, Gamio answered yes, explaining that the incorporation of the Indian would create a homogeneous nation by unifying language and culture. The Indian remained misunderstood, he said, because of the lack of communication between him and the dominant society, a problem that would be resolved only when an indigenist viewpoint prevailed. This bias pervaded Gamio's idea of Mexican history, the beginning of which, he argued, lay not with the arrival of the Spaniards but in the pre-Colombian era. Thus he thought that Mexican history should not be viewed as the growth of European institutions, but should be refocused to include knowledge relevant to Mexico as a whole and to each phase of its evolution. Many aspects of the country's social problems grew worse, he maintained, because the people knew nothing of themselves, and he concluded that the study of pre-Hispanic history was hindered by inadequate perspective and methodology. Discussing the conditions necessary for a viable national culture, Gamio listed ethnic homogeneity and stressed the role of *mestizaje* in shaping the popular acceptance of Mexican identity. Coupled with this emphasis on social process was the enjoinder to "know Mexico." Gamio lashed out at the sculptor who copied Olympus rather than finding inspiration in *lo mexicano*, and he took to task the armchair intellectuals who read Spencer and James and knew the problems of Europe but not those of Mexico. Contending that contemporary social science methodology did not apply to Mexico, Gamio urged the scholar to put

[46] Manuel Gamio, *Forjando patria*, pp. 129–132.

aside his foreign books, get out and "see the pueblo," and "peek into its soul."[47] Gamio's book was widely read in an age of uncertainty, and one who was inspired by its rational, populist message was Alvaro Obregón.[48]

The writers who gave direction to the Revolution in the years 1910–1920 found a Mexico still in the making, chaotic, but whose contours were becoming increasingly familiar. Amid the political uncertainty a sense of renewal was slowly binding the nation together, and clearly the Mexican of the pueblo was emerging. The educator Abraham Castellanos criticized the idea that the Mexicans were "Latin" in spirit and, supporting their cultural uniqueness, argued for a Mexican "species."[49] Yet the country remained as discrete fragments lying about like potsherds in the mound-studded valleys. Several regimes failed to cement them together, though all entertained the illusion of doing so. All proposed that nationhood be re-created, which for some intellectuals was a question not only of politics but also of history posed as social awareness and knowledge of self. If politics were to speak of a Mexican identity, ideas must be made to balance the disparate elements of the patria. Thus the notions of the "national soul," the "national character," the hypothesized relationships between education and native cultural and behavioral norms, between law and reality, between nationalism and cosmopolitanism would emerge in the forefront of the enlarged Revolution.

Lo Mexicano in a Revolutionary Decade

The interest in defining the national character, widespread from the eighteenth century on, was not substantially altered during the years 1910–1920, except insofar as the Revolution deepened that preoccupation by making the idea of the Mexican even more problematical. Mexican positivism, in the main ignoring selfhood, had

[47] Ibid., pp. 9–10, 64, 25–28, 97–99.

[48] See Linda B. Hall, "Alvaro Obregón and the Mexican Revolution, 1912–1920: The Origins of Institutionalization" (Ph.D. diss., Columbia University, 1976), pp. 296–298.

[49] Abraham Castellanos, *Discursos a la nación mexicana sobre la educación nacional*, p. 98.

supported concepts of nationality through the principles of evolution and had reinforced social values with Darwinian notions of racial inferiority. The Revolution infused neoromantic idealism into the dry formulae of positivism, and the synthesis was exemplified in Gamio's Mexicanist analysis structured on subjective as well as scientific criteria.

Thus the age-old concern with national character was given Revolutionary overtones and the trappings of contemporaneity once it could be made contingent upon the goals of national change. This new paradigm was contained in an essay by Joaquín R. Ortega, a positivist caught in the controversy of the Revolution, who wrote of the need to extirpate those aspects of the national character which inhibited reform.[50] In his classic essay, *La querella de México* (1915), written at the time the Revolutionaries were most depressed, Martín Luis Guzmán also pointed up the deficiencies of the Mexican character, analyzing Mexican institutions as reflections of violence and apathy. Appalled by the apparent senselessness of the Revolution, Guzmán suggested that Mexican politics could be explained as the unequal struggle between a fatalistic majority and an optimistic minority, noting that the masses were politically indifferent and reflected the national mood only during minority victories, when they became enthusiastic spectators. Guzmán thought that the formal causes of the Revolution were materialistic, yet he contended that the country suffered a malaise compounded of ambition, injustice, brutality, and the absence of real nationhood. Employing a stock criticism of social behavior, he assailed the Mexican for his bloody spectacles, his practice of summary execution, and for enslaving his reason to passion.[51]

While the Indian impinged on many aspects of Mexicanist thought in this decade, he elicited no uniform response from the intellectuals. Where Gamio saw the redemption of the Indian through indigenist programs, Guzmán focused on the complex factors that had largely destroyed the Indian. For Guzmán the Indian was already mutilated spiritually before the Conquest. Forced to become

---

[50] Joaquín R. Ortega, "El verdadero plan," *Revista Positiva* 12 (August, 1912), 411.

[51] Martín Luis Guzmán, *La querella de México, a orillas del Hudson, y otras páginas*, pp. 11–12, 79–82, 239.

a sacrificial warrior and virtually enslaved by caciques, he had no life of his own. Guzmán's cynicism was evident in his conclusion that the fall of Quetzalcóatl symbolized the decline of indigenous culture, a decline only aggravated by the Conquest.[52]

Other writers viewed the negative characteristics of Mexican behavior in terms of what came after the Conquest. For the educator Paulino Machorro Narváez, the national character had its roots in the colonial period, when prohibitions on New World development created apathy toward government affairs. At the same time that a native social psychology was evolving, Machorro explained, the Mexican was being alienated by those who ruled. In a line of reasoning similar to that of Guzmán, Machorro stated that from independence on, the majority of the people became mere spectators of the state, unaware of the important issues. Left skeptical by his negligible civil function, the Mexican saw politics not as the means to serve his country, but as a chance to rob and to tyrannize. Gradually the masses learned they could challenge authority only through social disruption and, for its part, elite power evolved into despotism.[53] Violence, of course, was the Revolutionary legacy that compounded the earlier historical experience of lurking hostility. Typical of the attacks on the morality of civil conflict was the complaint voiced by Carlos Trejo Lerdo de Tejada that ambition, resentment, and intolerance had led to an inferior level of culture and government. Resorting to the popular sanguinary metaphor, he called Mexico a collective monster with the furies of an animal, either killing for blood or dying at the hands of the enemy.[54]

Not every intellectual, however, approached the topic of national character to vent his political frustration. Justo Sierra turned to behavioral typology as a key to history, while Manuel Gamio used it as a point of departure for creating a sense of nationhood. As the Revolution wore on, the concept of Mexican selfhood endowed with distinctive traits was linked more frequently with the new educational goals, perhaps in tacit admission that social factors could slow the impetus to progress as much as "character." To the extent that

---

[52] Gamio, *Forjando patria*, p. 21; Guzmán, *La querella de México*, p. 18.
[53] Paulino Machorro Narváez, *La enseñanza en México*, pp. 75–76, 86–93.
[54] Carlos Trejo Lerdo de Tejada, *La Revolución y el nacionalismo*, pp. 105–106.

reform measures aimed at raising the consciousness of the masses, the intellectuals tried to provide answers to the questions concerning the unique cultural circumstances of the Mexican. Thus in a work that anticipated Gamio's idea of integrated society, Abraham Castellanos argued that before preparing an educational program for the Indians, it was necessary to consider their "psychic nature" and to adapt textbooks to their "racial peculiarities."[55]

The racial focus was common in educational theory of the time. One has only to compare *La sociología mexicana y la educación nacional* (1916) of Julio S. Hernández, a positivist educator, with his earlier writings during the Díaz period to grasp the transition in thought from the Porfiriato to the Revolution. Although its cohesion derives from a positivist framework, the work reeks of the new romantic ideals of the patria, the "Mexican soul," and the virtues of Mexicanism. It is the statement of a man identified with his country's problems, a document that testifies to the optimism and search for new values engendered by the Revolution. Using a speculative approach to understand random social and historical factors, the book is a critique of the national character for the purpose of improving education. Hernández wanted Mexican culture to reflect "racial idiosyncracies"; thus he stood midway between Chávez and Ramos. He called for the "bio-socio-psychological knowledge" of races, structuring his book on the sociology of Indians, creoles, and mestizos. Among the character types discussed in Hernández's study, the dissembler is noteworthy inasmuch as it prefigured the post-Ramos preoccupation with masks.[56]

The national character generally was treated in this decade as it had been for a century on the basis of the racial assumptions regarding the Indian, creole, and the mestizo, although most writers also illustrated the vagaries of Revolutionary politics as well as the intellectual tension generated by the forces of change. Reflecting upon the Indian, Pedro Lamicq, the *maderista* pamphleteer, concluded that Mexico did not have a true patria, because its society was divided between two antagonistic classes. Lamicq imbued the

---

[55] Castellanos, *Discursos a la nación mexicana*, p. 9.

[56] Julio S. Hernández, *La sociología mexicana y la educación nacional*, pp. 306–309, 240.

term *creole* with a psychosocial meaning, arguing that the "creole prejudice" was a prominent attitude of the middle- and upper-class intellectuals, businessmen, and bureaucrats, who deemed creole values superior to those of the Indian and the mestizo. The creole prejudice impeded progress, Lamicq explained; even the Indian might acquire this bias once he succeeded in white society and wished to forget his origins. If Mexico wanted to enter the twentieth century, Lamicq urged, it must divest itself of everything colonial or creole.[57]

While most social critics by this time agreed that the creole had had a pernicious effect in Mexican history and that the Indian, whose character was determined by historical circumstances, had "virtues" and was capable of being incorporated into national life, there was no consensus regarding the mestizo. Martín Luis Guzmán, for example, thought that the mestizo exemplified the revolutionary mystique and discussed a mestizo Mexico that was alternately peaceful and violent. Violence notwithstanding, it was mestizo Mexico that Guzmán poetized. The real Mexico, he wrote, was not found in its well-known extremes, but in the meeting of the two cultures that resulted in mestizo life in the small village.[58]

Luis Cabrera, on the other hand, thought the mestizo could not be typified. Arguing that the idea of the mestizo could not be static, Cabrera saw the evolution of the mestizo beginning with the Conquest and continuing into the twentieth century. There was, he contended, no mestizo population differentiated from the Indian or the white population, but a varied group that, depending on their degree of acculturation, might be classified as Indian or white. Emphasizing that Mexican social problems were not racial but educational, Cabrera maintained that the educated Indian was socially equal to the mestizo. If Gamio hinted at indigenism as the solution to the problem of nationality, Cabrera, echoing Molina Enríquez, looked to *mestizaje* and education to absorb the white immigrants into the population.[59]

[57] Pedro Lamicq, *Madero*, pp. 138–139, 369–371, 597.
[58] Guzmán, *La querella de México*, pp. 73, 173.
[59] Luis Cabrera, "México y los mexicanos," in *Tres intelectuales hablan sobre México*, pp. 8–9.

Thus in an age purported to be revolutionary, the national character was often seen as a factor in causal relationships. The Indian or the mestizo made plausible this or that social characteristic, event, solution, or program. The national character provided the hard-core symbols for change and buttressed the new identity that certified the aspirations of those wanting power and the opportunity to be Mexicans with a status superior to the limited enfranchisement of their predecessors. In a country still desperately charting the course of its affairs, the national character could be invoked to excuse error or to boost prestige. It was one way of generating a sense of Mexicanness, since the moral and the historical were thrust together in a palpable synthesis of the minute and the grandiose, the locality and the encompassing unit of sovereign achievement.

Mexico and the Outside World

One of the paradoxes of the Revolution was that it occurred at a time when the expansion of technology was reaching the distant regions of the earth and, in the name of progress or not, was inducing a leveling syndrome in the native cultural context. The Revolution catalyzed social action and created new forces of mobility and mechanization as well as the need for mass communication, and while these were necessary conditions for nationhood, they would, by replacing the patria chica with a patria grande, significantly diminish traditional life. As Mexico advanced toward modernity through the Revolution, it was inevitably brought into the sphere of world influence, and this required that identity be structured on external as well as internal factors.

Their awareness heightened by the Revolution, many thinkers argued Mexico's sensitive position vis-à-vis the outside menace. Explaining that his people had no intellectual autonomy and passively accepted foreign judgments on themselves, Martín Luis Guzmán bemoaned the fact that Mexico looked abroad for the answers to its problems. And Julio S. Hernández spoke of the selling out to alien values, a phenomenon later to be called *malinchismo* (after Cortés's Aztec mistress who advised him on native intrigue), evident among the country's leaders. Another writer, observing that during the

Revolution the wide-brimmed sombrero had been exchanged for the Stetson hat, saw *lo mexicano* disappearing before cosmopolitanism and mass consumption. The machine, usually associated with the spread of western technology, began to be included in the list of items contributing to the destruction of native traditions; therefore solutions were offered based on the myth of the return to native roots.[60] There was no escape from this burden forced on Mexico by the continuity of its past and the challenge to foment change under the guise of progress.

Just how serious this dilemma was could be seen in Antonio Caso's assessment of Wilson's Latin American policy and what that policy implied for the structure of Mexican history. Acknowledging that Wilson's presence had been felt in Latin America following his role in the Niagara Conference and in the downfall of Huerta, Caso shrewdly analyzed the shape of United States–Latin American relations midway between Big Stick and Good Neighbor. According to Caso, Wilson's puritanical vision of world affairs put him in the camp of the anti-imperialists, but his doctrinaire adherence to constitutionality as the determinant of democracy, though inherently reasonable, could have only disastrous results for Latin America. Caso's article was written not long after the overthrow of Huerta, during a time when Wilson's attitude toward Mexico was more circumspect than ever and when each caudillo knew that recognition by the United States meant arms, possibly loans, and probably victory for his faction.

However, Caso converted a rather superficial, political response into a statement of profounder diplomatic significance regarding the theme of imitation in Latin American history. He commented that the American president was perhaps unaware that Latin American constitutions seldom reflected their own national actualities but all too often copied foreign models. Since no Latin American country, Caso thought, could be fully constitutional, an inflexible United States policy toward Latin American government was unrealistic and could become an instrument of Yankee aggression. Nevertheless,

---

[60] Guzmán, *La querella de México*, pp. 14–16; Hernández, *La sociología mexicana*, pp. 20, 306–307; Jesús Villalpando, "Lo nacional, lo mexicano, lo pintoresco," *El Nacional*, November 18, 1917.

the facts of life dictated that United States tutelage was inevitable, and it therefore behooved Mexico to put its constitutional house in order.[61]

In a similar vein, Martín Luis Guzmán also viewed Mexican–United States relations in historical perspective, noting that World War I had refocused the problems caused by geography and unequal development. No nation, Guzmán contended, could afford to ignore another, but in the physical character of the relationship lay a spiritual crisis that was the real source of misunderstanding between the two countries. The United States, he argued, even though it was beginning to show signs of understanding Latin America, still displayed its ignorance regarding the area, in particular Mexico, which reacted with xenophobia toward the northern neighbor. But Mexico's attitude was self-defeating, Guzmán added, since geographical reality urged a greater identity with the United States. Conversely, Guzmán attacked the traditional policy of United States condescension toward Mexico and that country's ethnocentric evaluation of Mexican internal problems, although he lauded the idealistic tenor of Wilson's position on Mexico.[62]

Venustiano Carranza based his legitimacy on constitutionality and was recognized by the United States, yet by 1919, with his control over the country still precarious, one of his envoys, Toribio Esquivel Obregón, discussed the Mexican situation along Casonian lines and with prophetic overtones for post-Revolutionary Mexico. The Mexican government, he argued, essentially rested its consolidation on foreign recognition, in the process forgetting the social forces that had determined the origins of its struggle. Once entrenched in power, the government maintained itself by paradoxically relying on help from abroad and the resignation, not the support, of the masses, whose responses to problems were now viewed as crimes. This system of power was made palatable to the public by the government's hollow expression of sovereignty.

Esquivel thereupon outlined a history of Mexican dependency upon Europe and the United States, the gist of which was that the country had never honestly turned to itself for the secret of har-

[61] Antonio Caso, "La doctrina Wilson, sin Wilson," in *Obras completas*, II, 186–190.
[62] Guzmán, *La querella de México*, pp. 52–54.

monious progress. As a result, the Mexicans had become self-deprecating and doubted their capacity to sustain nationhood. But there was hope, Esquivel thought. If the Mexicans' energies had never been socialized to the extent necessary for the mass undertakings and cooperation in developed countries, the Mexican people were nonetheless the equals of others, and now with Mexico almost forced to become more resourceful, the way was open, Esquivel concluded, to improve national self-esteem.[63]

In examining the criticisms of the foreign influence on Mexico, one comes full circle. In suggesting, as Guzmán did, that the Mexican was deficient in self-awareness because he submitted easily to outside criteria, the tutors of national regeneration could continue to exhort their wayward compatriots to know themselves. The dialectic between the wider and the parochial cultures now becomes meaningful in light of the historical process. Through a keener perception of self, the Mexican could exorcise the alien bogeyman in his midst; conversely, the inexorable foreign pressure might determine the intensity of nationalism. Hence it is possible to see the unity between the political, economic, and cultural sectors of twentieth-century Mexico. Each dared to test the limits of nationalism; each at times felt the push of the foreign from behind and the pull of the native before. Mexico's historic struggle to be a contemporary in the Atlantic world could be consummated only if the country could balance within itself both native and western values. Theoretically the Revolution would implement this adjustment as it oversaw the nation's emergence from underdevelopment; however, the blueprint for change would yield results that would fall short of successful entry into the modern world.

Hispanism and Nationalism

A noteworthy example in this decade of how Mexican identity could be approached from a position outside the national context is contained in Alfonso Reyes's "Mindscape of Anáhuac," an essay written in Spain in 1915 and first published in 1917. Reyes had had

---

[63] Toribio Esquivel Obregón to Venustiano Carranza, May 3, 1919, in *Documentos históricos de la Revolución mexicana*, ed. Isidro and Josefina E. de Fabela, XVIII, 254–255.

ample preparation to absorb the Spanish thought fermenting since
the generation of '98 set new standards for literary and social analysis. A member of the Ateneo de la Juventud, the group that spearheaded the revolt against positivism and launched Mexico's intellectual revolution in the twentieth century, Reyes had already
expressed his Mexican orientation in discussing the poetry of Manuel José Othón.[64] Having left Mexico in the wake of his father's
debacle in the Decena Trágica in 1913,[65] he bore with him the seeds
of the new Revolutionary culture, and his easy acceptance of Hispanism would allow his creative perspective to be shaped by both
Spain and Mexico.[66]

Reyes's native cultural experience was now infused with Spanish
intellectual interest in Mexico. For several decades Spanish intellectuals had been kindling the fires of Hispanic reintegration. An ideal
community was envisioned based on blood, language, past glory,
trade interests, and spiritual kinship. A manifestation of the Hispanic liberal-conservative conflict, frequently uniting the two forces,
or perhaps the gesture of a dying empire, or playing on the Latin
American fear of United States encroachment, Hispanism, though
never successful in a practical way, was significant in the intellectual
life of Spain and the Latin American nations.[67] Thus when Reyes
arrived as representative of a New World rediscovering itself, the
Spaniards were at no loss to recognize him. One whose help was to
be consequential to Reyes's Spanish sojourn was the journalist and
philosopher José Ortega y Gasset, who in 1914 published *Medita-*

[64] Alfonso Reyes, "Los poemas rústicos de Manuel José Othón," in *Conferencias del Ateneo de la Juventud*, pp. 41–56.

[65] For Bernardo Reyes's part in the Revolution, see Charles C. Cumberland, *Mexican Revolution: Genesis under Madero*; and Peter Calvert, *The
Mexican Revolution, 1910–1914: The Diplomacy of Anglo-American Conflict.*

[66] See Alfonso Reyes, "Treno para José Ortega y Gasset," *Cuadernos
Americanos* 15 (January–April, 1956), 65–67; idem, "Rumbo al sur," in *Obras
completas*, II, 141–150. Reyes explained that exile had induced his reflection on
Mexico and that one day he would try to write a "history of the national idea"
in Mexico (Reyes to Guzmán, March 12, 1914, Archivo Alfonso Reyes; hereinafter abbreviated as AAR). Elsewhere he emphasized his promotion of Mexican literature in Spain (Reyes to Enrique González Martínez, April 23, 1917,
AAR). For Reyes's double perspective, see Barbara Bockus Aponte, *Alfonso
Reyes and Spain*, pp. 193–194.

[67] Fredrick B. Pike, *Hispanismo, 1898–1936*, p. 230.

ciones del Quijote, his first major effort to characterize the Spanish spirit. Ortega welcomed Reyes, giving him employment on his periodicals and sponsoring his projects. This contact between Reyes and Ortega marked the first instance of Ortega's influence on Mexican intellectual life and would establish a mutual affinity between the two nations for more than half a century and provide the basis for much of the theory of *lo mexicano*.[68]

Over the years "Mindscape of Anáhuac" has become Reyes's best-known piece, a curious distinction in view of the unoriginal nature of the essay. The plan was simple enough: a re-creation, or vision, of aspects of daily life during the conquest of Tenochtitlán based on accounts by the chroniclers. To sing the grandeur of Anáhuac had been a stock theme of Mexicanists for centuries; Cortés, Díaz del Castillo, Balbuena, Humboldt, Prescott, and Velasco had all spread the fame of the Valley. The latest effort had been that of Julio Guerrero. Reyes's essay, however, occupied a category of its own because it illustrated the convergence of historical, political, and esthetic factors during the Revolution and how Mexican identity could be construed from a Hispanist viewpoint. Moreover, the piece was like a prolegomenon to local history, a subject Reyes would quietly bring to the attention of historians in the 1950's.[69] Reyes's role was twofold: he would make Spain understand the New World, just as he would discover Mexico through Spain.[70] In "Mindscape of Anáhuac" Reyes fused Mexican nationalism with greater Hispanic civilization, in the reverse order of the sixteenth-century European who conveyed the New World to Europe. As writer, Reyes assumed the guise of New World man emerging from his colonial cocoon to show that he had body and color like the other species of the earth.

[68] See José Gaos, *Sobre Ortega y Gasset*, p. 102; Bockus Aponte, *Alfonso Reyes and Spain*, pp. 95–101. For a review of Ortega's influence on Mexican intellectuals, see Leopoldo Zea, "Ortega el americano," *Cuadernos Americanos* 15 (January–April, 1956), 132–145. Ortega's formal influence on Mexico can be dated from 1914 to 1969, the date of the death of José Gaos, one of Ortega's protegés exiled in Mexico. The works of Gaos's last students, however, illustrate the Orteguian-Gaosian influence in the study of ideas in Mexico. Among these see Javier Ocampo, *Las ideas de un día*; and Palacios, "La idea oficial de la Revolución mexicana."

[69] See Luis González, *Invitación a la microhistoria*, p. 73.

[70] Bockus Aponte, *Alfonso Reyes and Spain*, pp. 185, 193.

Here was the classic Hispanic humanism of Las Casas put in a new frame of reference that impelled the twentieth-century Mexican to enter the western world without loss of identity.

Reyes's essay is divided into four parts and begins with a discussion of the sixteenth-century literature of exploration and discovery, underscoring the Conquest as historical event and source of rich description. Significantly Reyes observes that the chroniclers saw the new lands through the eyes of their European readership, who responded to elements of surprise if not exaggeration. The New World mindscape emerges from the Ramusio collection of voyages, whose illustrations Reyes skillfully uses to establish the pictorial context of the essay. A panorama of geography and history unfolds in the "gradual conquest of shores" by men whom Reyes identifies as the "sons of Ulysses," suggesting the classical origins of European exploration. Describing the natives of "dream islands" and their uncomplicated daily life in coastal Africa, he recapitulates the European myth of a tropical paradise, his style redolent of the Columbian idyll in the Caribbean.

Approaching the New World, Reyes hints at the course of European penetration from the coast inland. Abruptly he concludes his perusal of the illustrations by turning to their images of plant life in Anáhuac, disarmingly applying the term *Mexican* for the first time to the cactus. Stating that the Valley of Mexico has a "new kind of nature," Reyes imparts to the essay a Mexican mood in his mythical description of the flora: the maguey, which draws its water from the rocks; the organ cactus, used to mark boundaries; the nopal, whose discs are an "emblematic flower" seemingly created to decorate a coat of arms. The harsh environment usually associated with the cactus perhaps led Reyes to focus on the willful desiccation of the Valley from the time of Netzahualcóyotl to Porfirio Díaz. Reyes employs this ecological disaster symbolically to explain three "monarchical regimes": Aztec Mexico, New Spain, and the Díaz regime, which he calls the "great political fiction that gave us thirty years of Augustan peace."

But this observation was national in content, and Reyes was writing the essay in Europe, so the "New World traveler," as he styled himself, had to answer the Europeans' naïve questions on Mexico. Yes, there are trees in America, and what is more, an "Ameri-

can Castile" higher than theirs, "more harmonious" and "less bleak."
Castile, he explains, brings forth ascetic thought and Mexico quick,
realistic thought—the one is essentially tragic, the other plastically
rich. Casting a barb at European writers who titillated their readers
with the tropical environment of the New World at the expense of
other regions, Reyes attempts to rectify this misplaced identity by
presenting Anáhuac as an alternative environment to the "poetry of
hammock and fan." Anáhuac was "better" and more "salutary" for
those who enjoyed a "responsive will" and "clear mind."

Nearing the end of the first section, Reyes makes some thematic
shifts that set the focus for the rest of the essay. He wants to single
out the environment of central Mexico as the most characteristic of
the country: "The most appropriate image of our nature is found in
the regions of the central plateau." He then praises the luminosity
of the air in the Valley, which, as established by the tag line to the
section ("Traveler: you have come to the clearest region of the air"),
works in support of the pictorial context. The reader sees the Valley
as the "transparent region." Thus the mindscape is built through the
intermediary airscape rather than through the direct visual impact of
the objects: "The mind perceives each line and enjoys each
curve...." Today one of the most famous metaphors in Mexican
culture, the idea of the Valley's luminous air found expression in
Humboldt, as Reyes acknowledges, and by the late nineteenth century formed a key motif in the paintings of José María Velasco.
Later Carlos Fuentes would use the metaphor in his well-known
novel *La región mas transparente*.

Significantly it is within this context that Reyes introduces the
arrival of the Aztecs—those "unknown men" who passed with a
"spiritual demeanor" under that "shining air." In this glowing description of the wanderers of Aztlán the poet got the better of the
ethnohistorian: in fact, the Mexica were a ragged band driven by
the god Huitzilopochtli and sneaking their way into the higher
civilization of the Valley. In a confusing sketch of Nahua settlement
in the Valley, Reyes resorted to stock natural symbols of Mexican
identity—nopal, eagle, and snake—to provide a backdrop to Aztec
history and the growth of Tenochtitlán. Reyes's historical bias is
Mexican as he refers to Moctezuma as "the Weak." This is a crucial
point in the essay, since through the word *weak* he summarizes the

Aztec state of mind on the eve of the Conquest. Then, masterfully, in the next sentence he switches to the mountains, and his mindscape conveys the reader into the eyes of Cortés gazing at the whole of Anáhuac.

The second section re-creates the conquistadors' amazement on beholding Tenochtitlán. Written in an era before the indigenous accounts of the Conquest were widely circulated, the viewpoint here is frankly Spanish, drawing on Cortés, Gómara, and Díaz del Castillo. Reyes is concerned solely with the esthetic effect of the city, although there is a naïve anthropological interest in social and political organization.

Nonetheless, so powerful were the impressions of the pre-Hispanic world that Reyes chose to emphasize the Indian at the expense of the Spaniard. To be sure, amid the paean to native craftsmanship are hints of the coming Spanish colonial role: the temple stones that will be used in the cathedral, the herbs that will be recorded by the botanist Francisco Hernández. But Reyes as a good writer knew that the exotic world of Moctezuma, not the European intrusion into it, made poetry of Anáhuac. In this instance Mexican identity lay in a vibrant Tenochtitlán and the indigenous sensibility. Aztec speech is a "cheerful song," the people's faces are "smilingly calm" with a "pleasing look," the Mexican woman's sensual figure merges with the pottery she sells. It is the baroque metaphor of Middle America, so rapidly visualized that it produces a magical effect. Each scene becomes more exotically palpable than the one before, all building toward the splendor of Moctezuma's way of life. Appropriately, Reyes ends the section with the conquistador overwhelmed by the spectacle, as hyperbole is used to isolate and intensify the identity.

In the third section Reyes turns from the external brilliance of Tenochtitlán to enter the inner world of the inhabitants of Anáhuac through their poetry, which is permeated by one of their principal symbols, the flower. Here Reyes's relationship with indigenous values is unequivocal. It is that professional admiration which cuts across political barriers: in this case a poet's acclaim for the muse as honored by another people. As Reyes explicates Náhuatl songs so as to evoke the indigenous genius, he observes that the Náhuatl metaphor has a non-European quality. The Spanish and indigenous elements are present as conflict, but again Spanish culture is foreshortened in

the mindscape. Indeed, Reyes quietly emphasizes the destruction wrought by the Spaniards rather than their preservation of the songs, and juxtaposes the imaginative native mind with the dull, pious mentality of the missionaries. By using the songs about the tragedy of Quetzalcóatl, Reyes may have been implying that the consequences of the Conquest were like an elegy for Anáhuac. The section closes with a line from a song referring to a poet's distress as that of a "last flower." The mood of the essay has changed from the ebullience of the marketplace to the spiritual commemoration of a civilization.

This metaphysical plateau becomes more meaningful when read in connection with the fourth and final section. A self-conscious postscript, this section makes the essay more relevant to the problem of national identity than if it had been written merely for the sake of poetry. Belying the issues of Hispanism and Revolutionary indigenism, Reyes explains that whichever historical theory one espouses— confessing that he was partisan to neither—the twentieth-century Mexican feels a bond with the "people of yesteryear." Racial aspects of identity were unimportant, Reyes argues, since ancient and modern Mexicans are united by their efforts to dominate the environment and by a "common soul" created by the impact of nature upon their sensibilities. Yet if one cannot accept this kinship, he adds, one at least can be responsive to the sense of history in contemporary Mexico, without whose "brilliance" the landscape is like a "theater without lights."

Reyes concludes the essay by returning to the panorama of the Valley but this time from a modern Mexican perspective. Skillfully recapitulating the civilization of Anáhuac by invoking the figure of Doña Marina silhouetted against the volcanoes, with its implications of Mexican history as tragedy, Reyes calls for the continual evocation of Anáhuac as a source of esthetic pleasure. Stating that Anáhuac is in "our hands," Reyes suggests that the search for identity is the responsibility of the modern Mexican.[71]

Is this essay nostalgia, kitsch, ideology, pure art, high-brow travelogue, or tour-de-force Mexicanism? Reyes molded his mindscape of Anáhuac as a writer would have done in the age of explora-

---

[71] Alfonso Reyes, "Visión de Anáhuac" in *Obras completas*, II, 13–34.

tion, conditioned by the political and attitudinal factors prevalent in his own contemporary history. One can almost see the Europeans eagerly pressing Reyes for images of Mexico, and one can almost see the Alfonsine reply forming in the lyrical penetration to the heart of New World history.

"Did the Indian have culture, sensibility, reason?" Las Casas answered these questions, and so did Reyes. Indeed, their political ends were similar: to define the Hispanic world. Only Reyes had a more developed Mexico to work with, finer symbols, and esthetic license. He had the Revolution at his back dramatizing the search for national identity. Reyes would later say that "Mindscape of Anáhuac" was the first in a projected series of essays on the "national soul."[72] In its mosaic of autochthonous life, the essay foreshadowed the Mexican mural of the 1920's; in its expression of the newness and freshness of Mexican history, it conveyed the renovating force of the Revolution in agrarian, social, and educational reforms. The multiple levels of consciousness in the years 1915 to 1920 were reflected in the essay, since, paradoxically, the Revolution had stimulated a colonial vogue as well as an indigenous one.

The essay made the point that in the new Revolutionary culture the past was not disjunctive to the present, but part of it. The indigenous and colonial experiences were linked to that of Revolutionary Mexico, telescoping the country's history. Thus the cosmopolitan and Hispanic circumstances in which "Mindscape of Anáhuac" was written helped focus the problem of national identity in relation to the Revolution as well as to the western world.

It was evident that the Revolution fostered the transition of Mexican identity from an era shaped by positivism to one that reinforced a nationalistic mystique whose symbols stressed the uniqueness of Mexican culture. Manuel Gómez Morín, the politician who belonged to the first intellectual generation formed by the Revolution, analyzed the impetus given to nationalism by the widespread sentiment in 1915 that the Revolution might fail after all. A "new orientation" grew out of the despair, he remembered. Forced into relative isolation from the rest of the world through the Revolution,[73]

---

[72] Reyes, "Carta a Antonio Mediz Bolio" in *Obras completas*, IV, 421.

[73] World War I was also a factor in Mexico's isolation at this time. See Frank Tannenbaum, *The Mexican Agrarian Revolution*, p. 175.

Mexico discovered itself in spite of the sordidness of the conflict, finding that its history was permeated by a "distinctive mode of being."[74]

It remains moot, however, whether the Revolution was unifying or disrupting the life of the mind. There was constant arrest, exile, dismissal, and bitterness in the intellectual community. Ezequiel Chávez said he was on the verge of organizing his psychology institute for the study of the Mexican but the Revolution forced a halt to his plans.[75] In 1911 Andrés Molina Enríquez was arrested for his role in the Plan of Texcoco (to oppose interim president Francisco León de la Barra), and the National Museum bemoaned the interruption of his ethnology class.[76] In 1913 Antonio Caso complained of the hard times, the dispersal of friends, and the necessity to sell his books in order to eat. Jesús Acevedo, on the wrong side of the political fence in 1915, lost his job in the Ministry of Public Instruction and Fine Arts after thirty-eight years of service and, three months behind on his rent, was in danger of being thrown out on the street. Julio Torri and Martín Luis Guzmán complained that the ideals of the Ateneo had ended in failure.[77] Externally, at least, the intellectuals pursued different goals; and it was logical that the earlier esthetic preoccupations of the *ateneístas* were redirected by the upheaval. For Manuel Gómez Morín technics provided the answers to Mexico's problems; for Antonio Caso solutions lay in resolving moral issues. With the consolidation of CROM (Mexican Workers' Regional Confederation) in 1918, Vicente Lombardo Toledano viewed culture in a labor context, whereas Antonio Castro Leal attempted to remain aloof from the Revolutionary process and cultivate a literary detachment from life.[78] José Vasconcelos fused a blend of activism and spiritualism, while Alfonso Reyes and Manuel Tous-

---

[74] Manuel Gómez Morín, *1915*, pp. 7–24.

[75] Ezequiel Chávez, "Notas," April 12, 1938, AEC, Caja 6.

[76] "Report," Museo Nacional de Arquitectura, Historia, y Etnografía, April 12, 1912, AGN, RIP & BA, Leg. 9, Exp. 170.

[77] Caso to Alfonso Reyes, December 14, 1913, AAR; Jesús Acevedo to Otilio Montaño, June 15, 1915, AGN, RIP & BA, Leg. 25, Exp. 38; Julio Torri to Alfonso Reyes, December 28, 1917, AAR; Martín Luis Guzmán to Alfonso Reyes, May 17, 1918, AAR.

[78] Enrique Krauze, *Caudillos culturales en la Revolución mexicana*, pp. 79–91.

saint gave an artistic focus to the pre-Hispanic and colonial periods of Mexican history. If the Revolution dissolved the unity of the Ateneo, it also exercised a controlling force over ideas by broadening the search for meaning in Mexican civilization.

As 1920 approached, critics who complained that Porfirism had not "dignified the popular soul"[79] could take note of the cultural achievements in the preceding decade. Besides the essays of ideas by Caso, Guzmán, Gamio, and Reyes, Mariano Azuela had written *Los de abajo*, Francisco Goítia had painted *Tata Jesucristo*, and Manuel Ponce had composed the Concierto para Piano y Orquesta; all reflected the growing interest in native themes. The nation was spent after years of violence, and it asked for renewed efforts from the people as reconstruction began to replace destruction. Mexico had "to think and to feel like a single, original being" and create an intellectual life "intensely Mexican in character."[80] The inaugural editorial of the newspaper *Excélsior* called for spiritual as well as material reconstruction, calm discussion, and a willingness to confront errors and dispose of prejudices. The nation was urged to strengthen its "national character," and the study of social behavior became a postulate for reconstruction.[81]

The formalistic, positivist-influenced thought of Sierra, Chávez, Guerrero, and Molina Enríquez had by 1915 become laden with multiple connotations—emotional, experimental, political, revolutionary, and esthetic. In part this shift corresponded to the changing concept of nationality from the individualism of the nineteenth century to the broad social context of the twentieth. The decade underwent a jarring of the national consciousness preparatory to the 1920's, when a new phase in Mexican thought would emerge.

[79] Gregorio A. Velásquez, "Los intelectuales," *El Pueblo*, May 22, 1918.

[80] Fernando Solís Cámara, *La reconstrucción de nuestra patria*, pp. 9–10.

[81] "Al comenzar," *Excélsior*, March 18, 1917; Gregorio A. Velásquez, "El carácter nacional constituye la fuerza de los pueblos," *El Pueblo*, August 23, 1918; Salvador Alvarado, *La reconstrucción de México: un mensaje a los pueblos de América*, I, 2.

4.
Nationalism and the Reorientation
of Thought: The 1920's

THE 1910 Revolution generated an unprecedented expansion of knowledge in Mexico. At the same time as it lessened the tensions of an unresponsive political system, it ushered in a new age of creation. If the post-Revolutionary political development cannot always be viewed favorably, the efforts to reorient thought toward a greater awareness of national conditions at least merit commendation. Thus the 1920's is known as the period of "reconstruction" and "renaissance," when the country, having undergone its most profound dislocation since the Conquest, attempted to consolidate the gains its people had struggled for since the waning of the Porfiriato.

A program based on a coalescing ideology associated with the Revolution had to be implemented in many areas of civic endeavor—constitutional law, labor, agrarian reform, and education. It was a time of rebuilding the shattered structures of a passing era, and it demanded continual policy formulation to meet the exigencies of the aftermath of violence and projected social change. Foreign recognition was needed, claims were a pressing issue, subsoil rights were argued, sources of revenue had to be found, loans floated, militarism checked, conflict between church and state resolved, and the national infrastructure developed. Revolutionary politics were to be organized and made representative of the pueblo; contending political factions had to be more tightly knit in a central party.

Intellectually and culturally, the 1920's witnessed an enthusiastic nationalism as scholars, critics, novelists, poets, painters, and composers captured the spirit of the Revolution.[1] Schools opened their doors to the pueblo, and "missionaries" attempted to establish

[1] See Frank Brandenburg, *The Making of Modern Mexico*, p. 70; Frederick C. Turner, *The Dynamic of Mexican Nationalism*, pp. 254–306.

a link between modernity and tradition. The arts flourished in concerts and ballets of native inspiration, in lectures, libraries, and the publication of books, in open-air schools of painting, and, most spectacularly of all, on the public walls, giving the Mexican a sense of identity with his history and the social community. This ambitious program was only partially successful.

The period under consideration begins as early as 1915, when the literature of reconstruction first appeared, and it reached a watershed in 1934 when the Revolutionary party, organized in 1929, had become the dominant factor in national politics. The 1917 Constitution was a major step toward reconstruction, but laws could not be written and administered without a reference to reality. Thus Mexico faced the double imperative of reconstruction and self-analysis, which triggered a search for criteria by which Mexicans could measure their worth and restructure their values to match Revolutionary ideology. It is only against the background of post-Revolutionary preoccupation with the meaning of Mexico that the ideas of the country's thinkers may be properly elucidated.

The Problematic 1920's

If Mexico had buckled down to the task of national redefinition, it also was enduring the ferment and confusion wrought by World War I, the Jazz Age, and the increasing liberation of irrational man. Rapid change was evident as traditional Mexican life was being modernized, mostly through American influence. The bob was replacing the classic braid of the Mexican woman. Jazz and chewing gum became popular, as did English-language phrases, parties, expensive cars, weekends, the beach, and women's sports. In the salons, a product of Porfirian Mexico, waltzes and mazurkas gave way to the saxophone playing the hit parade.

The new forces of the 1920's were manifested in *estridentismo*, Mexico's contribution to the international avant-garde. Despair at the Mexican situation, an outlook both universal and nationalist, and a rebellious attitude toward the status quo balanced by conformity to their own group and style characterized these practitioners of the unorthodox. Significantly, the movement took hold in the provincial cities where enthusiastic young intellectuals "made battle plans

against the academics, reactionaries, and traitors to the popular struggle." These visionaries wanted to provide Mexico with a "guide," someone who could orient the country in the crisis of destruction and lack of leadership, a goal made clear by *estridentista* Germán List Arzubide when he voiced the consciousness of his peers and stated that "we were the Revolution." In Vera Cruz General Heriberto Jara patronized their efforts, and they founded a magazine to serve as a "tribune of modern political, social, philosophical, and esthetic doctrines."[2] Communism and art now formed the ideological basis of the "syndicates" of painters and writers who strove for reform in Mexico,[3] yet the concept of "Mexican socialism" with its compelling native myth was to predominate in the battle between left and right during the years 1920 to 1940.

The Mexican polarization of the national and the international presented a challenge. Since the nineteenth century, western thought had been imbued with notions of the relativity of cultures, of the importance of concrete histories over global abstractions. If the Mexican were to hearken to universalist principles, he more than likely would be met with the dictum to know his country, thus finding himself forced back into a nationalist position by virtue of the influence of western ideas. The painters were the first to experience this tyranny of models, many of them making a pilgrimage to Europe in search of cultural salvation, only to find that it lay in their homeland. Thus nationalism grew concomitantly to the Revolution and with the internationalism that linked Mexico to the wider world. That this conflict extended beyond the cultural sphere was noted by a political analyst of the period who saw the issues in terms of the socioeconomic variables of the Revolution.[4]

On the other hand, the Mexican intellectual continued to find the foreign model useful, and European philosophy offering a neoromantic basis for cultural relativism was received enthusiastically in Mexico. Thus European thought supplemented a trend already developing in Mexico: a dual perception of reality gave an internal

[2] Germán List Arzubide, *El movimiento estridentista*, pp. 19, 42; idem, "Propósito," *Horizonte* 1 (April, 1926), 1.

[3] See Rosendo Salazar, *México en pensamiento y acción.*

[4] See Rafael Nieto, *Más allá de la patria: ensayos económicos y políticos,* pp. 119–125, 190–195; idem, *El imperio de los Estados Unidos y otros ensayos,* p. 15.

as well as an external configuration to the idea of Mexico. As one German scholar-traveler, whose account influenced the Mexican at the time, suggested, the unity of soul and nature, the inner dimension of the land and the people, must be sought in Mexico.[5] The Mexican artist, however, really needed no prodding in this direction. And if the problem of national identity in the 1920's was shaped by nationalism and cosmopolitanism, it was also colored by politics. One report from Mexico in 1921 describes the atmosphere of uncertainty that hung over most of the decade:

Uneasiness grows here daily. We are having sudden deportations of foreign agitators, street riots and parades of workers carrying red flags. A general was executed today for counterrevolutionary activities. There is fevered discussion in the newspapers as to the best means of stamping out Bolshevism, which is the inclusive term for all forms of radical work. Battles occur almost daily between Catholics and Socialists in many parts of the Republic: Morelia, Yucatán, Campeche, Jalisco. In brief, a clamor of petty dissension almost drowns the complicated debate between Mexico and the United States.[6]

The Revolution made it incumbent upon the Mexican people to provide political stability so that ideals spawned in its social upheaval might be given substance, yet as steps were taken to solve the country's problems, labor disputes, factional revolt, ideological differences, and a serious religio-political conflict marred the progress.

Indeed the years from 1928 to 1934 have been characterized as "most perplexing, . . . debased and clouded."[7] Power was assumed by the Revolutionary family, and some feel that the ruling clique of Plutarco Elías Calles known as the Maximato delayed the participation of the masses in the governmental processes and altered the course of the true Revolution.[8] By the late 1920's the Revolution was evident in the dispute between European and native ideals in literature as well as in government, and the discord in some measure motivated the Mexican intellectuals to plumb the meaning of their

[5] See Alfons Goldschmidt, *Mexiko*, p. 9.

[6] Katherine Anne Porter, "The Mexican Trinity," in *The Collected Essays and Occasional Writings of Katherine Anne Porter*, p. 399.

[7] Frank Tannenbaum, *Mexico: The Struggle for Peace and Bread*, p. 69.

[8] See Roger D. Hansen, *The Politics of Mexican Development*, p. 162; Albert L. Michaels, "Mexican Nationalism from Calles to Cárdenas" (Ph.D. diss., University of Pennsylvania, 1966), pp. 10–22.

society and political culture. What was the Revolution and how
should it be consolidated? And of course the eternal question: What
was Mexico and the Mexican? It was during these years that Bernardo J. Gastélum wrote his critical essays on the Revolution[9] and
Samuel Ramos wrote his Mexicanist "characterology." Magazines
like *Contemporáneos, Crisol,* and *Examen* reflected the problematic
situation of the country. Thus the intellectual and political crisis of
Mexico fed the introspective gloom that in part surrounded the
search for identity.

Yet the paradox of the period was that if the country was rife
with dissension, it was also beginning to be unified by nationalism.
As one intellectual put it in 1921: "We come out of the nightmare of
grief . . ; bloodied and abused, with a hesitant faith and dry ideal;
but . . . there is a precious virtue of rebirth. . . . Everything Mexican
has the marvelous power to renew faith and to invigorate . . . the
love of our country."[10] It was left for the poet Ramón López Velarde
to see most profoundly into the twenties. For him the suffering during the Revolution was necessary for the emergence of a patria less
"external" and more "modest." The concept of nationhood, he said,
was oriented "within," and the long period of independence had
revealed "a patria that was neither historical, nor political, but intimate" and as yet undefinable. For López Velarde and others the
course of Mexicanism was leading inevitably to the province.

The Mexican intellectual in the 1920's seldom conceived nationalism as deriving from anything but the Revolution. As Lucio
Mendieta y Núñez remarked: "In Mexico, we have come to the end
of the social disturbances that the old administrative systems pro-
voked. A new clarity dawns on the horizon, tracing new aspects of
our evolution. Among those aspects, the one which has the greatest
transcendence, the one which future generations will use to characterize this feverish epoch, is the rebirth of nationalism." Making a
plea for "constructive nationalism," he noted the prevailing taste for
lo mexicano. Similarly, educator Narciso Bassols observed that Mexico was steeping itself in cultural nationalism. The people, he noted,

[9] See Bernardo J. Gastélum, "La teoría del sufragio," *Contemporáneos*
(April, 1930), pp. 34–46; idem, "La Revolución mexicana," *Contemporáneos*
(February, 1931), pp. 140–151.

[10] José María Puig Casauranc, *Páginas viejas con ideas actuales,* p. 75.

were no longer disposed to think themselves inferior, nor did they wish to copy the foreign model that "disowns" Mexico's originality. And Pedro de Alba, one of the principal *pensadores* of the twenties, analyzed Mexico's problems in terms of its experience of conquest and violence, class prejudice, and the absence of cohesive ideals. If the Revolution was to make positive advances, he said, Mexico would have to "integrate its nationality," as a basis of "spiritual unification for all Mexicans."[11]

It was during the years 1920 to 1934 that the term *lo mexicano* became popularly associated with the idea of nationalism. One magazine emphasized *lo mexicano* in support of "healthy nationalism."[12] The Porfiriato was now blamed for inhibiting *lo mexicano*,[13] a stock attitude that would permeate Mexican thought until the fifties. It was in the arts that the term *lo mexicano* received its greatest currency, pointing up the nativist quality of Mexican painting or the treatment of national life in the literature that followed the Revolution.[14] In his letters from New York, José Clemente Orozco discussed the American response toward *lo mexicano* in art and noted that Anita Brenner and Jean Charlot were trying to promote *lo mexicano* in that city.[15]

Whether one emphasizes the optimism or the pessimism of the 1920's in Mexico, both stimulated the Mexican's awareness of self and nation. The Mexican now enjoyed two intellectual traditions that would shape his creative efforts. The social sciences would carry on the tradition of positivism without the positivist cant and with more

[11] Ramón López Velarde, "El minutero," in *Poemas completas y el minutero*, pp. 295–298, Lucio Mendieta y Núñez, "El renacimiento del nacionalismo," *Ethnos* 1 (January–February, 1925), 3–5; Narciso Bassols, *Obras*, pp. 12–13; Pedro de Alba, *Del humanismo y otros ensayos*, pp. 196–197.

[12] Editorial, *Azulejos* 2 (December, 1923), 11.

[13] See Moisés Sáenz, *México íntegro*, p. 241; and "Mexicanizacion," *Nuestro México* 1 (August, 1932), 7.

[14] See Magda Portal, "Panorama intelectual de México: la literatura mexicana," *Repertorio Americano* 16 (March 10, 1928), 158; "Exposición de arte mexicano," *El Nacional*, June 29, 1930; and Bernardo Ortiz de Montellano, "Esquema de la literatura mexicana moderna," *Contemporáneos* (June, 1931), p. 205.

[15] José Clemente Orozco, *El artista en Nueva York: cartas a Jean Charlot y textos inéditos, 1925–1929*, ed. Luis Cardoza y Aragón, p. 60; Orozco to Juan Crespo de la Serna, February 11, 1930, in Luis Cardoza y Aragón, *Orozco*, p. 23.

application to pressing needs, while the metaphysical flight from positivism, spurred in part by the Revolution, would sustain the mentality necessary for the growth of national identity.

The Rhetoric of Reconstruction

The term *reconstruction* expressed both the superficial concepts of the age and the pervasive ambiguities arising from the contradictions of contemporary history. To the extent that the Revolution worked as a leveling factor in Mexico, the government had to give a sense of purposive beginning to the people. Yet Mexico both repudiated and incorporated its past. Much has been written about the Revolution as a revolt against a neofeudalistic Hispanic heritage, less about its also being, indirectly, a protest against modern western development, especially along classical economic lines. Hence Mexico was forced to reject elements of both its past and its present. One of the political solutions to this dilemma was the growth of an intense nationalism that can best be described as a self-conscious process of selecting out the experience deemed inappropriate to Mexican evolution.

But nationalism became a Pandora's box for those who too eagerly espoused it. While leaders spoke against foreign economic involvement that compromised national integrity, the government encouraged such involvement as a means to hasten development. The capitalist ethic was officially condemned at the same time that it was built into the post-Revolutionary rationale. If reconstruction led to hierarchical control of political power in order to reduce endemic factional conflict, it did so at the cost of removing the government from the pueblo, for which the Revolution had just been fought. And Mexico's entry into modern western society meant sharing a cosmopolitan culture that did not always harmonize with officially sponsored native values. Thus nationalism attempted to sweep Mexico out from under its foreign domination and to steer the country on a path of self-contained nationhood, at the same time establishing conditions that invited outside penetration in business, culture, and behaviorial norms—the classical syndrome of underdevelopment in the twentieth century. Nationalism therefore was called upon to check what essentially it created.

In view of the disorder resulting from the Revolution together with the analysis of Mexico stimulated by that event, a rhetoric designed to cope with problems was necessary to sustain the public benedictions on progress, nationhood, and the postulation of personal identity. Madero's vision of a new patria was now translated by President Alvaro Obregón into the consequences of upheaval:

> After the prolonged civil war that has just passed, in which everything was inevitably destroyed, we say optimistically that the only problem facing Mexico is national reconstruction. National reconstruction is necessitated by the fact that almost all the sources of wealth in the country have been closed. More than half of the fields are abandoned, and the mines and the industries are paralyzed. National reconstruction cannot be achieved unless it is by a mandate from the people.[16]

Another political architect of the period, Plutarco Elías Calles, saw reconstruction as a problem of long-term policy making: "It is time that we define meaningfully and sincerely our ideology, that we know where we are going and that the country know it also."[17]

The course of ideology from Obregón to Calles became steadily more intellectual. As one student notes, under Calles the concept of the Revolution became the abstraction of the "national reality," the "resumé of Mexico" and its "singularity." By the time of the Calles regime (1924–1928) and the Maximato (1928–1935), the official view was that the Revolution had progressed from arms to ideas and had assumed a quality of "spiritual betterment." When Calles refuted the accusations of imitation of foreign political and social systems and emphasized the Revolution's relationship to the environment and the national character, he was predicating Mexican identity on the idea of national uniqueness.[18]

The unifying element in the politics of the twenties was the discovery that reconstruction required a more sophisticated manipulation of knowledge whether in the arts or in the economy. Knowledge of the Mexican circumstances was to be transformed through the Revolutionary mythos into a rationale for nationhood. The goal of the Partido Nacional Revolucionario (PNR) was to "penetrate the

[16] Alvaro Obregón, *Discursos del General Alvaro Obregón*, I, 119.
[17] Plutarco Elías Calles, "Los problemas del México de hoy," *Crisol* 10 (September, 1933), 135.
[18] Guillermo Palacios, "La idea oficial de la Revolución mexicana" (master's thesis, El Colegio de México, 1969), pp. 94–104, 129.

soul of the people and sculpt the heart of the patria. . . . arrive at the intimate . . . sentiment of the pueblo, to perceive its misfortune, its bitterness, interpret its joys, console it in its sorrows and help it to shake off the yoke of its errors and superstitions: this is the objective that the new leaders of the ideal propose to accomplish."[19]

Thus, as reconstruction became a pervasive attitude in the decade, it offered a framework for both action and revelation. In propagandistic fashion, Alfonso Teja Zabre praised the effect of re-construction on culture and education. The glory of the future patria, he said, was being prepared in lectures, games, excursions, archae-ology, scholarly monographs, the press, and the magazines of the avant-garde. The "doors of the eternal temples" must be opened to the pueblo and the names of the "authentic heroes" inculcated in the popular consciousness.[20] Indeed, Mexico at long last seemed on the verge of a shared sociocultural experience. As the government rein-forced nationalism, it sanctioned a variety of cultural and social pro-grams involving the masses, and their enthusiastic reception had a profound effect on the intellectuals. The older Arielist generation, which initially had proposed the possibility of national rebirth, realized that it must give way to the technically oriented leadership of men like Narciso Bassols, Miguel Palacios Macedo, and Daniel Cosío Villegas. The impulse to achieve something practical had be-come so strong, one scholar asserts, that there was even a decline in the quality of writing by the *pensadores*.[21]

Daniel Cosío Villegas recalled the vision and good will with which Mexico was trying to rebuild its society. When Alfonso Reyes made a brief trip to Mexico in 1923, his friends invited him to Vi-cente Lombardo Toledano's home, where, as Cosío put it, in order that Reyes could "see" Mexico and "love and admire it," they would give him the latest news. Excitedly, Cosío wrote, they told him of the "great new Mexico": the reorganization of the University, the publication of the classics, the reappearance of the Ministry of Public Education, the mural movement, public libraries, rural education,

[19] Vicente de P. Cano, "Las misiones culturales del PNR," *El Nacional*, June 30, 1930.
[20] Alfonso Teja Zabre, "Tópicos de actualidad: la campaña cultural," *El Demócrata*, July 15, 1924.
[21] Enrique Krauze, *Caudillos culturales en la Revolución mexicana*, pp. 146, 154–155.

farmers' banks, agricultural schools, an economics school, fiscal reform, a national bank, and a "thousand other marvels." Reyes, Cosío
added, was astonished by the display of fervor and faith.[22] But how
should one interpret this intense revelation by Cosío? In fact, it is an
excellent example of a reenactment of the creation myth of contemporary Mexico, an event that had become ritualized in the
1920's. Yet the conflict between cosmopolitanism and nationalism
lingered, and if in Cosío's recollection Mexico seemed to vibrate with
the sense of national culture, the search for selfhood remained incomplete, and in 1932 Salvador Novo noted that the Mexican was
still far from being defined.[23]

While the concept of reconstruction permeated political thought,
under the surface there was often despair and confusion. All did not
augur well as the objectives of the Revolution became distorted by
the inevitable bureaucracy, ideological conflicts, and greed. As one
editor bemoaned: "1915! when we were all better. We were fighting
for an ideal and nobody was concerned with low politics."[24] Reconstruction was Janus-faced: the creative impulse stood against chaos,
and the intellectual was forced to contend with the problem of
balance as well as of integration.[25] But in theory whichever political
alternative was to prevail had to be based on a nationalist rationale:

We who are aware of the singular environment of Mexico and the possibilities for contributing to the national well-being have taken from the international social question only those aspects which logically and justly
can be adapted to genuine and exclusive Mexican needs in order to create a social character, a truly national ideology that will permit us to work
freely toward progress and be independent of doctrines and systems foreign to our indigenous and Spanish manner of being.[26]

The implication here was that knowledge should control the formation of polity.

As the programs of reconstruction led to the institutionalization

[22] Daniel Cosío Villegas, "Justificación de la tirada," in *Ensayos y notas*,
I, 19–20.
[23] Salvador Novo, "Nota de la provincia," *Nuestro México* 1 (July, 1932), 6.
[24] "Vamos entrando . . . ," *Crisol* 5 (January, 1931), 3–4.
[25] Javier Vivanco, "La integración nacional," *Universidad de México* 1
(November–April, 1931), 44–45.
[26] Tranquilino Torres, "La cuestión social mexicana," *Crisol* 3 (May,
1930), 337–338.

of the Revolution, they were accompanied by reflection and criticism, and the more perceptive intellectuals looked at Mexico to see where it stood or what had gone wrong. It was in this pessimistic but critical atmosphere that the concepts of nationhood and selfhood became important. What was Mexico after the third "revolutionary" change in a hundred years of national history? Why were the ideals people had fought for so hard to maintain? How did history shape the national character? Mexico seemed to be discovering itself, yet a full understanding of the unique culture evaded everyone. The need for deepened consciousness of national problems was paramount. However, Bernardo J. Gastélum went so far as to caution against excessive preoccupation with the country, if events were to be properly understood.[27]

But few doubted that a radical change in the mental life of the nation was necessary. Jesús S. Soto called for a comparative study of the ideology of the twenties and previous periods and in effect issued a plea for the history of ideas in Mexico. Mexican thought, he maintained, was now respectable and should be studied as a historical phenomenon in its own right. A "careful reinterpretation" should be made of the scientific, philosophical, and religious underpinnings of Mexican society in order to synthesize the "true national ideology."[28] In a similar revisionary tone, Manuel Gómez Morín stated that Mexicanism should be grounded in cultural authenticity and that it was necessary to elucidate the desire for national self-fulfillment. "If there really is an esthetic, a morality, an internal quality that creates an art, a form of life, a society, and a religious spirit that are Mexican, let's not waste time with explanations and systems of thought that are foreign to our native essence." Gómez wanted a criticism that would offer the Mexican standards for distinguishing between the national and the foreign basis of culture.[29]

Educational institutions and curricula began to be modified in accordance with nationalistic attitudes. One scholar observed that in the National University there was a growing desire "to know the national personality which had been ignored throughout Mexican

[27] Bernardo J. Gastélum, "Democracia asimétrica," *Contemporáneos* (November, 1928), p. 244.
[28] Jesús S. Soto, *Aspectos de la nueva ideología mexicana*, pp. 1, 6.
[29] Gómez Morín, *1915*, pp. 49–50.

history." The Mexican of the 1920's, he said, remained insecure; thus he was trying to understand himself and his world. This search for identity was interpreted as the guiding principle behind the monographs dealing with national problems and the professional training necessary to cope with the social environment.[30] In a discussion of the newly created Institute for Social Research of the National University, the themes of nationalism and reconstruction were underscored:

So that the University might pursue this lofty objective, it needs to know, above all, how the people of the country's different regions live . . . ; their diet; their physical resistance and capacity for work; the nature of their social relationships, religious sentiments, and economic activities; their mutual protection and cooperation for the common good; how meteorological phenomena impress them; how they amuse themselves; the causes of their joy and sorrow; how they express their feelings artistically; their hopes and fears, spiritual values and creations . . . ; if they have anything in common, and if not, how their differences may be reduced. . . . In sum, the University needs to know . . . what is unique in our people so that . . . it may provide a philosophical orientation based on our ethnological essence for the purpose of creating our ideology.[31]

The central image here is that of knowledge providing a framework for national unity with the implication that a cultural pluralism was to be amalgamated into a monolithic ideal of nationhood.

A Mexican studies program whose rhetoric harked back to Sierra was outlined by educators. One rector of the university noted that research seminars were developing a knowledge of land and people for the purpose of solving problems as well as for affirming Mexico's "true nationality." Another rector stated that the organization of higher learning should reflect the emergence of Mexicanist themes in history. Thus nationalism was to inform a new scholarship, whose assumptions were at least partially independent of foreign models.[32]

The constellation of attitudes associated with the reorientation

---

[30] Beatriz Ruiz Gaytán, "La Facultad de Filosofía y Letras y sus postulados," *Historia Mexicana* 30 (April–July, 1970), 578–581.

[31] Tranquilino Torres, "El genio de la raza," *Crisol* 4 (August, 1930), 112.

[32] Ignacio García Téllez, "Informe del rector al H. Consejo universitario," *Universidad de México* 4 (May, 1932), 3; Roberto Medellín, "Informe del rector al H. Consejo universitario," *Universidad de México* 6 (May–June, 1933), 6; Bassols, *Obras*, p. 23.

of thought had its origins in a broadly conceived sociohistorical rationale. In his theory of the integral study of culture, Manuel Gamio argued that society could not be examined in isolation but had to be seen in relation to its total environment. This entailed a multidisciplinary approach to a historical spectrum ranging from the archaeological to the contemporary horizons, methods Gamio employed in his monumental study of Teotihuacán. Of particular importance to the growth of nationalistic thought was the tenet developed in Gamio's applied anthropology linking knowledge and the efficacy of the state.[33]

Clearly the enlargement of the idea of Mexican study sought to break down conventional criteria controlling the manipulation of data. Thus, it was argued, the Mexican was traditionally steeped in the legendary and tended to conceive history as the picturesque, tragic, and heroic. But contemporary Mexico, it was advised, should be viewed against its own history starting with the colonial period, and not studied as discrete episodes with connotations of the fabulous.[34] Similarly, in order to analyze institutional failure, it was necessary to get behind the formal structure to the obstacles preventing the growth of public opinion.[35]

Mexico, then, as editorials of the day indicated, was frenetically pursuing its "intimate life" and proclaiming self-analysis as a didactic tool.[36] Reconstruction generated the feeling among intellectuals that they were suddenly grappling with unknown factors in their country's history and social organization and that to implement constructive measures extensive knowledge was required. As one critic expressed it, the armed conflict had to be followed by intellectual evolution.[37] For some the racial preoccupation was foremost. It was

[33] Manuel Gamio, *Introducción, síntesis y conclusión a la población del Valle de Teotihuacán,* p. ix.

[34] Pedro de Alba, "La realidad y la fábula en nuestra historia," *El Nacional,* October 30, 1930.

[35] Fernando González Roa, "Discurso leído por su autor ante el tercer congreso jurídico nacional reunido en esta ciudad al mes de octubre del año 1924," *Revista de Ciencias Sociales* 3 (February, 1926), 20.

[36] See "Nuestros propósitos al comenzar Crisol," *Crisol* 1 (January, 1929), 3.

[37] Ricardo Parado León, "Después de la Revolución," *Crisol* 2 (February, 1929), 38.

necessary to define the mestizo and relate governing institutions to him.[38] Yet even in a discussion of the direction of literature, the expanded horizons of the nationalistic quest for Mexican "individuality" did not illuminate the landscape and popular culture merely, but the total historical experience.[39]

Reconstruction signaled a special phase in the Revolutionary process; as the armed conflict wound down, the reasons for which the struggle was waged were still present, but instead of mobilizing men for warfare, they now generated a battle of minds. The idea replaced the bullet, though power remained eternally couched in force. Thriving on the tasks presented by the sense of responsibility to the new cultural values, intellectuals intensified their preoccupation with selfhood and national identity in the twenties. In the broadest meaning of these objectives, the long-alienated people of Mexico were to achieve a dignified station in life, first in the national sphere and then perhaps in the international one. To a considerable extent reason was now expected to balance the fervor of the Revolution; hence the years 1920 to 1934 saw the real emergence of modern nationalistic inquiry in Mexico, though it had been adumbrated during a long preceding period.

The Outside Model

The criticism of foreign influence remained broadly interrelated with the theme of nationality. The Mexican intellectual, it was said, conjured up an image of government based on European or North American circumstances. An example was the Reform, a reflection of European ideas ill-suited to Mexican realities.[40] On the other hand, Mexican self-esteem was considered to be improving as modern science destroyed the myth of Anglo-Saxon superiority, thereby easing the inferiority complex that gripped "the Mexican soul." Thus the Mexican, who had been denigrated for his "insolence, lassitude, technical incapacity, kleptomania, and a sanguinary in-

[38] Flavio Aguirre Cárdenas, *El problema de la heterogeneidad racial de México, ensayo sociológico*, pp. 13–14.

[39] See Rafael Ruiz Díaz, "Restalla el cohete: ¿cuál es el problema fundamental de la literatura mexicana?" *Bandera de Provincias* 1 (May, 1929), 1.

[40] Soto, *Aspectos de la nueva ideología mexicana*, p. 13.

stinct," was now viewed as redeeming himself in the struggle for ethnic egalitarianism.[41]

The foreign influence was cited constantly as a force undermining nationhood. Elaborating Bagehot's idea that an incipient nationality needed isolation to strengthen itself, one critic pointed to the necessary parochial basis of national character. Foreign elements slowed the national process, and an example was the English language via American "talkies." If Mexico were to survive as a cultural entity, it was argued, it would have to beware of absorption by North America, whose capital bought the country and whose ideals permeated the national weal.[42] France no less than the United States was seen as a source of antinational influence in Mexico. Unlike the United States, however, France was not accused of cultural imperialism; in fact, criticism was leveled primarily against the Mexicans for imitating French forms: romantic imagery, naturalism, architecture, and landscaping. To root out this French influence became one objective of nationalism.[43]

Not infrequently the dangers involved in adapting the culture of the outside world to Mexican circumstances were discussed in the problematic context of the Reform. Narciso Bassols saw Mexico turn to France and the United States in the nineteenth century for the democratic principles that resulted in the destruction of the juridical integrity of the Indian and his subjection to a liberal legal status that made him theoretically equal to the European. In an analysis of marginal classes, which anticipated the work of Pablo González Casanova, Bassols stated that 75 percent of the population lived isolated from the core activities of the country, and that the Indian and the mestizo could not effectively relate to the European cultural system in Mexico. The origins of this situation, he maintained, lay in the fact that an economically powerful minority had imposed its will on the country.[44] In keeping with the visionary New World blends of socialism and nativism prevalent in the 1920's, Bassols looked for

[41] Agustín Aragón Leyva, "Futuro de la nación mexicana," *Nuestra Ciudad* 2 (September, 1930), 22–23.

[42] Genaro Fernández McGregor, "La universidad y el vitáfono," *Universidad de México* 1 (November, 1930), 39–40.

[43] Héctor Pérez Martínez, "Escaparate: I: La influencia francesa," *El Nacional*, November 22, 1930.

[44] Bassols, *Obras*, pp. 26–27.

Mexican civilization in the fusion of indigenous and technological values:

Our education is concerned with achieving a synthesis of two cultures, keeping the positive values of the indigenous peoples and taking from western civilization (with its technical resources and the possibilities the machine offers) everything that will strengthen our Indians, making them into a vigorous and mechanically apt race capable of producing greater wealth. If we are going to triumph, it will be because we succeed in conserving the spiritual structure of the Indians at the same time that we give them the indispensable aid of scientific technique. We want to obtain the external forms rather than the spiritual elements of the European utilitarian civilization—the enormous power it offers for the material well-being of man. . . . But we try to save in the soul of the Indian all the virtues that beyond doubt surpass the morality of contemporary capitalism.[45]

Thus, central to the post-Revolutionary mythos was a nationality to be fashioned from select elements of foreign as well as native culture.

If Bassols stood midway between cosmopolitanism and nationalism, other intellectuals spoke for the external factors in Mexican history. A penetrating counter-criticism of the foreign influence was offered by the poet and essayist Jorge Cuesta, who pointed to the historical misconceptions regarding French culture in Mexico. As he expressed it, "The influence of French culture has been so constant and profound in Mexico that whoever disavows it is running the risk of repudiating the most personal part of his essence." Cuesta looked at the scope of Mexico's national history and concluded that independence, the Reform, and the 1910 Revolution showed traces of French radicalism; thus, in contrast to most thinkers of the decade, he advocated the search for the French element in Mexican civilization.[46]

Society and the National Character

The new preoccupation with reorienting thought in the wake of the Revolution sustained the older interest in the national character. A variety of behavioral and cultural phenomena were now being

45 Ibid., pp. 178–179.
46 Jorge Cuesta, *Poemas y ensayos*, ed. Miguel Capistrán and Luis Mario Schneider, II, 147–154.

grouped under the rubric *lo mexicano*, although some intellectuals wanted to avoid deterministic frameworks for this subject. The educator and anthropological theorist Moisés Sáenz stated that the concept of *lo mexicano* was not fixed, and that the incorporation of the Indian did not depend on acculturation but was linked to a biological process whose factors were always changing. He defined *lo mexicano* as a social variable that shifted in relation to its context.[47] In another discussion of *lo mexicano* Enrique Martínez Ulloa, one of the principal Guadalajara intellectuals in the twenties, explored the much-publicized need to transcend the negative aspects of the Mexican psychology.[48]

Social analysis was often interwoven with the idea of national character for the purpose of a moral and political solution to specific problems. Thus the young novelist Agustín Yáñez lashed out at the provincial mentality that limited reading habits, stunted curiosity, and kept *abajeño* from knowing *jarocho*, and *yucateco norteño*. He argued that increased travel would improve social relationships, underscoring a geographical determinism to show that isolation still hindered national unity. In another view of social conduct, rebellion against authority was explained by the fact that the people were forced to disobey the arbitrariness of leaders. Generally speaking, the Mexicans came down hard on themselves, describing their behavior as "destructive" and "suicidal."[49]

The facile invocation of the national character as the cause of public ills and individual aberrations reflected the dearth of cultural and historical methods available at the time, precipitating the reliance on obsolete concepts to grapple with contemporary challenges. Thus the Mexican was credited with a special nervous system that yoked his reason and left him with the illusion of creating great works. The Mexican failed to follow through on his admirable plans, it was said, for fear of not succeeding. Cultural selectivity was controlled by imitation, the critics concluded, while a position midway

[47] Sáenz, *México íntegro*, p. 231. This book included several essays written by Sáenz before 1934.

[48] Enrique Martínez Ulloa, "Dimensión de lo mexicano," *Bandera de Provincias* 1 (October, 1929), 1.

[49] Agustín Yáñez, "Notas criollas," *Bandera de Provincias* 1 (April, 1929), 5; Carlos Félix R., "¡Mexicanos! ¿Por qué somos rebeldes y gritones?" *La Antorcha* 1 (January 24, 1925), 10; Gilberto Loyo, XYZ, pp. 40–55.

between cosmopolitanism and nationalism was not in evidence. The social profile was also circumscribed by the regional context, and the patria chica elicited the appropriate response in psychology and history.[50]

The themes of machismo and sexual differentiation remained central to the preoccupation with the national character. A Don Juan complex, based on self-love and oneupmanship unified the racial interpretation of history. *Tantear*, or "to put it over" was linked to the hypothetical mestizo cunning, and although Don Juanism traditionally concerned sexual conquest, its jokester associations were extended to the loss of national territory, dependence on the United States, poverty, middle-class frustration, and an unresponsive government. The woman, however, was considered to invite the *tanteada* by provoking the man and feigning denial while giving herself. On the other hand, the widespread abandonment of the woman by the man was thought to be a factor in a broad range of problems from the economy to public health. In effect, the theory of the *tantear* complex anticipated the later *chingar* concept, since the Don Juan was seen as the forcer whose method was physical, monetary, and verbal.[51] Often the solitary existence of woman was viewed as perpetuating a bourgeois atmosphere at the domestic level, and thus she was ripe for a normative relationship to society with the options made available by the Revolution.[52]

Racial themes continued to shape the Mexicans' images of themselves and now helped establish a post-Revolutionary context for the national character. Hence Andrés Molina Enríquez equated the nationalism of the twenties with the emergent cultural significance of the mestizo, while Luis Cabrera employed the socioracial

[50] Luis Rubio Siliceo, "Nuestra pasión," *La Antorcha* 1 (November 8, 1924), 41; Soto, *Aspectos de la nueva ideología mexicana*, p. 51; Javier Sorondo, "Necesitamos mexicanizarnos," *Revista de Revistas* No. 1166 (September 18, 1932), p. 3; Enrique Martínez Ulloa, "Guadalajara: fragmentos de una interpretación," *Bandera de Provincias* 1 (July, 1929), 1, 6.

[51] Armando Monteverde, "El don juanismo mexicano," in *El desastre moral de México: la bancarrota del pudor*, with Rodrigo Cifuentes, pp. 113–117.

[52] María del Refugio Azores, "Las mujeres mexicanas," *La Antorcha* 1 (February 14, 1925), 33; Guadalupe Gutiérrez de Joseph, "Psicología de la mujer mexicana," *Nuestra Ciudad* 1 (April, 1930), 38.

triad for demographic analysis.[53] The historian Toribio Esquivel Obregón discussed the syndrome of humility, obedience, and indifference hidden behind "democracy," judicial organization, the railroads, and banks. Historians, he maintained, preoccupied as they were with the narration of external events, ignored these forces. In an analogy similar to the one that inspired Samuel Ramos and much later Octavio Paz to posit pre-Hispanic survival in Mexican civilization, Esquivel stated that Huitzilopochtli patiently awaited the successors of Cortés.[54]

The negative stereotype of the creole was based on the familiar elements of affluence, arrogance, privilege, and the capacity of whiteness to invest one with status. Seen in a favorable light the creole was sober in mind and hard-working, qualities that allowed him to adapt to the New World environment and to exploit its wealth.[55] The mestizo was analyzed increasingly in a socioesthetic context in which his temperament and expressive skills were becoming the subject of novelists and essayists impelled by the post-Revolutionary search for authentic Mexican behavior. Moisés Sáenz relied on an emotive framework to explain how the Indian's repressed feelings were contained in the mestizo's boasting and cynicism. If rebelliousness and bitterness as conveyed in the *corrido*, or ballad, were the mestizo's lot, Sáenz thought, melancholy was not. Romantic in temperament, he quickly found surcease through action, avenging himself with a laugh or a boast, deceiving himself and the world. Defeat only triggered his self-confidence; when he was trapped, he turned from being victim to being executioner: "If you are going to kill me tomorrow, kill me right now."[56]

The Mexican character was given passing but significant treatment by Ezequiel A. Chávez in *Ensayo de psicología de la adolescencia* (1928). Chávez had been one of the first in the twentieth century to approach the psychology of the Mexican, and this work

[53] Andrés Molina Enríquez, *Esbozo de la historia de los primeros diez años de la Revolución agraria de México*; Luis Cabrera, *Los problemas transcendentales de México*.

[54] Toribio Esquivel Obregón, "El indio en la historia de México," *Boletín de la sociedad mexicana de geografía y estadística* No. 41 (1929), pp. 297–298.

[55] Querido Moheno, *Sobre el ara sangrienta*, p. 103.

[56] Sáenz, *México íntegro*, p. 43.

demonstrated his abiding concern with the subject. Interestingly, he applied Alfred Adler's theory of the inferiority complex to Mexican behavior, thus prefiguring, and possibly influencing, Ramos, although the latter did not acknowledge it. Chávez argued that the Mexican inferiority complex was rooted in a history of conquest whose cruel heritage generated a lack of self-esteem, compelling the Mexican to exaggerate his personal worth. Thus such alleged character defects as dissimulation, hypocrisy, and adulation had their origins in historical determinants and in the social structure. Like Ramos, Chávez had a didactic purpose in mind, hoping that his study would help "remake" education and society.[57]

Clearly the 1920's provided a propitious setting for the search for national identity, and the Mexican responded by engaging in an extensive moral inquiry of his society. The strident nationalism in the arts and in the government programs of reconstruction, which redirected thought to the problems of Mexico, were reasons why the idea of *lo mexicano* came to the fore and would be crystallized in the essays of Samuel Ramos. If some of the writings surveyed here were those of lesser luminaries, considered together they illustrate the diffusion of *lo mexicano* thought from 1920 to 1934. Their themes had become woven into the fabric of attitudes that tidied up the dubious certainties of a youthful age given to philosophical speculation ranging in style from the bombastic to the acutely analytical. Samuel Ramos would emerge as the most persuasive arbiter of the specifically Mexican perception, yet between him and the dozens of intellectuals who polished the images of identity in the newspapers, magazines, and forums, stood several major thinkers whose scattered writings in the twenties revealed their exceptional affinities with the problem of defining Mexico.

[57] Ezequiel A. Chávez, *Ensayo de psicología de la adolescencia*, pp. 408–409, 14.

5.

Antecedents to Samuel Ramos: Vasconcelos, Caso, Reyes, and Cosío Villegas

IF the Revolutionary endeavor included the classic experiments in painting, the novel, education, anthropology, agrarian reform, and indigenism, it also must be credited with producing a new breed of intellectuals, public men who rose to prominence through their creative abilities and government service. Four such men who helped shape the age in which Samuel Ramos matured were José Vasconcelos, Antonio Caso, Alfonso Reyes, and Daniel Cosío Villegas. All were *pensadores*, writers who interpreted society and politics with the hope of correcting misplaced prestige and distorted values.[1] Their varied careers could converge in reaction to the United States presence in Mexico, the dilemma of socialism, or the apathy surrounding the development of Mexico's potential in the modern world. As contemporaries and mentors of Samuel Ramos, their essays reveal those clusters of ideas which influenced Ramos's intellectual growth, thus providing a background for understanding his book as well as underscoring Mexico's search for itself during the transition from upheaval to the institutionalization of the post-Revolutionary order. To the extent that these four anticipated or reinforced Ramos's themes, their writings are immediately precursory to his analysis of Mexican identity.

José Vasconcelos: "Children of the Pueblo" and Americanism

José Vasconcelos (1881–1959) was the classical Hispanic vital man and one of the key figures in the "renaissance" of the twenties.

[1] For a discussion of the *pensador* in the Latin American context, see François Bourricaud, "The Adventures of Ariel," *Daedalus* 101 (Summer,

Continuing Justo Sierra's work in nationalistic education, he was, like many of the early Revolutionaries, exuberant and seemingly tireless. Philosophical in mind, he was a man of action as well, and his role in education and in politics was notable for its drive and idealism.[2] Of the major intellectuals of the period, he was the most political and was involved in some of the most important issues of the decade. With Antonio Caso he shared the intellectual leadership of the twenties, though the decade really belonged to him. His exiles, travels, and studies took him through the Latin American experience, and for him *lo mexicano* was conceived as the problem of *lo americano*. At the center of his quest was the meaning of Mexico and Latin America, which he sustained in a romantic nationalism imbued with the concepts of newness, discovery, creation, and historical destiny.

To understand Vasconcelos' Mexicanist stance, one has to consider his idea of Latin America, with which he achieved his greatest fame as a writer. Vasconcelos was Mexico's chief spokesman for Americanism in the 1920's.[3] The roots of this movement stretched back into the national period of Latin American history, and its ideology included cultural differentiation from Europe, a belief in native values, and a sense of emergence into world civilization. An older Arielism was giving way to either Hispanism or indigenism in an attempt to contain the social atomization resulting from the rise of the masses in Latin America.[4] If revolution were to be avoided, it would be necessary to spiritualize the patria, and this would best be done by reconstructing national experience so as to create an idealistic buffer between the materialism of the modern age and the older organic unity of a hierarchical polity. The Americanism of the 1920's amplified themes articulated by such earlier writers as the Venezuelan César Zumeta, the Peruvian Francisco García Calderón,

---

1972), 109–136. The *pensador* in the Mexican context is treated by Peter Calvert, *Mexico*, pp. 207–212.

[2] For an introduction to his philosophy, see Patrick Romanell, *Making of the Mexican Mind*, pp. 95–138.

[3] The term *Americanism* will be used in this discussion to mean "New Worldism" or "Latin Americanism."

[4] Fredrick B. Pike, *Spanish America 1900–1970: Tradition and Social Innovation*, pp. 15–28.

the Bolivian Alcides Argüedas, and the Argentinian Manuel Ugarte.[5] For our purpose, it is important to know that this phase of Americanism culminated in such cultural and social analyses as Gilberto Freyre's *Casa-grande e senzala* (1933), Ezequiel Martínez Estrada's *Radiografía de la Pampa* (1933), and Samuel Ramos's *El perfil del hombre y la cultura en México* (1934). The study of national ethos contained in these works reflected both the history of ideas of a particular country and intellectual currents common to all of Latin America.

In the 1920's Mexico found itself becoming a leader in Latin America by virtue of its agrarian Revolution and cultural nationalism that promised to redeem the Indian.[6] The circumstances favored a Vasconcelos. His country incarnated a form of Americanism, and Latin America was ripe for his vision. Throughout the western world, during his periods of exile, he carried the message of Mexico and Latin America, often tailoring his remarks to fit the occasion. In Vienna, he spoke of an eclectic nationalism that emphasized the European contribution to Latin America; in Austin, Texas, he called for love between the United States and Latin America; elsewhere he cautioned Latin America against "Texanization."[7] In Mexico several of the magazines Vasconcelos was associated with—*El Maestro, La Falange*, and *La Antorcha*—supported the theme of Americanism.

Thus, while Vasconcelos wrote articles on the defects of the Mexican social character,[8] his Mexican analysis was frequently launched from a Latin American perspective. For instance, his discussion of the "spiritual" challenge of Mexico was based on the idea

---

[5] See Martin S. Stabb, *In Quest of Identity*, pp. 12–33.

[6] See Humberto Tejera, "México y el indolatinismo," *Repertorio Americano* 8 (March 31, 1924), 17–20; Pedro Henríquez Ureña, "El hermano definidor," *Repertorio Americano* 7 (October 29, 1923), 81; and Emilio Uribe Romo, "Oportunidad de Hispano-América," *Crisol* 4 (December, 1930), 407–410.

[7] José Vasconcelos, "El nacionalismo en la América Latina," *Repertorio Americano* 12 (March 1, 1926), 129–132, and (March 8, 1926), 148–150; idem, "Mensaje a Norte América," *Repertorio Americano* 9 (September 15, 1924), 17–19; idem, "El genio en Ibero-América," *Repertorio Americano* 17 (July 7, 1928), 8–9.

[8] Vasconcelos, "¿En dónde está la salvación?" *La Antorcha* 1 (October 11, 1924), 1–2.

of Latin American emergence from colonialism.[9] The emblem he designed for the National University illustrated his attempt to fuse his Mexican and Latin American visions. He explained that while the University must have a national direction, the Mexican patria must nevertheless be coterminous with that of the "great Hispanic-American patria." Thus in the center of the emblem a map was drawn of Latin America with an eagle and condor on either side, symbolizing Mexico and South America. The emblem's motto "Through my people the spirit will speak" signified a "new" and "free" culture.[10]

Vasconcelos treated Latin America and Mexico extensively in *Indología* (1927), a more theoretical statement of his earlier *La raza cósmica* (1925). The book crystallized the second period of Latin American nationalism—the twentieth-century emphasis on the Indian, the mestizo, the pueblo, and native expression. Vasconcelos' purpose was to characterize the "collective Ibero-American essence," and his term *indología* referred with visionary overtones to a study of Latin American social history. Offering the perfect rhetorical response to the political growth of national self-awareness behind Latin American development, the Mexican seer chose the symbol of the sphere to elaborate a philosophy of life potential. The sphere at the same time represented the great age of exploration, which had brought Latin America into world history. Falling back on the Hispanic legacy to the New World, Vasconcelos argued that Columbus had discovered a land that could create a universal civilization.

This was Vasconcelos' vision: that Latin America could become the cradle of future man whose development, aided by racial mingling, would result in the "cosmic race." He urged the Latin Americans toward a unitarian consciousness that would determine their identity.[11] While Vasconcelos held that philosophy should be universal and thus did not believe in a specifically Latin American

[9] See Wenceslao Blasco, "Entrevista: con el Licdo. José Vasconcelos," *Repertorio Americano* 2 (July 20, 1921), 369–370; Vasconcelos, "Discurso," *Repertorio Americano* 5 (January 8, 1923), 216–218.

[10] Vasconcelos, "El nuevo escudo de la Universidad Nacional," *Boletín de la Universidad* 2 (July, 1921), 91.

[11] Vasconcelos, *Indología*, in *Obras Completas*, II, 1116–1129.

philosophy, he nonetheless thought that a country should constantly examine its values in order to safeguard its progress.[12]

If *Indología* presented Vasconcelos at his most theoretical, his speeches often revealed him as a man of action, quixotically attempting to implement his ideas of spiritual regeneration. When he accepted the rectorship of the National University in 1920, he said he did not intend to meditate in an ivory tower but to do battle, to share responsibility with faculty and students, and to respond to the "national mood." Reflecting the educational dynamism of the twenties, Vasconcelos urged the intellectuals to leave their studies and join the Revolution, and insisting that elitist art had no meaning for those times, he described himself and kindred spirits as "children of the pueblo."[13]

His discourse exuded nationalism, and he decried the century of French and English influence that implied the Mexican was incapable of selfhood. Reinforcing the ideal of mestizo culture, he sought the origins of Mexican identity and outlined a creation myth based on the towering figures of pre-Hispanic Mexico and New Spain such as Quetzalcóatl, Netzahualcóyotl, Vasco de Quiroga, Pedro de Gante, Motolinía, and Antonio de Mendoza.[14]

If Vasconcelos was role playing, he did it well, combining a flair for publicity with his convictions about teaching the masses. The man who had been a member of the Political-Social Plan of 1911 and had served as minister of education from 1914 to 1915 found himself in 1920 in a position to apply his ideas to the post-Revolutionary consolidation, with its emphasis on popular culture. For example, when a recipient of a government stipend to study music in Europe wrote Vasconcelos to report on his progress, he made the mistake of saying that he was moving in upper-class Parisian society, whereupon Vasconcelos sternly answered that social success detracted from the creative experience and that the life of the common people was the source of modern reform.[15]

[12] Ibid., pp. 1205–1284.
[13] Vasconcelos, *Discursos*, pp. 8–11.
[14] Ibid., pp. 63–111.
[15] José Vasconcelos to Antonio Gómez Anda, August 31, 1920; Gómez Anda to Vasconcelos, November 19, 1920; Vasconcelos to Gómez Anda, December 7, 1920, all in AGN, RIP & BA, Leg. 8, Exp. 370.

It was Vasconcelos who set the intellectual orientation for the 1920's by his ability to generate practical responses to his vision. By circulating in newspapers a notice calling for local help in a campaign against illiteracy, he demonstrated the line of communication he hoped to open. The enthusiasm of Vasconcelos and the people is evident in the correspondence relating to the project. Diplomas, books, and school supplies were sent throughout Mexico and to the southwestern United States. From Arizona, Mexicans wrote of their efforts to further education through mutualist societies. A paymaster for Mexican railroad workers in Texas told how the men could not sign for their checks and were ridiculed by the North Americans.[16]

Vasconcelos' mystique of the pueblo embraced his definition of the revolutionary as one who dreamed and succeeded, one who formulated a theory of social progress and dedicated his life to its cause. While some believe that Vasconcelos betrayed his Revolutionary ideals in an attempt to secure personal power,[17] one cannot fault his work in the 1920's, especially his support of the mural movement when he was minister of education under Alvaro Obregón. Among his lesser-known achievements is the influence he exercized through the magazines he founded and thus the role he played in advancing the writing careers of Daniel Cosío Villegas, Samuel Ramos, and others.

Vasconcelos was the creative generalist of Mexico in the 1920's. His New World theory, based on his philosophy of sphericity and man's unlimited possibilities, characterized the optimism of the Revolution that had attempted to destroy an older life structure and to face reality radically and immediately. A creeping counter-force would alter the spherical course of Mexican life, however, as institutionalization, professionalism, and specialization—the linear syndrome—led to the establishment of power, elitism, and the loss of revolutionary praxis. Yet the spherical motif of the Vasconcelian doctrine was part of the flowering of the metaphysical revolution of

[16] Eliseo A. Pérez to José Vasconcelos, June 26, 1920, AGN, RIP & BA, Leg. 5, Exp. 207; Vasconcelos to Alfonso A. Sosa, July 12, 1920; Vasconcelos to Juana Quiñones, November 10, 1920, Exp. 206; Vasconcelos to Juan I. Cedillos, August 18, 1920; José Ernesto Segura to Vasconcelos, August 30, 1920, Exp. 208.

[17] See Daniel Cosío Villegas' comment, *Ensayos y notas*, I, 19.

Mexico in which Ramos and Paz would bloom, the one with his "new humanism" and the other with his "metaphor."

In summary, Vasconcelos was the archetypal Revolutionary intellectual, fusing esthetic, political, and educational ideals and presiding over a Mexican rebirth into innocence and utopia through a flight from the sophistication and corruption of the old regime. Swept along in the dynamism of the twenties, he illustrates how contemporary events converged in the thinker who fashioned a new consciousness for his country, synthesizing its history, judging it morally, and envisioning its possibilities.

Vasconcelos' ideas were often muddled and contradictory, but they reflected the Mexican mind impelled beyond its previous limits in the rush of Revolutionary experimentation and national euphoria. He saw the basic problems facing the Mexican intellectual: the Indian heritage, the colonial past, the origins of national identity, the polarization of nationalism and universalism, and the entry of Mexico into the modern world. In many ways his thought resembled the pictorial history of Mexico he sponsored in the mural movement. Like Antonio Caso's, his was a singular voice of the decade, but unlike Caso's his conveyed the spontaneity and turbulence of the period.

Antonio Caso and the "National Ideology"

From 1915 to 1945 Antonio Caso (1883–1946) probably influenced every notable Mexican figure in the humanities and many in the social sciences. Largely through his teaching, philosophy, a "ghost ambling about the corridors" as Justo Sierra described it in 1910, was restored to a place of eminence in Mexican intellectual life. His Bergsonian neoromantic revolt against positivism established a current of thought that prevailed for half a century, created the circumstances for such allied preoccupations as the history of ideas, and broke the ground for the arrival of the Spanish Orteguians in 1939. His anti-intellectualist philosophy of love and charity corresponded in part to the idealism spawned by the Revolution.[18]

[18] For an introduction to Caso's philosophy, see Rosa Krauze de Kolteniuk, *La filosofía de Antonio Caso.*

However, Caso at first did not support the Revolution, because he could not reconcile its violence with his philosophy.[19] Probably the least political of the intellectuals of this period, he did not go into exile but remained in Mexico, teaching his Christian-humanist idealism during the years 1910 to 1920. Like Vasconcelos, Caso developed an Americanist position as goodwill ambassador to South America under Obregón and as rector of the National University. As poor with the pen as he was gifted with the spoken word, his writings on Mexico are thin and disorganized, yet they represent a more significant portion of his works than is usually recognized. Given his eminence in Mexican intellectual life in the first half of the twentieth century, it is easy to see why his writings influenced Ramos and others.

A major medium for Caso, as for all intellectuals of this era, was the journalistic essay, which provided a forum for advancing the latest ideas of Latin American nationalism. Thus we discover him writing that Latin America represents the flowering of Latin civilization; that the New World has potentiality; that Mexico's wealth is controlled by foreigners; that the machine-oriented United States would never understand romantic Mexico; that the United States is the secret force in Mexican politics. Or we find him explaining his telluric vision of the Mexican patria.[20]

Much of Caso's defense of Latin America undoubtedly stemmed from his participation in post-Revolutionary politics and was dramatically crystallized in his debate with Francisco Bulnes in 1922. The third of eleven interchanges to take place between Caso and leading intellectuals, each dealing with an important issue in the history of ideas, the debate concerned the future of Latin America

[19] Apparently he was arrested by *zapatistas* and was on the verge of being shot for his suspected anti-Revolutionary bias. See Juan Hernández Luna, *Antonio Caso: embajador extraordinario de México*, pp. 64–65.

[20] Representative articles are "En América dirá su última palabra la civilización latina," *Repertorio Americano* 4 (May 22, 1922), 113–114; "Simpatía, sin raza, sin ideal," *Repertorio Americano* 4 (May 29, 1922), 134–137; "¿Por qué somos tan pobres?" *Repertorio Americano* 7 (January 28, 1924), 276–277; "La opinión de América," *Repertorio Americano* 8 (March 24, 1924), 13–14; "Nos compran la tierra," *Excélsior*, June 14, 1924; and "La tierra y la patria," *Repertorio Americano* 16 (March 24, 1928), 177.

as viewed by the older positivist and the younger optimistic nation-alist.[21]

The debate touched on both the universal and national levels, with such themes as classical civilization, Christianity, the Renaissance, and the meaning of Latin America bandied back and forth. Bulnes and Caso shared a respect for European culture but diverged on its relationship to the New World. Although Caso manifested a pro-Spanish bias, he also accepted responsibility for the problem of Latin American identity, whereas Bulnes fled from it.

For Bulnes, "Latinity" brutalized rather than humanized the New World; thus in neo-Buffonian fashion everything was wrong with Latin America. Nationalism was nonexistent because the Indians were not yet civilized, while Latin America had produced no writers or philosophers of international merit. The art of the "inferior races," he contended, such as the Chinese, Japanese, and Aztec, was devoid of esthetic value, but the statue of Cuauhtémoc was effective because of its Helenized demeanor. Latin America held little promise for the future because of its unfavorable climate, the pressure of the United States, and a weak economic structure. Bulnes's social prognostic was just as bleak; he harped on his interpretation of the tropical portion of Latin America as degenerate and therefore lacking the potential to contribute to progress.[22]

Caso was attracted by the cultural uniqueness of Latin America and in the case of Mexico sought to define its Spanish, French, and indigenous origins. Calling Bulnes passive before the encroaching power of the United States, Caso argued that a new Latin American sense of nationhood would counter the Yankee menace. Writing in an age when the decline of the West was being prophesied, Caso spoke of a future shift of power away from Europe to Asia and Latin America.[23] In spite of the fact that Bulnes and Caso were engaged in unfounded generalizations and that both represented the elite culture of their respective eras, Caso obviously was more imbued with the populist nationalism of the 1920's.

[21] See Juan Hernández Luna, Introduction to Antonio Caso, *Obras completas*, I, 84.
[22] Caso, *Obras completas*, I, 110–112, 117–119, 120.
[23] Ibid., 89–94, 108, 107.

Some of Caso's Mexicanist essays were collected in books during the twenties, and they testify to that decade's concern with national identity. History, social psychology, and moral commentary were the interwoven themes in his analysis of the state of affairs resulting from the violent struggle to achieve political stability and socioeconomic reform, an experience from which many intellectuals had not recovered. The historical perspective provided Caso with the necessary background to view specific political and social issues. In *El problema de México y la ideología nacional* (1924), he noted that Mexican problems were never fully resolved but were allowed to accumulate, resulting in civil war. He traced the origins of this situation to the Conquest, which had enlarged the horizons of western civilization, albeit at the expense of the Indians. The Spaniard placed the Cross on the *teocali* and thereby created a social dilemma: the commingling of two peoples whose cultures were in different stages of evolution.[24]

Buttressing his rationale with liberal social theory, Caso explained that the consequences of the Conquest became apparent when Mexico borrowed a theory of government such as democracy, which was inapplicable because of the lack of a homogeneous society. He pointed out that socialism, which he called the latest imitation of European ideologies, was being discussed while the problems of the Conquest and democracy were still unresolved. For Caso this was the intellectual pattern of Mexico: the continual acceptance of imperfectly developed theses not rooted in the internal conditions of the country but originating in the extension of the European mind to Mexico. To mitigate the effects of this, Caso exhorted the country to national self-awareness.[25]

If patriotism encouraged national identity, as Caso thought, the social character still had its shortcomings. With an air of philosophical superiority, Caso argued that the Mexicans gave free rein to their passions and were contentious because of the scramble for hierarchical supremacy. Thus with his typical Christian approach to social psychology, he called for compassion to replace passion, sympathy to dissolve antipathy, and intelligence and forgiveness to

[24] Caso, *El problema de México y la ideología nacional* pp. 11–13.
[25] Ibid., p. 68.

transcend the affront.[26] But the superficiality of his essays on the psychology of the Mexican was offset by his pioneering attitude toward the subject. Falling into the trap of stereotypes, he produced an image of the national character based on the shallow assumptions of indigenous indolence and Spanish arrogance. Yet he was aware of his limitations and indicated that his work was merely exploratory.[27] He extended his social criticism to the intellectual sphere and called for an improved study of history, a "pragmatic history" that would not distort truth and would be written without partisanship, religious prejudice, or anger. The task of the historian was to reconstruct the patria from the Conquest to the Revolution.[28]

Caso's reactionary Mexicanist ideology was never rigorously formulated but remained ancillary to his meditation on Mexican history. Thus what he said is of less importance to the age than the fact of his having said it. With his doubt concerning the viability of political thought, his search for national meaning, and his faith in moralistic solutions to social problems, Caso, like his fellow intellectuals of the twenties, put the question of Mexico under review. The Revolution had quickened the Mexican mind, and the intellectual took stock. Caso looked at the indigenous and Spanish strains of Mexican history and balanced each in a judgment influenced by the Revolution. He saw the Mexican conflict between idealism and actuality and in the consensus of the period sought at least a partial solution in nationalism.

His famous French influence notwithstanding, Caso was fond of writing about the "collective soul," a concept he drew from his reading of nineteenth-century German psychologists like Wundt and Steinthal.[29] This gave him at best a thin purchase on social analysis. If his interpretation of the national character was colored by his pessimism, Caso nevertheless believed that through self-awareness, understanding, and love, Mexico could enhance its identity, and that a nation could be built that would transform the social enmity and fragmented culture. Like his predecessors and successors who delved into the meaning of Mexican society, Caso pointed up behavioral

[26] Ibid., pp. 76–79.
[27] Caso, "Psicología del pueblo mexicano," *Excélsior*, June 8 and 15, 1925.
[28] Caso, *Discursos heterogéneos.*
[29] See Caso, *Sociología genética y sistemática*, p. 136.

128 Roots of *Lo Mexicano*

defects in order to root them out, and in his discussion of imitation and passion as national characteristics he anticipated Ramos. This moral control of the negative aspects of the social character lay at the heart of Caso's "national ideology."

Alfonso Reyes: "In Search of the National Soul"

After Vasconcelos and Caso, Alfonso Reyes (1889–1959) was probably the most important figure in Mexican intellectual life during the first half of the twentieth century. Primarily an influence on writers—his style and subject matter making him a successful essayist and poet—his voice was also heard in the search for national identity. With Caso and Vasconcelos he was one of the Ateneo de la Juventud who rebelled against positivism, and his works reflect his youthful experience: free, imaginative, and romantic. He was Mexico's grand cosmopolite during the twenties, spending most of his time outside the country in diplomatic service. Often accused of a lack of interest in Mexican themes, he was nonetheless attracted by Spain and the New World in his literary endeavors.[30] Scattered pieces illustrate a preoccupation with Mexican identity that would not go unnoticed by Ramos. Reyes liked to write about the relevancy of the "national soul,"[31] and although he never continued his projected series of essays beyond "Visión de Anáhuac," he did touch on the subject in treating the Americanism of the twenties. As with Vasconcelos, it is necessary first to view Reyes's Americanist position in order to understand his Mexicanist reflections.

For Reyes the significant aspect of New World history had been the growth of national self-discovery, an experience that revealed the "American imagination" and identified *lo americano*.[32] In outlining the "American complex" Reyes saw New World man suffering anxiety because, not ethnically unified, he was forced to live in an imported culture at the same time as he was impelled by an "American consciousness" to grapple with native circumstances. This com-

[30] For a discussion, see Barbara Bockus Aponte, *Alfonso Reyes and Spain*, pp. 193–194.
[31] Alfonso Reyes, "Carta a Antonio Mediz Bolio," *Obras completas*, IV, 421–422.
[32] Reyes, "Sobre folklore," *Obras completas*, VIII, 55.

plex produced a sense of inferiority, Reyes concluded, and, noting the growing literature dealing with the problem, he summarized the writers' attempts to find *lo americano* and trace the profile of the New World mind.[33] Thus Reyes, like Vasconcelos, tended to see the search for Mexican identity from a continental perspective.

Nonetheless, Reyes dealt with specifically Mexican topics. In "México en una nuez," he offered an interesting model for the literary synthesis of Mexican history, one that would increasingly appear during the *lo mexicano* movement in the post-Ramos period. Elsewhere he made a plea for the study of Mexican culture and called for a return to *lo propio* (that which is characteristic of or pertinent to the self). In "A vuelta de correo," he denied that he had ignored Mexico and discussed his concern with *lo mexicano*. For him the folkloric and the *costumbrista* strains in Mexican culture were interesting but could not effectively explain *lo esencialmente mexicano*. *Lo nacional*, he thought, was only beginning to be clarified psychologically, and calm and time were needed to discover the national mind, which he termed a "secret chemistry," not always evident on the surface of Mexican life. In his arguments Reyes borrowed Jungian and Freudian concepts of the subconscious but cautioned that national character was not the sole determinant of national culture.[34]

Reyes's approach to Mexican identity was visionary; he had more in common with Vasconcelos than with Caso, Cosío Villegas, or Ramos. If Reyes conceived his thought in poetic perspective, he nevertheless grounded it in his country's history and social problems. Like Vasconcelos, he committed the error of mixing his ideas on Mexico and Latin America, although this is understandable in light of the traditional position of the Latin American intellectual who speaks for his country as well as for his continent. Like Ramos, Reyes wanted to free Mexico and the rest of Latin America from their "inferiority complex." "America" was to fulfill its potential, create an original culture, and hearken to a mythic historical destiny.

Representative of the Mexican mind as it turned inward, Reyes

[33] Reyes, "Los ojos de Europa," *Obras completas*, VIII, 304.
[34] Reyes, "México en una nuez," *Obras completas*, IX, 42–56; idem, "Discurso por Virgilio," *Obras completas*, XI, 159–161; idem, "A vuelta de correo," *Obras completas*, VIII, 441–443.

thus was expanding the psychological dimension of national identity opened by Sierra, López Velarde, and others. In effect he poetized and philosophized upon Sierra, whom he greatly admired, and helped tip the balance of historical thought from the factual to the interpretive and the moral, a shift of emphasis important to the Mexican intellectual, whose cultural multiplicity left his identity a maze of contradictions and uncertainties. Reyes's New World outlook, which subsumed his Mexicanism, was an attempt to provide a rationale for national emergence from the psychological implications of a convoluted historical development. Reyes wanted the creative experience to crystallize Mexican identity by offering a mystique of land and history that conveyed a sense of being amid the ephemeral tug-of-war of politics. His full weight as a writer was not felt until the 1930's and 1940's, and he was more important in the 1920's for his influence on such younger writers as Cosío Villegas and Ramos.

Daniel Cosío Villegas and the Critical Attitude

Daniel Cosío Villegas (1898–1976) is regarded as one of the independent spirits who brought maturity and respect to the world of ideas in the post-Revolutionary period. Best known today as the chief author of a monumental study of the Porfiriato, his role as political critic was equally important and underscored his whole career as an intellectual. His seldom-read writings of the twenties reveal his response to the Revolution in the form of a critical attitude that encompassed the gropings of a nation searching hither and yon for the mainspring of social progress and meaningful identity. In a country where criticism has been called the "original sin,"[35] the attempt to penetrate the complexities of a history noteworthy for political fictions masking underdevelopment is essential to the vocation of the ideologue, statesman, and seer. Like Ramos, his contemporary and friend, Cosío was a protegé of Antonio Caso and Pedro Henríquez Ureña and was endowed with a perspicacity and irony that well qualified him to hold the reins of intellectual power in his country. Like Ramos, Cosío would improve upon the Mexicanist thought of

[35] See Jorge Hernández Campos, "La crítica como pecado original: México ante la crisis de la cultura universal," *Excélsior*, April 30, 1972.

Caso and Vasconcelos, and he may be included among the immediate precursors to Ramos because of his earlier publications dealing with national identity.

Cosío left Toluca as a student and arrived in Mexico City in 1915, shortly thereafter entering the Law Faculty of the National University. He received his baptism into Mexican intellectual life through literature and politics, writing prose poems and assuming leadership in student organizations. Within a few years he had settled into the experience of open creation that was Mexico in the 1920's. Soon he was filling in along with Ramos for a busy Vicente Lombardo Toledano in his ethics class in the National Preparatory School. Eventually his activities included translating the classics for the University; writing literary reviews, articles on Mexican culture, and current events commentary; editing journal notes and the *Revista de Ciencias Sociales*;[36] serving as director of extension for the University; and succeeding Antonio Caso to the chair of sociology in the Law Faculty. He would serve in various administrative posts and would study in the United States, France, and England. Like that of Ramos, his cosmopolitanism would balance his nationalism; in a spoof on the pretensions of his age, he expressed the Revolutionary consciousness in a setting of the Parisian 1920's.[37]

Cosío evolved a cynical but flexible idea of Mexico to underpin his analysis of post-Revolutionary problems, advising his readers to be skeptical of what the government promised, in view of what was actually delivered. It was a creaky history he drew forth to support his premise that Mexico was lacking in rigorous policy-making and cohesive action.[38] Thus he strove to give form to a wayward polity,

[36] Daniel Cosío Villegas, "Repertorio," *México Moderno* 2 (June, 1923), 250–254; idem, "La resurrección de Arévalo Martínez," *La Antorcha* 1 (April 18, 1925), 18; idem, "La pintura en México," *Cuba Contemporánea* 34 (April, 1924), 331–339; idem, "La universidad zoológica," *La Antorcha* 1 (January 24, 1925), 3–4; idem, "Notas bibliográficas: Don Juan Ruiz de Alarcón," *Revista de Filología Española* 10 (April–June, 1923), 192–193.

[37] Cosío Villegas, "BA-TA-CLAN," *La Antorcha* 1 (February 25, 1925), 29. Biographical data taken from idem, *Ensayos y notas*, I, 17–18; Enrique Krauze, "Datos personales," in *Extremos de México: homenaje a don Daniel Cosío Villegas*, pp. 5–10; and Guillermo Ochoa, "El gobierno debe mantener el avance," *Excélsior*, November 29, 1971.

[38] Cosío Villegas, "El renacimiento agrarista," *La Antorcha* 1 (June 6, 1925), 4.

and such efforts became the cornerstone of his civic relationship to his country. His life became a microcosm of contemporary Mexican intellectual history as he moved from a period of romantic searching toward the professional and institutional concerns of later years. The transition was evident in his contribution to the organization of the National School of Economics, the Fondo de Cultura Económica publishing house, the journals *El Trimestre Económico* and *Historia Mexicana*, El Colegio de México, and his crowning achievement— directing and co-writing the multi-volume *Historia Moderna de México* (1955–1971). One of the handful of intellectuals who made criticism a meaningful endeavor, Cosío as *pensador* in the twenties reflected the temper of the age and contributed to the growth of national identity.

The key to Cosío's mind is found in one of his first publications, a book of prose poems entitled *Miniaturas mexicanas* (1922).[39] Cultivating a favorite genre of Hispanic writers, he penetrated reality through the poetic image. Examining his writings more than a half-century later, one finds the same mind at work: the careful, intimate expression, the distinctive combination of adjectives and nouns classical in tone yet never forced, and a rugged syntax that makes Cosío's writing unmistakable among that of his contemporaries. He delighted in pointing out that the first requirement of good writing was discipline, not inspiration.[40] Obviously he was carving out a literary career for himself, yet he never fully pursued it and ultimately turned away from it.[41] Perhaps he found the altitude of literary creation too rarefied and, as one of his short stories suggested, there may have been an element of the frustrated creator in his life. In any case, as the title of his story indicated, he "returned to reality."[42]

By 1925 Cosío had written "Nuestro pobre amigo: novela mexi-

---

[39] For a discussion of the genesis of this work, see Cosío Villegas, *Memorias*, pp. 80–81.

[40] Cosío Villegas, "Prólogo," in Xavier Icaza, *Gente mexicana*, p. 11.

[41] By 1923 Cosío was listed among the leaders of the contemporary literary generation (Pedro Henríquez Ureña to Alfonso Reyes, November 17, 1923, AAR).

[42] Cosío Villegas, "El retorno a la realidad," *Repertorio Americano* 11 (December 14, 1925), 213. For another example of his creative writing, see "El hilo se rompe," *La Antorcha* 1 (June 20, 1925), 15, 18, 19.

cana," a mature example of his tight, clear style and an interesting treatment of the Mexican themes of humor, death, and family life.[43] Yet before too long, he was writing on banking, displaying his historical consciousness and his ability to handle hard data.[44] It was clear that his "return to reality" was to become a lifelong critique of institutional Mexico, primarily of the Porfiriato and post-Revolutionary development. Of special interest to him was the relationship between rhetoric and reality, between aspiration and accomplishment. If Mexico should become enmeshed in its rhetoric, he reflected prophetically, how could the achievements of the Revolution be justified? Would they cease to exist in time? Reconstruction was being tested, said Cosío, by the person who recognized that problems existed and tried to solve them.[45]

Nothing so epitomized the challenges posed by the twenties and the intensified search for nationhood as Cosío's interpretation of the Revolution. In a seminal essay that established the precepts for his *Historia Moderna de México* and for his political analysis up until his death, Cosío saw that the evaluation of the Revolution rested on an understanding of the Porfiriato. Already he was addressing the question of whether the Revolution had failed. The Revolution's critics, he noted, came in three varieties: the "radicals," who wished to advance solely for the sake of success; the "snobs," whose cult of newness caused them to view the status quo contemptuously; and the "dilettantes," whose worship of the foreign impelled them to import the Russian revolution. However, Cosío alternately affirmed the Revolution and doubted its achievement. It was this Cartesian methodology which allowed him to bypass fixed assertions regarding contemporary events and to explore at the deepest rational level the essence of the Revolutionary transfer. The result was a sagacious rejection of political rhetoric that changed the course of Mexican intellectual history and opened the Revolution to scrutiny within a historical process by freeing it from a framework of appearances. Thus Cosío explained how the "triumph" and "prestige" of the

43 Cosío Villegas, "Nuestro pobre amigo: novela mexicana," in *La Novela Semanal de El Universal Ilustrado*, January 1, 1925.

44 Cosío Villegas, "Los bancos y la moneda," in *México económico, 1928–1930*, pp. 141–157.

45 Cosío Villegas, "El ABC de las cosas," *La Antorcha* 1 (April 25, 1925), 4.

Revolution stemmed in great part from the *bola*, the violence and arbitrary action that underlay the destruction of the old regime.

A comparison of the two epochs was now inevitable, and it emerged as an analysis of the shifts in political style and public attitudes, revealing Cosío's attraction to the Díaz period. By the 1920's the myth of the Porfiriato as a negative chapter in Mexican history was providing much of the basis for Revolutionary ideology, but here Cosío departed from the tacit assumptions of his fellow intellectuals. He argued that the Porfiriato was not debased but employed discretion to hide the sordid workings of government. Astute and deft, Díaz, he maintained, was never implicated in the unseemly aspects of his rule; instead he perpetuated a system—which Cosío called intelligent—whereby he appeared not as tyrant but as benevolent patriarch. It was difficult for Cosío to accept the public clamor of the Revolution. While he acknowledged that the "noisy, savage outburst" had demolished the "false theory" of Díaz, arrogance had become the order of the day and was corrupting politicians. But the Revolution had generated self-esteem and a sense of freedom, and that was worth consolidating, he said.

Cosío's ambivalence regarding contemporary Mexico, however, was to furnish him with the stuff of a fruitful intellectual synthesis. If he could not conceal his admiration for the Porfiriato, he also could not deny the sincere motivations of the Revolution; thus he was led both ways and could remain ironically detached from an official position, making a backward appraisal of the Porfiriato while contemplating the forward thrust of the Revolution.[46] Cosío's historiography meant that the Revolution could no longer be seen as the monolithic bulwark of nationhood, nor could the Porfiriato be viewed as an interruption in the course of progress. The implications of this approach would rewrite Mexican history in the modern and contemporary periods, establishing a framework for the evaluation of continuity and change.[47]

The Revolution posed questions that led Cosío to reflect upon

[46] Cosío Villegas, "La escuela del servilismo," *La Antorcha* 1 (June 13, 1925), 19, 20.

[47] For an example, see Lorenzo Meyer, "Continuidades e inovaciones en la vida política mexicana del siglo XX: el antiguo y el nuevo régimen," *Foro Internacional* 16 (July–September, 1973), 37–63.

the conflict between the traditional and the modern. Speaking on the Revolution at the University of Havana, he referred to a Mexican culture with an indigenous base, clearly differentiated from the European. Using the automobile as an example of an imported cultural artifact, he noted that while it was not a Mexican product, it was nonetheless comfortable and practical and that there was no reason why the Mexican should not use it. He added, however, that the automobile should not be equated with civilization.[48] Here his statement embodied the twentieth-century concern with *malinchismo* and *pochismo* (a Mexican culture debased by North American influences) and their inhibiting effects on the growth of native culture.

Cosío's early criticism contained a sociological reference for the twenties in which, as outlined in Ortega's *El tema de nuestro tiempo* (1923), history was conceived as the idea of generations—a rhythm of ages of senescence and rejuvenation. Influenced by Fichte's *The Characteristics of Our Age*, Ortega discussed the problems of culture and life in the modern era and argued that a new generation came into being when a "vital sense" was altered, and there was a new way of judging history.[49] It was not difficult for Cosío to apply the Orteguian concepts to Mexico: the Porfiriato could be viewed as senescence and the twenties as rejuvenation.

In an essay in which Cosío expressed his debt to Ortega, he said that his sociology course in the University reflected contemporary ideas and explained that while some of his conclusions might be alarming, they were at least sincere. In analyzing Mexican society he told his students that he would speak the truth and that he was not worried about repercussions abroad or at home. These seemingly naïve remarks cannot go unattended, for they point to the role of the Revolution in creating the modern critical consciousness in Mexico. Just as the raggle-taggle armies had ripped the façade off Porfirian Mexico, so would the thinkers, once the violence had ceased, see through the false images of the country.

The new generation, changed by the Revolution, Cosío asserted, was aware of the troubles ahead and was more pessimistic than the

[48] See the summary of Cosío's lecture in Rafael Heliodoro Valle, "Ideario mexicano," *Repertorio Americano* 13 (September 4, 1926), 143.

[49] José Ortega y Gasset, *El tema de nuestro tiempo*, pp. 3–11.

older generation. Thus it was necessary to be rigorously critical, and Cosío surmised that the country would be found wanting once its history and society were judged. To illustrate his point he proceeded to destroy the myth of Mexican wealth and resources, which he concluded had been created through the uncritical acceptance of ideas.[50] For Cosío the twenties was a period of re-evaluation and renewal, marked by a revolutionary attitude widespread in western civilization: radical man wanted to revivify an unresponsive establishment and time-worn values.[51] His Orteguian essay, it may be noted, was one of the first expressions of the impact of Germano-Hispanic thought on Mexico.

Cosío's main critical work of the twenties is the curious *Sociología mexicana* (1924–1925), which consists of three short volumes of notes taken by a student in the sociology course Cosío had inherited from Caso.[52] Divided into three parts treating land, people, and education, the book is a rambling analysis of Mexican history and the national character. In the introduction, which reflects the intellectual atmosphere of the times, Cosío stated that he did not fear failing as a professor but rather in providing his students with a "warm human idea of Mexico" and explained that his teaching was a question of proselytism. He said that if the students felt what he did—a "vague restlessness," an impression that something "profoundly mysterious" was happening—then he would not worry about Mexico's future.

In elaborating his critical rationale, Cosío stated that, since it was necessary to remedy the ills of Mexico, he would emphasize the negative aspects of the country. And although he observed that life in the twenties in Mexico and in the rest of the world contained an element of euphoria, he maintained that he would not deviate from his pessimistic approach, since the insignificant events of the day

[50] The myth of great wealth in Mexico was still current among the country's leaders in the 1920's. Earlier, Francisco Bulnes had pursued the same line of attack as Cosío. See Moisés González Navarro, *Población y sociedad en México, 1900–1970*, II, 24–25.

[51] Cosío Villegas, "La riqueza de México," *La Antorcha* 1 (May 30, 1925), 8. See also his "La tierra madre única," *La Antorcha* 1 (May 16, 1925), 7–8.

[52] Ortega's *El tema de nuestro tiempo* (1923) was also written in part from the class notes of one of his students. It is possible that this was the influencing idea behind Cosío's work.

might have repercussions years later. Cautioning that the development of Mexico would be slow, he warned that if the country proceeded badly, it would have to answer for its mistakes.[53] Cosío proposed to examine the social vices of Mexico and worked from the premise that man did not resolve many of his problems, because he did not confront the important issues.

Faithful to his purpose of rigorous criticism, he drew a bleak profile of Mexico, illustrating many of the themes recurrent in Mexican thought from the Revolution on. Implicit in his argument was the role of national self-examination in creating the true patria by educating the people to their problems, one of which was the clear perception of reality. Thus, while it was standard to focus on the idea of national uniqueness, Cosío remarked that the term *idiosyncracy* was used by Mexicans to explain what they did not understand, adding cynically that the term should read "everyone's bad luck."[54]

Loosing his barbs at the Mexican façade, he punctured some myths about the national character. Among the traits he singled out was the Mexican's courtesy, which foreigners interpreted as a natural gregariousness. He explained that the courtesy was perfunctory, a veil for the Mexican's intimate sociability that led him to prefer solitude and the company of family and friends to the world at large. Cosío shattered the image of the happy Mexican by arguing that his life was monotonous with little public diversion. Woman, educated to fulfill a submissive role, tended to remain aloof to the outside world, even though the fiesta erased the barriers between the sexes for a short duration. And echoing an environmentalist approach to social psychology, Cosío pondered the harmful effects climate could have on personality and social patterns. The cold afternoons dampened the Mexican's enthusiasm, he said, and, overcome by a feeling of sadness, he went home bored or to the cantina.[55]

Mexican society was riven by what Cosío saw as the consequences of historical disunity. Following the racial precepts still in vogue in the twenties, he dwelled upon the triad of Indian, creole, and mestizo. The creole was ambitious and disciplined and had in-

[53] Cosío Villegas, *Sociología mexicana*, I, 7–8; II, 9.
[54] Ibid., III, 13–17.
[55] Ibid., II, 22–27.

herited an elaborate cultural framework; the mestizo, who was also ambitious, was astute and energetic. The Indian was exploited by both, and Cosío concluded that all three did not have a shared patria. Pointing out that the lack of communication and education hindered the development of nationhood, he maintained that the problems of Mexico could thus be viewed from the standpoint of diverse and conflicting peoples. This was the origin of the perpetual absence of peace in Mexico, the "eternal revolution."[56]

Like most critics of his time, Cosío emphasized the disjunctive forces of Mexico: the revolutionary momentum supported by an ideology that could break down at any moment; the national character as a reflection of socioeconomic ills; and the indigenous basis of Mexico that contrasted with the country's need for modernity. Yet over against his pessimism, Cosío posited the new sensibility of the post-Revolutionary generation that sought intellectual integrity for the future. The problem was how to reconstruct Mexico and achieve modernity without sacrificing the country's essential humanity, which was made up of Hispanic and indigenous elements that did not harmonize well with the machine age. The solutions, he held, could be found only in a critical approach to the tasks confronting the nation.

Cosío represented Mexican thought typified by analysis rather than by intuition. Though the influence of Caso is evident in his writings of this period, he was more incisively critical than his mentor. In discussing reconstruction, the challenge of education, and the moral purpose of intellectual activity, he summarized the age and its preoccupation with national identity. Samuel Ramos was to elaborate a theory of Mexican society and its relationship to the wider world. Yet his Mexicanist study was not original to the extent that it reflected the preoccupations of the thinkers presented in this chapter. All shared a philosophical approach to history, the concept of the duality of Mexican culture, the realization that Mexican nationhood was an equation of internal and external factors, a distrust of the United States, a healthy skepticism regarding the national character, and the sense of directed change consonant with the goals of the Revolution.

[56] Ibid., III, 11–18.

6.

Samuel Ramos and the Mexican

By 1929 when Samuel Ramos (1897–1959) had begun his serious analysis of the Mexican character, the country was in turmoil, the Revolution precarious. The political situation following the assassination of Obregón the year before had presaged military revolt. Reconstruction was by no means complete, and Emilio Portes Gil took office promising to consolidate the Revolution. Yet the newly organized Partido Nacional Revolucionario (PNR), separated for a time from Calles and pressured by *vasconcelistas*, hardly looked like the solution to political problems that in fact it would become.

Mexico witnessed major outbreaks of violence: first in the Escobar revolt, which took two thousand lives, and then, after the attempt on Ortiz Rubio's life by a suspected *vasconcelista*, the massacre at Topilejo. And although the Cristero War was concluded in 1929, it would be more than a decade before the church and the government would be reconciled. To many the Revolution was betraying itself as the social and agrarian ideals of earlier years were pushed aside by business and military interests. Calles became the *jefe máximo* of the Revolution and was accused of dictatorship. Then the Maximato was burdened by the world depression, which caused a withdrawal of capital from Mexico and contributed to the curtailment of land distribution. And the recurrent intrusion of the United States in Mexican affairs emphasized the country's internal weakness. Many young intellectuals were distraught by these events.

In this strained atmosphere Ramos began writing the essays that would recapitulate many of the themes of the 1920's: reconstruction, the idea of *mexicanidad*, the transition from positivism to Orteguian perspectivism, the critique of social psychology, and some of the Mexican topics treated by Vasconcelos, Caso, Reyes, and Cosío Villegas. In short, it was the multifaceted preoccupation with the meaning of Mexico and the Mexican that influenced Ramos and was

in turned synthesized by him, yet by 1934 Ramos could actually say little on the problem of national identity that had not been said since 1920 and hinted at since 1900 and earlier. However, the cosmopolitan-nationalistic duality that molded his intellectual growth from his adolescent experience with philosophy to his entry into the Mexico City circle of thinkers provided Ramos with an expressive power and breadth of comprehension unequalled for his times, giving him the distinction of being the first modern student of *lo mexicano*. Thus his classic interpretation of the national behavior, *El perfil del hombre y la cultura en México* (1934), brought to fruition a Mexicanist preoccupation that spanned a decade; it is only within this context that his work can be meaningfully explicated.

From Province to Capital

Born of middle-class parents in Zitácuaro, Michoacán, Ramos at an early age moved with his family to Morelia. A center of learning since colonial times, Morelia followed the pattern of provincial culture in Mexico. Intellectual life was focused in the atheneum, which stimulated the exchange of ideas and fostered creative aspirations under the sponsorship of a patron, usually a prominent teacher, a military man, or a leading politician, while a small magazine often was produced as an outlet for local talent.

It was in such a tradition and in such a magazine, *Flor de Loto*, that Ramos entered the intellectual world. *Flor de Loto*, published from 1909 to 1911, was one of the noteworthy small magazines of the period and numbered among its contributors such future national figures as the physician Ignacio Chávez, the journalist Rafael Heliodoro Valle, the novelist José Rubén Romero, the historian Jesús Romero Flores, the president Pascual Ortiz Rubio, the general Francisco J. Mújica, and Ramos, whose first contributions dealt with literature and photography.[1] Ramos was preparing for a career in medicine, but as a student of José Torres Orozco, who taught philosophy, psychology, and sociology at the College of St. Nicholas and

---

[1] According to Juan Hernández Luna, Samuel Ramos was fourteen or younger when he was associated with this magazine (*Samuel Ramos: su filosofar sobre lo mexicano*, pp. 20–22).

who was, according to Ramos, Mexico's greatest positivist, he gradually turned to philosophy. To some scholars Torres is one of Mexico's least recognized intellectuals, and revisionist historians of ideas have attempted to disseminate his work in order to correct the image of positivism as supportive of the Díaz regime and as a corrupting force in Mexican culture.[2] Ramos pursued the three major preoccupations of his mentor: medicine, philosophy, and psychology. Because of Torres's presence in Morelia, Ramos received a rigorous initiation into the life of the mind and arrived in Mexico City already substantially prepared. The closing of the medical school in Morelia in 1917 during the Revolutionary upheaval together with the death of his father had made Ramos decide to go to the capital to continue his medical studies. Once there, however, political difficulties at the Military Medical School after the fall of Carranza and the effect of hearing the impassioned Caso induced him to abandon his career in medicine.[3]

Contact with such prominent thinkers as Antonio Caso, José Vasconcelos, and Pedro Henríquez Ureña opened new vistas to Ramos, and his philosophical vocation deepened. Conversations with other literati stimulated his preoccupation with esthetics and with Mexico.[4] Soon he was involved in the scholarly pursuits of that period: teaching philosophy in the National Preparatory School, translating the classics for Vasconcelos' literature programs, and writing. When he inherited the editorship of *La Antorcha* from Vasconcelos with the April 25, 1925, issue, he had earned a place in the intellectual community and the respect of his peers.

Vignettes of Ramos by his contemporaries are revealing. Daniel Cosío Villegas wrote that Ramos was a philosopher even before he knew it, one of the few young intellectuals whose path was clearly marked. Cosío reported that Ramos lived in poverty and solitude for two years studying constantly, while Eduardo Villaseñor regarded

[2] See Samuel Ramos, "José Torres: el primero y el último positivista," *La Antorcha* 1 (June 20, 1925), 6–7; Juan Hernández Luna, *José Torres Orozco: el último positivista mexicano*, pp. 13–14.

[3] Hernández Luna, *Samuel Ramos*, pp. 33–39.

[4] See Salvador Azuela, "Samuel Ramos abrió el camino a los trabajos que se han hecho sobre la filosofía cultural de México," *El Sol de Puebla*, July 25, 1959.

Ramos as a figure to reckon with. In speaking of Ramos, Villaseñor urged Mexico to follow Argentina's example of synthesizing its identity through the medium of the essay and the knowledge of national and foreign values. He further stated that although it would come as a surprise to many, Ramos was the leader of the new generation, adding that he hoped it would be Ramos who would take the first step in the rigorous formulation of a Mexicanist critique. Thus Ramos had earned the esteem of two of the principal architects of institutional development in post-Revolutionary Mexico.[5]

By his own admission Ramos had been struggling since 1916 to overcome a deep spiritual crisis caused by a conflict between positivism and scholasticism inherited from his provincial background.[6] He had clearly been turning inward as he searched for a solution to the dilemma posed by the passing of one era of thought in Mexico and the beginning of another, a transition he himself was going to hasten. If Caso had broadened Ramos's philosophical horizons, Vasconcelos provided him with the means to express himself as well as to play an active role in shaping the flow of ideas in Mexico. As editor of *La Antorcha* Ramos acknowledged that his generation was indebted to Caso and Vasconcelos but pointed out that it was also "new" and admonished it to substitute "methodical reflection" for rhetoric.[7] He conceived his task as shaping a "popular awareness" of western intellectual trends, and in this role his cosmopolitan interests took precedence over his nationalistic ones. Thus his dialogue on love opened against a 1920's background of jazz, Freudian thought, and "sexual electricity."[8] But Ramos had by no means consolidated his philosophical position. If he had succeeded in transcending the materialist thought of the nineteenth century,[9] he nevertheless could

[5] Daniel Cosío Villegas, "Libros y revistas," *La Antorcha* 1 (May 16, 1925), 18; Eduardo Villaseñor, "Intenciones sobre la cultura en México," *La Antorcha* 1 (January 17, 1925), 16.

[6] Samuel Ramos, "Mi experiencia pragmatista," in Agustín Basave Fernández del Valle, *Samuel Ramos: trayectoria filosófica y antológica de textos*, p. 108.

[7] Samuel Ramos, "Incipit vita nova," *La Antorcha* 1 (June 13, 1925), 5.

[8] Ramos, "Notas editoriales," *La Antorcha* 1 (May 23, 1925), 4; idem, "El simposio," *La Antorcha* 2 (October, 1925), 5.

[9] Ramos, "Del siglo XIX, líbranos señor," *La Antorcha* 1 (February 21, 1925), 13.

not accept the intuitive and pragmatic synthesis Caso offered in its place. Here was the root of the next phase of his intellectual growth.

Ramos Challenges the Master

In 1927 Ramos denounced Casonian thought in two issues of *Ulises*, a leading avant-garde magazine of the period. His arguments were well-balanced, and he placed Caso within the perspective of intellectual history, starting with the thesis that positivism had justified liberalism at the expense of social progress. The "base interpretation of positivism," he maintained, had limited education to practical ends, while a bourgeois elite masked its power motives behind a false rationale of national legitimacy. Caso drew his praise for leading the attack on positivism and for arousing public interest in ideas. Nonetheless Ramos assailed Caso's pontification and accused him of continuing to the point of monotony his lectures on charity and disinterest—the philosophy of the spirit that had made him famous and had helped loosen the hold of positivism on the country. Arguing that Caso resorted to sentimentality and anti-intellectualism to compensate for analytical deficiency, Ramos suggested that Caso relied too heavily on accepted truths and had become as dogmatic as the positivists.[10] Caso's function as a thinker was diminished, Ramos declared, by his hero worship and by his histrionic style.[11]

Although Caso was by now an old hand at the polemical art, his reply to Ramos was little more than an exercise in self-commemoration, citing the flattering reviews of his South American speaking tour and referring to an autographed picture of a European philosopher as proof of his own eminence. His rebuttal was as unconvincing as his conclusion that Ramos was unfit to teach philosophy. Controversy flared following the exchange between the older philosopher and his younger rival. The one was accused of a lack of clarity, and the other of opportunism. Ramos felt constrained to respond to Caso's remarks and took him to task for unprofessional behavior.[12]

---

[10] Ramos, "Antonio Caso," *Ulises* 1 (May, 1927), 12–19.
[11] Ramos, "Antonio Caso: (Conclusión)," *Ulises* 1 (June, 1927), 5–6.
[12] Antonio Caso, "Ramos y yo: un ensayo de valoración personal," in

But what was the deeper meaning of Ramos's attack on Caso? If it represents a philosophical coming of age for Ramos, does it not also illustrate a watershed in Mexican thought? At stake here was not only a specific critical problem, but ultimately a new Latin American framework for ideas.

The background of the debate should be weighed as carefully as the results. One scholar traces the origins to the salon of Antonieta Rivas Mercado, where Ramos and some of his students gathered to discuss the articles of the *Revista de Occidente* and to lay plans for the magazine *Ulises*. A contemporary of Ramos views the debate as merely the expression of a young man wishing to bring attention to himself and impatient to explore new ideas. Another scholar notes that as Vasconcelos' star went up in the twenties, Caso's seemed to decline, and thus Ramos may have been reacting to a shift in intellectual leadership.[13] One also must consider the influence on Ramos of his mentors José Torres Orozco and Pedro Henríquez Ureña. In the early twenties Caso and Vasconcelos were still involved in dismantling positivism, mostly in educational circles. Torres had come to Mexico City and, although dying of tuberculosis, heroically spent his time refuting Bergson's philosophy of intuition, which Caso had popularized in Mexico. To the end an unreformed positivist, Torres censured Caso and Vasconcelos in a manuscript he left to Ramos. According to Torres, positivism had been subverted for political purposes, its true message of a socialized polity misunderstood. While Ramos disavowed positivism, he nevertheless wrote an eloquent tribute to his mentor, and Torres's example must have bolstered his confidence to challenge Caso. Further precedence was established by Henríquez Ureña, who wrote one of the first evaluative studies of Caso, which Ramos cited in his *Ulises* article.

Obras completas, I, 142–157; Jorge Cuesta, "Antonio Caso y la crítica," in *Poemas y ensayos*, ed. Miguel Capistrán and Luis Mario Schneider, II, 52–57; Luis Garrido, "Un censor inoportuno," *Mástiles* 1 (September, 1928), 7–8; Ramos, "Antonio Caso," in Caso, *Obras completas*, I, 158–159.

[13] Hernández Luna, *Samuel Ramos*, p. 64; Eduardo Villaseñor, *Memorias— Testimonio*, p. 36; Patrick Romanell, *Making of the Mexican Mind*, p. 72. Romanell also observes that because Ramos identified with Vasconcelos' educational program, he did not attack him for his romanticism (p. 143). More significantly, Vasconcelos had become a mentor to Ramos in his writing career.

Later Ramos admitted that Henríquez Ureña had introduced him to the new European ideas he claimed Caso ignored. Finally, not the least motivation behind the joust with Caso was Ramos's desire to change the image he had created of himself as being excessively preoccupied with foreign thinkers.[14]

The Dilemma Resolved

Ramos now stood on the threshhold of a new philosophical synthesis for Mexico. Positivism had lost currency but so had emphasis on intuition, and in the vacuum Ramos and his generation turned to the cultural existentialism of Germano-Hispanic thinkers. Under the stimulus of José Ortega y Gasset, whom Ramos called the Spanish bridge between German and Latin American thought, the conflict between life and the intellect was resolved in the concept of "vital reason," of particular appeal to the Mexicans because it was associated with a historical justification of national culture.[15] Ortega's unique journalistic philosophy derived from a cultural analysis that was to become especially attractive to Ramos—the fusion of abstract principles and the details of daily existence together with the notion of national character.[16] Ramos must have viewed with approval Ortega's judgment that Latin American philosophy was imprecise and superficial, causing it to be dependent upon Europe.[17] Ortega not only offered a solution to the philosophical issues of the age, but also provided a focus for Latin American culture vis-à-vis Europe; in

[14] José Torres Orozco, "La crisis del positivismo," reprinted as "Prólogo," in *Filosofía, psicología y ciencia*, ed. Juan Hernández Luna, pp. 7–30; Ramos, "José Torres," pp. 6–7; Pedro Henríquez Ureña, "El positivismo independiente," in *Horas de estudio*, pp. 40–60; Ramos, "Mi experiencia pragmatista," pp. 113, 116.

[15] Ramos, "Notas editoriales," p. 3; José Ortega y Gasset, *El tema de nuestro tiempo*, pp. 58–59. For a discussion of Ortega's influence on Ramos, see Patrick Romanell, "Samuel Ramos on the Philosophy of Mexican Culture: Ortega and Unamuno in Mexico," *Latin American Research Review* 10 (Fall, 1975), 81–102.

[16] See Ramos, "El espectador," *La Antorcha* 2 (September, 1925), 18; and José Ortega y Gasset, "Vitalidad, alma, espíritu," in *El espectador*, pp. 670, 681.

[17] Ortega y Gasset, "Carta a un joven argentino que estudia filosofía," in *El espectador*, pp. 491–498.

writing a sociopsychological analysis of Argentina, he broke a path for Ramos to follow in Mexico.[18]

In cultivating Orteguian thought Ramos found a crutch at a time when his reputation was on trial. He emerged, however, as an intellectual to be reckoned with and he continued the polemic with Caso by emphasizing reason over intuition as the controlling force in the human order.[19] Ramos's claim to intellectual leadership was based on a universal rather than a Mexican problem, yet the results transcended the theoretical issue at hand, reorienting Mexican culture, as one critic observes, from a literary to a philosophical viewpoint. The age of Caso had now become synonymous with the lack of intellectual rigor in Mexico, and Ortega's advice to the Argentine student was heeded as a warning against irrational adventurism.[20]

Between 1925 and 1927 Ramos carved his niche in the world of ideas by assuming the editorship of *La Antorcha* and discrediting the intuitionism and pragmatism in vogue. He had undergone a deepened intellectual experience, and whatever stress it might have caused him was partially alleviated by the Nietzschean example of mental liberation and by the myth of the prophetic mission of the "unknown genius" who, laboring in solitude, moves "faster than time," presumably a veiled reference to himself.[21] His departure for Europe during this period to explore more fully the cosmopolitanism on which he had established his identity symbolized the pattern of his intellectual awakening.

The European Roots of Ramos's Thought

Ortega was not the only source of the philosophy of culture and life Ramos was developing. Contemporary European thinkers figured prominently in his writings: Georg Simmel, Max Scheler, Ernst Robert Curtius, Hermann Keyserling, Oswald Spengler, Salvador de Madariaga, Alfred Adler, and Carl Jung. Most of these were intro-

[18] See Ortega y Gasset, "Hegel y América" and "El hombre, a la defensiva," both in *El espectador*, pp. 809–830, 926–966.

[19] See Ramos, "El irracionalismo," *Ulises* 1 (August, 1927), 5–13.

[20] See José Romano Muñoz, "Ni irracionalismo ni racionalismo, sino filosofía crítica," *Ulises* 1 (October, 1927), 4–10.

[21] See Ramos, "Una confesión absurda," *La Antorcha* 1 (May 30, 1925), 7; idem, "El genio desconocido," *Sagitario* 9 (February 15, 1927), 9–10.

duced to the Hispanic world by Ortega in his *Revista de Occidente*, and Ramos of course was among the first in Mexico to become aware of what Ortega was doing in Spain. Of these influences, Simmel's may be singled out as contributing substantially to Ramos's intellectual experience. When Simmel died in 1918, he was regarded as one of the leading philosophers in Germany. Nevertheless, his academic career was a struggle, which is attributed variously to his uningratiating personality, antisemitism among his colleagues, and the charge of dillettantism leveled against him because he wrote on everything from coquetry and ruins to sociology, philosophy, and history. One of the thinkers published by Ortega in the *Revista de Occidente*, where Ramos undoubtedly learned of him, Simmel was a spokesman for *Lebensphilosophie*, and his ideas and writing style appealed to the Hispanic world. He influenced Ramos directly, and the latter's choice of models does not now seem eccentric; over the years scholars have drawn closer to Simmel.[22]

Simmel maintained that the philosopher determined his presuppositions in accordance with his own purposes. "There was no access to the concept of philosophy from the outside; for only philosophy can decide what philosophy is. . . ." Only when a thinker tried to place himself beyond external preconception, Simmel argued, did he begin to philosophize. This "autonomy of thought," as he labeled it, went beyond "momentary particulars" and was concerned with the whole of knowledge and life. Thus at the heart of the creative act for Simmel was the "imminent objectivity of the personality which is obedient exclusively to its own law." Through this personal experience the mind achieved unity in multiplicity. Simmel developed the notion of a "third something in man," a position that, transcending subjectivity and objectivity, was the ideal order the philosopher imposed upon his materials.[23]

Ramos absorbed Simmel's concept of the "third something" in his quest to achieve a synthesis of the intuitive method of Caso and the historical analysis being advocated by Ortega. It was meaningful in philosophy, said Ramos, to relate to the "totality of essence" and

---

[22] For a study of Simmel's life and work, see Rudolf H. Weingartner, *Experience and Culture: The Philosophy of Georg Simmel.*

[23] See Georg Simmel, "On the Nature of Philosophy," trans. Rudolf H. Weingartner, in *Georg Simmel, 1858–1918*, ed. Kurt H. Wolff, pp. 282–309.

to rely on personal rather than external postulates.[24] This assertion led Ramos to explain that culture did not consist of mechanically acquired knowledge but encompassed the spiritual life of the individual; he added that the man who aspired to a high degree of perfection had to remake culture as the embryo reproduced the species. Thus for Ramos culture became a creative act controlled more by self than by history.[25] In essence this was the Kantian imperative. The importance of Simmel's influence on Ramos lay in the personal and psychological approach of the thinker to history and culture. Ramos stated that he had practiced philosophical criticism without any method or, rather, without preconceived ideas.[26] If we now consider several of the works of other thinkers who were intermediate between Ramos's general philosophical position and his Mexicanist writing, we may better understand the presence of the Simmelian paradigm in Ramos's thought.

The few authors to whom Ramos referred in his book all wrote philosophical interpretations of history and culture, except for the two psychologists Jung and Adler, who provided Ramos with his notions of the collective soul and the inferiority complex. From these disciples of Freud, Ramos, like many other western intellectuals, derived the humanistic implications of the unconscious. Against a neoromantic background to social psychology, the German traveler and philosopher Hermann Keyserling analyzed European culture in *Europe* (1928) and influenced Ramos through his *Meditaciones suramericanas* (1933), an interpretation of the South American national character.[27] Also contributing to the formulation of Ramos's Mexicanist approach was Salvador de Madariaga, who in *Englishmen, Frenchmen and Spaniards: An Essay in Comparative Psychology* (1928) attempted to illumine contemporary world problems through an understanding of national character.[28] Madariaga was himself influenced by Ortega's meditations on Spain, especially Ortega's idea of Spanish passion.

The writer who, next to Simmel, most significantly shaped

[24] Ramos, "La tercera dimensión del conocimiento," *La Antorcha* 1 (February 14, 1925), 6.
[25] Ramos, "Un concepto de cultura," *La Antorcha* 2 (August, 1925), 7–8.
[26] Ramos, "Mi experiencia pragmatista," p. 116.
[27] See Ramos, *El perfil del hombre y la cultura en México*, pp. 59, 69.
[28] Ibid., pp. 25, 27, 29.

Ramos's thought was probably the German student of French culture, Ernst Robert Curtius, whose *Civilization of France* (1930) offered Ramos a model.[29] Influenced by Keyserling's approach to Europe, Curtius based his book primarily on Max Scheler's ideas of cultural study. Working in the vein of *Geistesgeschichte*, which had entered German thought with Herder, Curtius strove for the moral and psychological interpretation of civilization. One critic summarized Curtius's method: "Perception, penetration, integration—this is the rhythm that becomes the critical act. . . . The intuitive discovery of significant facts over the broad field of inquiry . . . and the subsequent search for interrelationships among them. . . ."[30] Curtius thus paralleled Simmel in his philosophical position.

These indications point to the conclusion that Ramos was responsible for the main Mexican variant of Germano-Hispanic humanism and marked the departure from the more French-influenced thought of Caso. Nonetheless, while the 1920's was a period when German, Spanish, and Mexican thought found affinities, Ramos emphasized a Hispano-Mexican humanism that corresponded to, yet remained distinct from, the Germano-Hispanic one. Significantly, the Mexican work Ramos most extensively drew from was Justo Sierra's synthesis of Mexican history.[31] In effect, Ramos completed the interpretation of Mexican history begun by Sierra, shifting the problem of Mexico, as one critic has explained, from the concrete and physical to the psychological.[32] Following the century-old formula, Ramos made use of European thought to elucidate the nationalistic context and in so doing cloaked his exposition in a Mexicanist rhetoric.

The Young Intellectual and Mexico

Before his break with Caso, Ramos indeed was primarily concerned with universal philosophical problems rather than with the nationalist issues of the day. However, much of his preoccupation

[29] Ibid., pp. 56–58, 164–166.
[30] See Arthur R. Evans, Jr., "Ernst Robert Curtius," in *On Four Modern Humanists: Hofmannstal, Gundolf, Curtius and Kantorowicz*, ed. A. R. Evans, Jr., pp. 138–139.
[31] For references to Sierra, see Ramos, *El perfil del hombre*, pp. 19, 21, 33.
[32] See Abelardo Villegas, *La filosofía de lo mexicano*, pp. 135–136.

with foreign thinkers stemmed from a dissatisfaction with Mexican intellectual life, as he emphasized in his critique of intuitionism. Thus his interest in Giovanni Papini originated in what he saw as a shallow comprehension in Mexico of the Italian thinker, and he saw further evidence of Latin American "philosophical dilettantism" in the neglect of Plotinus.[33] Mexico, he complained, had become anti-intellectual because it exalted work over theory, deeds over words; further, he implied that among some there was an unwillingness to exercise their full mental faculties.[34] In another pessimistic moment, as if he were harking back to Caso, he saw the death of Ariel (symbolic of the Latin American quest of spirituality) in the midst of growing materialism.[35] Likewise, the problem of the National University was not its divorce from reality, as critics maintained, but its very immersion in the sociopolitical situation, which, as a result of the Revolution, made improvisation the order of the day, much to the detriment of education.[36]

Even while Ramos struggled to formulate a critical framework independent of both positivism and intuitionism, there were indications of his underlying concern with the questions posed by the course of Mexican history. His job as editor enabled him to broaden himself beyond formal philosophical questions, since the magazine's political orientation forced him to become aware of national issues. Thus, in contrast to his usual Olympian heights, he could express xenophobia toward the United States or invoke "Indolatinism" (the Latin American vision of *mestizaje* in the 1920's) as a check on Yankee encroachment.[37]

In one of his earliest Mexicanist writings, which contributed to the history of ideas and which would be reworked into his essay on creole culture in *El perfil del hombre y la cultura en México*, Ramos treated the growth of the Latin American mind in the nineteenth

[33] See Ramos, "La evolución de Giovanni Papini," *La Antorcha* 1 (January 17, 1925), 11; idem, "Plotino," *La Antorcha* 1 (March 7, 1925), 16.

[34] Ramos, "El evangelio de la inteligencia," *La Antorcha* 1 (April 18, 1925), 3.

[35] Ramos, "El ocaso de Ariel," *La Antorcha* 1 (July 4, 1925), 14.

[36] Ramos, "El pecado original de la Universidad Mexicana," *La Antorcha* 1 (January 31, 1925), 13–14.

[37] See Ramos, "Notas editoriales," *La Antorcha* 1 (May 16, 1925), 3; and (June 27, 1925), 3–4.

century. In view of the fading Spanish colonial ideal, he said, the continent had adopted rationalism to justify its national independence. Scholasticism was replaced by rational inquiry and the resulting knowledge that could be adapted to the national circumstances. European ideas were good only to the extent that they met the needs of Latin America, and once in the New World, they were metamorphosed by the environment. Ramos thought these "lessons" of intellectual history should induce Latin American leaders to consider not only universal culture when toying with an idea, but also nationality and "concrete life." It was not the thinker preoccupied exclusively with foreign themes who gained stature, but the one who shaped culture to national contingencies. This was the achievement of Gabino Barreda, who, according to Ramos, responded to the times by introducing positivism in Mexico, thus strengthening the secular position against scholasticism and contributing to national unity.[38]

In another of his early writings, Ramos focused on the relationship between social psychology and politics, discussing the leader who was motivated not by a desire for the well-being of the country but by his own instinctual cruelty. In an argument condemning aspects of the social character, Ramos contended that the Mexican could pose as public servant for the same reason he might be an aficionado of the bulls: because he was a descendant of a people who sacrificed in the temple of Huitzilopochtli and sadistically enjoyed seeing a man destroyed in politics or in the bull ring.[39] The solution, Ramos concluded, was to develop a critical attitude and a sense of irony that would free the Mexican from fanaticism.[40] It is interesting to observe Ramos transforming the older idea of atavism into the concept of the relationship between machismo and the political system that later would be explored by social scientists.[41]

[38] Ramos, "Ideas filosóficas en México después de la Reforma," *México Moderno* 2 (August, 1922), 35–38.

[39] Compare Octavio Paz on the relationship between the Aztec ethos and modern Mexican political culture in *Posdata*, pp. 99–149.

[40] Ramos, "A guisa de prólogo," *La Antorcha* 2 (August, 1925), 6.

[41] See Evelyn P. Stevens, "Mexican Machismo: Politics and Value Orientations," *The Western Political Quarterly* 18 (December, 1965), 853; idem, *Protest and Response in Mexico*, pp. 224, 295, 299; and Martin C. Needler, *Politics and Society in Mexico*, p. 80.

Throughout most of the 1920's, then, Ramos evinced a concern with *lo mexicano*. For example, a student in Ramos's ethics class at the National Preparatory School in 1927 later recalled a discussion of the validity of a Mexican philosophy, indicating, according to the student, Ramos's attention to the problems of national culture.[42] When Ramos returned from Europe, he immersed himself immediately in his Mexicanist preoccupations.[43] At the University of Guadalajara he lectured on creole culture. That he was now able to shift smoothly between his cosmopolitan and nationalist meditations is illustrated by his essays on Stravinsky and Diego Rivera. In 1930 he completed an article entitled "Nacionalismo y cultura" for *Bandera de Provincias*, the Guadalajara journal founded by Agustín Yáñez and his group.[44] In 1931 he published his article on creole culture.[45]

Attuned to the prevailing criticisms and offering his own in a cogent variation, Ramos followed the pattern of intellectual success in the twenties. An issue central to his Mexican studies now was the debate being waged in the literary world between nationalism and cosmopolitanism, fostered in part by the Revolution. A summary of the conflict is useful. By the 1920's the concern with historical synthesis had generated a certain acceptance of European cultural values at the same time that it had stimulated a Mexican response; thus intellectuals were often polarized around the two concepts. Jorge Cuesta represented the cosmopolitan currents and hated anything nationalistic. José Goroztiza, Ermilio Abreu Gómez, and, to some extent, Ramos, spoke for the nationalists. The cosmopolitan school contended that nationalism was parochial and denied the universal; the nationalists argued that cosmopolitanism ignored the native sources of creativity.[46]

---

[42] Roberto Carrillo, "Comentando a Samuel Ramos," *Letras de México* 2 (December 16, 1940), 9.

[43] See Hernández Luna, *Samuel Ramos*, p. 96.

[44] See Ramos, "El caso Strawinsky," *Contemporáneos* (1929), pp. 1–22; idem, "El sueño de Diego," *Contemporáneos* (1930), pp. 113–126; idem, "Nacionalismo y cultura," *Bandera de Provincias* 1 (January, 1930), 1, 6. For a discussion of the journal see Emmanuel Palacios, "Bandera de Provincias," in *Las revistas literarias de México*, pp. 13–34.

[45] Ramos, "La cultura criolla," *Contemporáneos* (1931), pp. 61–82.

[46] For a review of Cuesta's position, see Luis Mario Schneider, "Prólogo," in Cuesta, *Poemas y ensayos*, ed. Capistrán and Schneider, I, 28–32; and Octavio Paz, *Labyrinth of Solitude*, trans. Lysander Kemp, pp. 160–162.

There were other aspects to the debate. Nationalist painters were enjoying more success than cosmopolitans, and the fact that painting was generally the most acclaimed field of Mexican creative endeavor at the time, ahead of literature, philosophy, and music, favored the argument for nationalism. Moreover, many European writers, to whom the cosmopolitans looked, made the case for an essentially nationalistic approach to literature. One such writer, André Gide, who influenced the young Mexican writers of the period, thought artistic experience should start with the local and work toward the universal.[47] Cuesta, however, thought the concept of the "return to *lo mexicano*," the key phrase in the argument, was not Mexican in origin but a European attitude traceable to the discovery of the New World and the concept of America as a refuge from the evils of Europe. Cuesta called it an "antipatriotic" attitude of "Europe against Europe."[48] One of the positive effects of the debate was that in the criticism leveled against the Europeanists, some writers—Alfonso Reyes[49] and Ramos for instance—were forced into a Mexicanist position that proved productive in their careers. Nevertheless, as Abreu noted, the question was basically not literary but philosophical in nature and implied a reevaluation of Mexican culture.[50] Like all major Mexican intellectuals Ramos realized that he belonged to the greater western tradition as well as to a national culture, and the best review of the 1920's, *Contemporáneos*, in which Ramos published, convincingly illustrated the fusion of cosmopolitan and nationalistic currents.[51]

Toward a Mexicanist Methodology

Ramos approached the problem of national identity philosophically and traced it out in a historical synthesis. In an essay that

[47] André Gide, *Nouveaux Prétextes*, p. 74.

[48] Cuesta, "La literatura y el nacionalismo," in *Poemas y ensayos*, II, 96–98.

[49] For Reyes's influence on Ramos, see Ramos, *El perfil del hombre*, pp. 23, 30–31, 104.

[50] Ermilio Abreu Gómez, "¿Existe una crisis en nuestra literatura de vanguardia?" *El Ilustrado*, April 28, 1932, p. 49.

[51] See Edward J. Mullen, "*Contemporáneos* in Mexican Intellectual History, 1928–1931," *Journal of Inter-American Studies and World Affairs* 13 (January, 1971), 121–130.

would be revised and incorporated into his book under the heading of the "abandonment of culture," he outlined a conflict between nationalism and culture, the latter signifying cosmopolitanism. Culture determined what he called the "consciousness of self," a phenomenon created by resentment against the colonization that had left Mexico politically and socially unstable. The loss of morale resulting from the imitation of foreign culture forced Mexico to become aware of its national character, and from that time on, Ramos stated, the Mexican became introspective, a condition Ramos regarded as a sign of maturity. Here Ramos was summarizing the growth of national self-analysis characteristic of intellectual history in Mexico from 1900 on. However, Ramos wanted to balance the forces of cosmopolitanism and nationalism. Mexico, he thought, had accepted the notion that European culture repressed the national spirit, which should therefore be isolated from all foreign influence. On the other hand, he maintained that European culture should be assimilated into the Mexican circumstances, if indeed Mexico differed that much from Europe. He concluded that Mexico, feeling itself incapable of supporting the demands of high culture, had looked for the line of least resistance and was content with a superficial nationalism.[52]

As a result of the debate over nationalism and cosmopolitanism and because *Contemporáneos* ceased publication, the magazine *Examen* was created in 1932 expressly to delve into the meaning of *lo mexicano*. Its issuance coincided with increasing disillusionment over the Maximato, one of the most problematic moments in the Revolution since the year 1915; thus, it was meaningful that some of Mexico's best minds undertook the analysis of national problems. Although it consists of only three numbers, *Examen* is one of the classic small magazines of Mexico. Ramos wrote two articles for it, "Motivos para una investigación del mexicano" and "Psicoanálisis del mexicano," both incorporated into his 1934 book. The articles were Ramos's latest expressions of his preoccupation with national identity, which by then had lasted a decade. It is worth reviewing the content of the article dealing with his rationale of Mexican study.

During the first fifteen years of the twentieth century, Ramos

---

52 Ramos, "Nacionalismo y cultura," 1.

noted, the Mexican had looked to Europe rather than to his own country for cultural norms. After 1915, however, the Mexican turned inward on himself, which Ramos attributed to the effects of the Revolution and World War I. But the Mexican had gone too far in his break with Europe and had lost the intellectual techniques necessary to cope with his problems. As a result, he had become negative in his attempt to give his life its native shape. Ramos blamed this state of affairs on the Mexican's refusal to pursue self-knowledge and contended that national regeneration would be frustrated if the Mexican did not come to grips with his "mode of being." Convinced of the necessity of national self-awareness, Ramos insisted that he would be the first to treat the psychology of the Mexican. Influenced by Jung,[53] his analysis of the national character was to go beyond the "frontiers of individuality" to the "collective unconscious," in which realm he would study the Mexican spirit.

Ramos stated that he approached the psychology of the Mexican by ridding himself of preconceived notions. There was no noteworthy antecedent upon which to base his study, he claimed, and to give his observations in an unexplored field some objective validity, he would use ideas from contemporary psychology, especially those of Adler.[54] As Cosío Villegas had done before him, he stressed that he would not praise the Mexican but would try to perform him a service by discovering his behavioral defects and their causes. For Ramos the study of the Mexican character was a moral problem insofar as it implied a sociopsychological ideal based on the potential development of the Mexican. Perhaps to excuse the lack of rigorous scholarship in his essays, Ramos admitted that he would not rely on sociological data in determining *lo mexicano*, since the national ethos was not yet sufficiently crystallized. He emphasized that he was not demonstrating a new psychological theory, but merely utilizing one in order to draw a social profile for the first time. Ramos's analysis centered on the hypothesis that the Mexican was beset by a sense of inferiority; he admitted the hypothesis was not new, but explained that it had yet to be developed systematically.

Borrowing Adler's concept that the inferiority complex had its origin in infancy as a result of the child's confrontation with the

---

[53] For references to Jung, see Ramos, *El perfil del hombre*, pp. 108, 170.
[54] Ibid., p. 67.

adult world, Ramos maintained that during the colonial period the Indians and mestizos had felt helpless under Spanish domination, and when Mexico achieved its independence, it found itself as a child before its parents.[55] However, Ramos suggested that if the Mexican had a more positive attitude toward life, such problems would serve to strengthen him, but since he shrank from the facts, any failure on his part impelled him to falsify his circumstances. The way to correct this situation was to lessen the Mexican's sense of inferiority by making him aware of it. The trouble arose, Ramos explained, when the Mexican measured himself on a scale of values that did not correspond with that of his own culture.[56]

Thus Ramos delved into the nature of the Mexican character—a topic that had attracted thinkers since Chávez, Guerrero, and Sierra at the turn of the century and after them Gamio, Caso, Cosío Villegas, and others. Although much of the preceding intellectual history had worked its way into Ramos's thought, the question remains as to why Ramos assumed a singular role in the study of the Mexican character. The obvious answer is that he treated the subject more rigorously than any of his predecessors. If Ramos did not acknowledge serious antecedents to his work, it should be remembered that he was primarily an essayist rather than a scholar and probably had not read extensively in Mexicanist literature.

The response to Ramos's essays in *Examen* did not go unnoticed by the intellectual community. Héctor Pérez Martínez took Ramos to task for treating only the symptoms and not the causes, noting that psychoanalysis dealt with the etiological as well as the symptomatic.[57] Another critic, Rubén Salazar Mallén, accused Ramos of pointing up only the inferiority complex in the Mexican and ignoring his opposite complex of grandeur, which could be observed in paired or "contradictory" behavioral responses. As Octavio Paz would do much later, Salazar explained that the national character was to be viewed in its dual function of contending extremes. With joy went hate, with the fiesta, death; on All Soul's Day there was

---

[55] For a discussion of Adler's influence on Ramos's thought, see Martin S. Stabb, *In Quest of Identity*, pp. 190–191.

[56] Ramos, "Motivos para una investigación del mexicano," *Examen* 1 (August, 1932), 7–11.

[57] Héctor Pérez Martínez, "Sobre el psicoanálisis del mexicano," *El Nacional*, September 4, 1932.

fighting as well as weeping. The origin of this contradiction lay in the Indian's humiliation stemming from the Conquest, which Salazar claimed Ramos did not sufficiently examine. The Mexican, Salazar thought, remembered the grandeur of the pre-Hispanic past but doubted his contemporary identity. Hence his explosive nature: fearful and unable to express himself confidently, he invented words without any meaning, as evidenced in the language of the *pelado* (double-talking, streetwise pariah). Salazar concluded that Ramos's essay was "ingenuous and simplistic."[58]

These criticisms of Ramos illustrate how one essay on *lo mexicano* begat another. Clearly Salazar merely used Ramos's essay as a point of departure to elaborate his own theory of national behavior. By 1932 *lo mexicano* was becoming an important topic, and the long accretion of symbols surrounding Mexican selfhood awaited earnest explanation. Aware of the growth of the problem of national identity in the twenties and early thirties, Ramos published his scattered essays on the choices facing the Mexican as, locked up in the uncertainty of a post-Revolutionary present, he confronted his past.

Ramos in Retrospect

For a work that has been of transcendent importance in the history of ideas and is read by all who enter Mexican studies, Ramos's uneven analysis of the mental patterns of culture does not demonstrate the requisites usually associated with such a grand purpose and such unqualified success. Much in the work is repetitive. The same ideas are expressed in almost identical terms in various chapters, and many sections are inadequately developed. The book is casually structured on the interwoven topics of social psychology, nationalism, cosmopolitanism, and progress as the resolution of psychological conflict, yet the author avoids objectifying his methodology. However, its contribution to the literature of national identity lay in its synthetic power that intensified the national diagnostic. The central points of reference of the study illustrate how Ramos shrewdly assessed the long-standing concerns of the intelligentsia as a series of problems whose answers were lodged on the

[58] Rubén Salazar Mallén, "Conocimiento del mexicano," *Revista de Revistas* No. 1164 (September 4, 1932), p. 42.

threshhold of ideology. In basing his explanation of the Mexican character on the country's historical development, Ramos thus did not deviate from the main thrust of this argument, which rested on an implicit *mestizaje*. In the logic of this behavioral typology, the creole had to appear as conservative and reactionary, an element of rigidity in the evolution of social attitudes. The image of the Spaniard was fashioned from the creole's former indictment of the peninsular as unprogressive, although in this instance Ramos looked to the indigenous as well as to the European origins of the obstacles to social improvement.[59] The price paid for these historical misfortunes was the urban Mexican's lack of confidence in himself and societal relationships.[60] In this vein Ramos set about to draw a bleak profile of the Mexican.

The technique of internalizing behavioral traits Ramos now exploited to the fullest, frequently invoking a dubious rationale that did little more than give a brilliant aura to his stock conclusions. Thus the Mexican was impassioned and aggressive because he lacked self-control, while the psychology of the Mexican bourgeois simply stemmed from his being a "Mexican." A bitter bias often prevented Ramos from developing the logical implications of his cultural insights. His contention that the Mexican was satisfied with his false self-image, though partially correct, failed to take into account the attitudinal context of the Revolution. In discussing the element of egomania in the Mexican character, for example, Ramos resorted to the stock sanguinary image of the Aztecs for his historical underpinnings rather than offering an analysis based on accessible contemporary factors. The Mexican, he maintained, was locked up in himself, distrustful of others, and thus indifferent to the collective aspects of society.[61]

If Ramos's rationale for Mexicanist analogy was stretched thin at the abstract and historical levels, his objectives were more persuasively stated when he approached a topic that touched upon the tacitly accepted realities of the age. Hence his interpretation of the national character centered on the *pelado*, the social type whose behavior was readily described in terms of the inferiority complex.

[59] Ramos, *El perfil del hombre*, pp. 26–37.
[60] Ibid., pp. 79–82.
[61] Ibid., pp. 84–91.

Ramos achieved a breakthrough in Mexicanist analysis by linking the testicular imagery of the *pelado's* language to the theme of machismo, even though his moralizing intruded on an otherwise noteworthy observation. The phallic symbol, Ramos argued, represented the patriarchal and authoritarian elements in Mexican history and did not, as in some cultural contexts, refer to creation, but to the demeaning aspects of power.[62] The fact that Ramos felt constrained to defend his use of these materials indicated the attitude the search for national identity was taking toward the concrete, earthy manifestations of *mexicanidad.*[63]

Like every serious Mexican thinker of the twentieth century, Ramos brooded ceaselessly on the inevitability of nationalism and cautioned against uncritical acceptance. Disdainful of the chauvinistic criteria that compromised the Mexican's relationship to a broader humanity, Ramos always sought to balance nationalism and cosmopolitanism, suggesting that Mexico could be understood only by means of a directing idea derived from European thought. Yet a knowledge of the Mexican mind was essential if European culture was to be cleansed of elements unassimilable to the Mexican experience.[64] The dilemma of Mexico's national and international position continually shaped the context of Ramos's thought and is apparent in his argument that if European civilization must be put to a Mexican process of selection, the country must also seek equality with the outside world through the creation of universal values, which would facilitate the absorption of the European influence. Derivative of the modernist philosophies in vogue at the time was Ramos's admission that although Mexico had been formed within a European framework, a disjunction between culture and life had prevented the successful articulation of its identity. By this he meant that it was necessary to relate the principles of universal study to the concrete observation of Mexican circumstances,[65] an obvious echo of the Mieran-Vigilian-Sierran dicta. Ramos aimed for rapprochement

---

[62] Ibid., pp. 71–74.

[63] In broaching the themes of dissimulation, machismo, solitude, and the relationship between Aztec ritual and the contemporary social character, Ramos was establishing much of the critical mythology later elaborated by Octavio Paz.

[64] Ramos, *El perfil del hombre*, p. 149.

[65] Ibid., pp. 150–151.

of the two antagonistic forces in Mexico. Attacking those who thought *lo mexicano* was manifested only in local color, he maintained that the ideal was to unite the national with the universal; nationalism was to accentuate Mexico's native life without lowering the level of universal value. The essential challenge for Ramos remained the recently revealed, rich, but unrealized potential of the country. Still disoriented and in search of its identity, Mexico must generate a new being so that the Mexican could free himself from his sense of inferiority and, his mask stripped from him, be no longer tormented by self-denigration.[66]

Ramos couched his Mexicanist analysis in racial terms designed to moderate controversy. Thus, in a period that had begun to emphasize indigenism, Ramos could shift from a universal position and interpret cultural conflict from the standpoint of the Indians, whom he viewed as psychologically unable to assimilate technology, since they did not share the white man's attitude toward the machine. Ramos went a step further and argued that the white man posed a threat to the country should it prove incapable of political stability and economic development; he therefore suggested that the Mexican try to adapt modern civilization even if it was not consonant with his way of thinking. It was Ramos's ability to see the complex factors at play in the development of Mexico that made his insights truthful indicators of the age. In discussing the subjugation of man by the machine, a theme not uncommon to the pessimistic analysts of the 1920's, he found ample room to pursue the Mexican dilemma of reconciling tradition with modernity. Calling for a wise use of technology to obviate the excesses of other countries, Ramos was persuaded that its intelligent application would give Mexico many of the good things of a non-modern life, which, he added, the Mexicans still knew how to enjoy. Humanistic education could counteract the "deceitful civilization" of the "machine age."[67] The Ramosian distortion in interpreting the psychology of the Mexican is most satisfactorily explained by the didactic purpose of the study, undoubtedly undertaken to establish a proper framework for social regeneration but limiting the choice of materials and denying them a scholarly rationale. This is especially noticeable in the final two chapters of the

[66] Ibid., pp. 157–162.
[67] Ibid., pp. 167–178.

book, in which Mexico was assigned the task of overseeing its future by discharging its burden of self-denigration and its need to imitate foreign culture, especially the French.

Evaluating Ramos's work against the background of the age produces mixed conclusions. Certainly his intellectual growth indicates a shift in elitist thought following the Revolution. While the Revolution contributed to the dismantling of positivism, it also generated a conflict between social values and a humanism that masked the resurgence of the ego threatened by the leveling tendencies of the masses. This partially explains why Ortega, the elitist philosopher par excellence, was a guiding spirit at this time. Thus in a sense Ramos and his group were creating a new aristocracy of thought.

Yet Ramos's study of Mexican attitudes has continued to elicit scholarly interest because its philosophy of selfhood, linked to national identity, underscored a major preoccupation of the country's thinkers. For more than a decade Mexico had turned inward in the search for political solutions and artistic forms forceful enough to convey a sense of Mexicanness. Ramos's analysis completed in the realm of ideas the nativist permeation of painting, music, and the novel. Its very sophistication accentuated the universal ideal, ever fashionable in liberal Hispanic culture, while emphasizing the national context intensified by the Revolution. Written during a new era of western pessimism, the book was underlaid with the detachment and irony of ultra-civilized introspection. Ramos's thought had evolved with almost formulaic precision in a pattern of Mexican history burdened with a cosmopolitan legacy and an exotic localism that left abstraction absurdly naked unless manipulated by a disarming consciousness of authenticity within tradition.

Postscript

THE search for national identity in Mexico between the years 1900 and 1934 points to a romantic phase in the country's intellectual history. The elements of Mexican civilization are separated from their factual order and transposed speculatively into a continuum where the temporal is subordinated to the moral perception of history. At this level the structure of the writing is fashioned, and although the content may be patriotic or critical, the mind becomes pragmatic and fluid within the circumstances of experience. Determinism is left on the shoals of a chance universe, and the individual as receiver gathers in the life forces and imparts meaning to them. This is what we call the creative act in any age.

Mexico's preoccupation with a national consciousness has been motivated not only by the necessity for solving its problems and assuming an identity denied it for four hundred years; it has also been stimulated by the desire to enter the larger world, to emerge from its isolated, colonial status, and to convey an image of equality with other nations. To do this Mexico has had to offer something more than raw products and foreign investment opportunities; it has had to build a political stability linked to social justice, a viable economy, and an educational system capable of advancing the aspirations of the people. The failures and the successes of these endeavors become the summary of post-Revolutionary history. In short, Mexico has had to hasten its development commensurate to the criteria of power that have shaped national policies in the twentieth century. Fortunately its agrarian revolution was novel, and it had the luck to produce an artistic movement that was considered original. Its literature made its mark abroad, and the nation learned that its culture enchanted tourists and scholars. It would begin the struggle for industrial self-sufficiency, while its social and political progress would remain in doubt.

But does the search for identity fit neatly into this national teleology? Does it conform, as one scholar would argue, to the utopian objectives of Mexican history?[1] The preoccupation with Mexicanness could be viewed as a conservative return to the creole values of the eighteenth century, with the Porfiriato supplying the liberal theme. Thus post-Revolutionary indigenism could be seen as a parallel to the creole identity with the Indian as a means of reinforcement against foreign intrusion. However, this analogy breaks down in light of the fact that in the creole ethos the mestizo was usually denigrated, whereas one achievement of the 1910 Revolution was to generate an identity whose constructs were established on *mestizaje.*

The search for national identity also could be explained by the fact that the majority of the intellectuals who displaced those of the Porfiriato were of the middle class, and they formed a new elite to manipulate media information by adapting the prevailing attitudes of nationalism as Porfirian intellectuals had done with economic liberalism. Moreover, the *lo mexicano* movement of the period 1900 to 1934 could be placed in an international context and related to the Pan-Latinism and the New Worldism then in vogue.

Indeed, Mexico received the intellectual recognition it wanted from the outside world when Spengler and later Toynbee granted historical autonomy to the ancient land for the purpose of countering European ethnocentricity.[2] The search for national identity was an aspect of the revolt of the New World of which one scholar writes, "Where European historians once wrote with the confidence born of an innate sense of European superiority, they now write burdened with the consciousness of European guilt."[3] Or as Claude Lévi-Strauss has written, "For those of us who are earthbound Europeans, our adventurings into the heart of the New World have a lesson to teach us: that the New World was not ours to destroy, and yet we

[1] For a discussion of the connection between national identity and utopian aspirations, see Jacques Lafaye, "La utopía mejicana: ensayo de intrahistoria," *Diógenes* 20 (April–June, 1972), 28.

[2] Toynbee wrote of Mexican civilization as a special entity within a western framework in numerous instances in *A Study of History.* See especially IV, 80–81, and XII, 65–67, 673. See also Oswald Spengler, *The Decline of the West,* I, 18.

[3] J. H. Elliott, *The Old World and the New, 1492–1650,* p. 4.

destroyed it. . . ."[4] Thus the probing of Mexican history reflected the redemption of the New World, and the Acostan tradition was once again reaffirmed.

But internal forces provide us with our safest avenues to understanding. The Mexican intellectual in the late nineteenth and early twentieth centuries perceived his country's history as endless controversy; hence his negative focus on an inferred behavioral evolution. Change in social attitudes was necessary, but only if it contributed to a more cohesive nationhood. So Mexico was in large measure considered to be a failure, and the analysis of its problems became an alternative to national self-esteem. Here the intellectual's position presupposed his alienation from the disruption of the Conquest and the subsequent elitist economy and government. Thus the themes of exploitation and falsehood in Mexican history from Aztec despotism to today's "internal colonialism" are emphasized in a body of literature ranging from the indigenous accounts of the Conquest to the structuralist analyses of society. The purpose of this endeavor has been to postulate a Mexican community, the "other Mexico" as Octavio Paz calls it,[5] where national identity may be completed.

In 1900 intellectuals were approaching some of the sensitive issues of Mexican history through the concepts of evolution and character analysis that originated in European science, but, though leaving their residue in Mexican thought, these formulae gradually gave way to the more vital preoccupations of the thinkers influenced by the Revolution. The years 1920 to 1934 saw the growth of Orteguian perspectivism in Mexico, when the search for national identity had been expanded by the Revolution and the country had become more aware of its rich and difficult history. It was the perfect philosophy for the times, justifying Mexicanist curiosity and closing any breach between a strayed academic appeal and the necessities of the age. Much of the pseudoanthropology and racial bias of these writers would disappear in the post-Ramos period, indicating that the search for national identity before Ramos was often descriptive and naïve, while after him it would become interpretive and self-conscious. Ramos's most significant contribution to Mexican thought lay not in ·

[4] Claude Lévi-Strauss, *Tristes Tropiques: An Anthropological Study of Primitive Societies in Brazil*, p. 392.
[5] Octavio Paz, *Posdata*, p. 103.

his summary of the themes relating to national identity, but in his exhortation to transcend the nationalistic-cosmopolitan conflict in Mexican history. He thus reaffirmed Mexico's humanity in a universal context, which has been the goal of the country's major thinkers ever since.

In the period 1900–1934 a national consciousness was finding its *raison d'être* in mere self-expression; hence the unevenness and diversity of the Mexicanist meditations. There was no program, no submission to progress as in the old Porfirian positivism. Rather, for the intellectual participant, Mexican civilization had become a fiesta, with its famous duality of grief and joy but always with its powers of renewal. All who witnessed the rite became sacred, having touched some sanctified part of a hypothetical national destiny. They enjoyed the illusion of fusing consciousness and reality in the mythopoeic generation of Mexican man and history.

Bibliography

Bibliographies and Archival Guides

Archivo General de la Nación. *Inventario de Ramo Instrucción Pública y Bellas Artes.* México. n.d.

Bibliografía histórica mexicana. México: El Colegio de México, 1967–.

Carreón, Ana María Rosa. *"Inventario de Fondo Jesús Díaz de León."* Manuscript (1969). Archivo Histórico. Universidad Nacional Autónoma de México.

García y García, J. Jesús. *Guía de Archivos.* México: Universidad Nacional Autónoma de México, 1972.

González, Luis. *Fuentes de la historia contemporánea de México: Libros y folletos.* 3 vols. México: El Colegio de México, 1961–1962.

Maciel, David R. *"Introducción bibliográfica a la historia intelectual de México." Aztlán* 3 (1973), pp. 83–132.

Ross, Stanley R. *Fuentes de la historia contemporánea de México: Periódicos y revistas.* Vols. 1 and 2, México: El Colegio de México, 1965–1967. Vols. 3 and 4, México: Universidad Nacional Autónoma de México, in press.

Archival Material

Archivo Alfonso Reyes. México.

Archivo Ezequiel Chávez. Universidad Nacional Autónoma de México. México.

Archivo General de la Nación. México.

Archivo Jesús Díaz de León. Universidad Nacional Autónoma de México. México.

Works Discussed

NOTE: Includes materials used as primary sources of thought.

Acosta, José de. *Historia natural y moral de las Indias.* México: Fondo de Cultura Económica, 1940.

Aguirre Cárdenas, Flavio. *El problema de la heterogeneidad racial de México, ensayo sociológico.* México: Talleres Gráficos de la Nación, 1929.

Alamán, Lucas. *Disertaciones sobre la historia de la república mejicana.* 3 vols. México: Editorial Jus, 1942.

————. *Historia de Méjico.* 4th ed. 5 vols. México: Editorial Jus, 1942.

Alba, Pedro de. *Del humanismo y otros ensayos.* México: Universidad Nacional Autónoma de México, 1937.

————. "La realidad y la fábula en nuestra historia." *El Nacional,* October 30, 1930.

Altamirano, Ignacio M. *Crónicas de la semana.* México: Secretaría de Educación Pública, 1969.

————. *La literatura nacional.* México: Porrúa, 1949.

Alvarado, Salvador. *La reconstrucción de México: un mensaje a los pueblos de América.* 3 vols. México: J. Ballesca, 1919.

Aragón, Agustín. "Elogio de don José Antonio Alzate y Ramírez." *Revista Positiva* 4 (October, 1904), 564–572.

————. "Juárez: su obra y su tiempo." *Revista Positiva* 6 (March, 1906), 187–191.

————. "México." *Revista Positiva* 14 (May, 1914), 246–251.

————. "Notas políticas." *Revista Positiva* 11 (December, 1911), 637–644.

————. "*Pacotillas*: novela mexicana por el Doctor Porfirio Parra." *Revista Positiva* 1 (January, 1901), 24–26.

Aragón Leyva, Agustín. "Futuro de la nación mexicana," *Nuestra Ciudad* 2 (September, 1930), 22–23.

Arriaga, Ponciano. Speech given at Constitutional Congress, 1856. In *Historia Documental de México.* 2nd ed. Edited by Ernesto de la Torre Villar, Moisés González Navarro, and Stanley R. Ross. 2 vols. México: Universidad Nacional Autónoma de México, 1974.

Balbuena, Bernardo de. *Grandeza mexicana.* México: Universidad Nacional Autónoma de México, 1963.

Barba González, Silvano. *Ponciano Arriaga, Andrés Molina Enríquez, Luis Cabrera, Pastor Rouaix.* Vol. 3 of *La Lucha por la tierra.* 4 vols. México: Editorial del Magisterio, 1963.

Barreda, Horacio. "Estudio sobre 'el femenismo'. VI: Del 'femenismo' en México." *Revista Positiva* 9 (June, 1909), 263–293.

Basave Fernández del Valle, Agustín. *Samuel Ramos: trayectoria filosófica y antológica de textos.* Monterrey: Centro de Estudios Humanísticos de la Universidad de Nuevo León, 1965.

Bassols, Narciso. *Obras.* México: Fondo de Cultura Económica, 1937.

Blasco, Wenceslao. "Entrevista: con el Licdo. José Vasconcelos." *Repertorio Americano* 2 (July 20, 1921), 369–370.

Bulnes, Francisco. *El porvenir de las naciones latinoamericanas ante las recientes conquistas de Europa en Norteamérica: estructura y evolución de un continente.* México: Sociedad de Artistas y Escritores "Generación del Segundo Cuarto del Siglo," n. d.

Bustamante, Carlos María. *Cuadro histórico de la revolución mexicana.* 5

vols. 1926. Reprint. México: Comisión Nacional para la Celebración del Sesquicentenario de la Proclamación de la Independencia Nacional y del Cincuentenario de la Revolución Mexicana, 1961.

Cabrera, Luis. "México y los mexicanos." In *Tres intelectuales hablan sobre México*. México: n. p., 1916.

————. *Obras políticas del Lic. Blas Urrea*. México: Imprenta Nacional, 1921.

————. *Los problemas trascendentales de México*. México: Editorial Cultura, 1934.

Calles, Plutarco Elías. "Los problemas del México de hoy." *Crisol* 10 (September, 1933), 133–136.

Campo, Angel de. "El Portero del Liceo Hidalgo. Los del porvenir: Micrós." *El Siglo Diez y Nueve*, November 3, 1894.

El Campo. Aguascalientes, 1895–1896.

Cárdenas, Juan de. *Primera parte de los problemas y secretos maravillosos de las Indias*. 2nd ed. México: Museo Nacional, 1913.

Caso, Antonio. *Discursos a la nación mexicana*. México: Porrúa, 1922.

————. *Discursos heterogéneos*. México: Herrero, 1925.

————. "En América dirá su última palabra la civilización latina." *Repertorio Americano* 4 (May 22, 1922), 113–114.

————. "Nos compran la tierra." *Excélsior*, June 14, 1924.

————. *Obras completas*. 8 vols. México: Universidad Nacional Autónoma de México, 1971–1975.

————. "La opinión de América." *Repertorio Americano* 8 (March 24, 1924), 13–14.

————. "¿Por qué somos tan pobres?" *Repertorio Americano* 7 (January 28, 1924), 276–277.

————. *El problema de México y la ideología nacional*. México: Editorial Cultura, 1924.

————. "Psicología del pueblo mexicano." *Excélsior*, June 8 and 15, 1925.

————. "Simpatía, sin raza, sin ideal." *Repertorio Americano* 4 (May 29, 1922), 134–137.

————. *Sociología genética y sistemática*. México: Secretaría de Educación Pública, 1927.

————. "La tierra y la patria." *Repertorio Americano* 16 (March 24, 1928), 177.

Castellanos, Abraham. *Discursos a la nación mexicana sobre la educación nacional*. México: Librería de la Vda. de Ch. Bouret, 1913.

Castro, Rosa. "¿Qué es y cómo es lo mexicano?" *Hoy* (April 14, 1951), 36–39, 66.

Cervantes de Salazar, Francisco. *México en 1554*. México: Universidad Nacional Autónoma de México, 1952.

Chávez, Ezequiel A. *Ensayo de psicología de la adolescencia*. México: Secretaría de Educación Pública, 1928.

———. "Ensayo sobre los rasgos distintivos de la sensibilidad como factor del carácter mexicano." *Revista Positiva* 1 (March, 1901), 81–99.

Columbus, Christopher. *Four Voyages to the New World: Letters and Selected Documents.* Translated and edited by R. H. Major. New York: Corinth, 1961.

"Al comenzar." *Excélsior,* March 18, 1917.

Cortés, Hernán. *Letters from Mexico.* Translated and edited by A. P. Pagden. New York: Grossman, 1971.

Cosío Villegas, Daniel. "El ABC de las cosas." *La Antorcha* 1 (April 25, 1925), 4, 32.

———. "Los bancos y la moneda." In *México económico, 1928–1930.* México: Editorial Cultura, 1932.

———. "BA-TA-CLAN." *La Antorcha* 1 (February 25, 1925), 29.

———. *Ensayos y notas.* 2 vols. México: Hermes, 1966.

———. "La escuela del servilismo." *La Antorcha* 1 (June 13, 1925), 19, 20.

———. "El hilo se rompe." *La Antorcha* 1 (June 20, 1925), 18, 19.

———. "Libros y revistas." *La Antorcha* 1 (May 16, 1925), 18.

———. *Memorias.* 2nd ed. México: Joaquín Mortiz, 1977.

———. *Miniaturas mexicanas.* México: Editorial Cultura, 1922.

———. "Notas bibliográficas: Don Juan Ruiz de Alarcón." *Revista de Filología Española* 10 (April-June, 1923), 192–193.

———. "Nuestro pobre amigo: novela mexicana." In *La Novela Semanal de El Universal Ilustrado,* January 1, 1925.

———. "La pintura en México." *Cuba Contemporánea* 34 (April, 1924), 331–339.

———. "Prólogo." In Xavier Icaza, *Gente mexicana.* Jalapa, Ver.: Lara, 1924.

———. "El renacimiento agrarista." *La Antorcha* 1 (June 6, 1925), 4–5.

———. "Repertorio." *México Moderno* 2 (June, 1923), 250–254.

———. "La resurrección de Arévalo Martínez." *La Antorcha* 1 (April 18, 1925), 18.

———. "El retorno a la realidad." *Repertorio Americano* 11 (December 14, 1925), 213.

———. "La riqueza de México." *La Antorcha* 1 (May 30, 1925), 8–10.

———. *Sociología mexicana.* 3 vols. México: Talleres Linotipográficos "Mayab," 1924–1925.

———. "La tierra madre única." *La Antorcha* 1 (May 16, 1925), 7–8.

———. "La universidad zoológica." *La Antorcha* 1 (January 24, 1925), 3–4.

Cuéllar, José T. de. *Ensalada de pollos y baile y cochino.* México: Porrúa, 1970.

Cuesta, Jorge. *Poemas y Ensayos.* Edited by Miguel Capistrán and Luis Mario Schneider. 4 vols. México: Universidad Nacional Autónoma de México, 1964.

Díaz de León, Jesús. *Disertación sobre la importancia de el estudio de la agricultura en los establecimientos de instrucción pública.* Aguascalientes: Jesús Díaz de León, 1894.

Díaz y de Ovando, Clementina. *La Escuela Preparatoria: los afanes y los días, 1867–1910.* 2 vols. México: Universidad Nacional Autónoma de México, 1972.

Documentos y discursos alusivos a la solemne inauguración de la Escuela Nacional de Altos Estudios. México: Fidencio S. Soria, 1911.

Editorial. *Azulejos* 2 (December, 1923), 1.

Eguiara y Eguren, Juan José de. *Prólogos a la biblioteca mexicana.* México: Fondo de Cultura Económica, 1944.

Esquivel Obregón, Toribio. "El indio en la historia de México." *Boletín de la Sociedad Mexicana de Geografía y Estadística* No. 41 (1929), pp. 293–321.

"Exposición de arte mexicano." *El nacional,* June 29, 1930.

"Exposición nacional de los artistas pensionados en Europa." *Arte y Ciencia* 18 (January, 1907), 169–172.

Fabela, Isidro, and Josefina E. de Fabela, eds. *Documentos históricos de la Revolución mexicana.* 27 vols. México: Fondo de Cultura Económica, 1960–1973.

Fernández de Lizardi, J. Joaquín. *El pensador mexicano.* México: Universidad Nacional Autónoma de México, 1962.

Fernández McGregor, Genaro. *El río de mi sangre: memorias.* México: Fondo de Cultura Económica, 1967.

———. "La universidad y el vitáfono." *Universidad de México* 1 (November, 1930), 38–41.

Flores Magón, Ricardo. "La Revolución." In *Antología.* Edited by Gonzalo Aguirre Beltrán. México: Universidad Nacional Autónoma de México, 1970.

———. *La Revolución mexicana.* Edited by Adolfo Sánchez Rebolledo. México: Grijalbo, 1970.

Freyre, Gilberto. *Casa grande e senzala: formaçao da familia brasileira sob o regime de economia patriarcal.* Rio de Janeiro: Maia and Schmidt, 1933.

Gamboa, Federico. *Diario, 1892–1939.* Edited by José Emilio Pacheco. México: Siglo XXI, 1977.

Gamio, Manuel. *Forjando patria.* 2nd ed. México: Porrúa, 1960.

———, *Introducción, síntesis y conclusión a la población del Valle de Teotihuacán.* México: Secretaría de Educación Pública, 1924.

García Téllez, Ignacio. "Informe del rector al H. Consejo universitario." *Universidad de México* 4 (May, 1932), 1–15.

Gastélum, Bernardo J. "Democracia asimétrica." *Contemporáneos* (November, 1928), pp. 224–256.

———. "La Revolución mexicana." *Contemporáneos* (February, 1931), pp. 140–151.

———. "La teoría del sufragio." *Contemporáneos* (April, 1930), pp. 34–36, and (February, 1931), pp. 140–151.

Gide, André. *Nouveaux Prétextes*. Paris: Mercure de France, 1921.

Goldschmidt, Alfons. *Mexiko*. Berlin: E. Rowohlt, 1925.

Gómez Morín, Manuel. *1915*. México: Editorial Cultura, 1927.

González Roa, Fernando. "Discurso leído por su autor ante el tercer congreso jurídico nacional reunido en esta ciudad al mes de octubre del año 1924." *Revista de Ciencias Sociales* 3 (February, 1926), 20.

Guerrero, Julio. "El fin del cesarismo." *La República* 1 (June 7, 1901), 5–13.

———. *La génesis del crimen en México: estudio de psiquiatría social*. México: C. Bouret, 1901.

———. "La humedad atmosférica: los delitos de ira: crónica de la sociedad positivista." *La República* 1 (June 7, 1901), 19–25.

———. "Transiciones pasionales del ebrio mexicano." *La República* 1 (June 22, 1910), 1–7.

———. "Trascendencia política de los estudios nacionales." *La República* 1 (June 22, 1901), 15–29.

Gutiérrez de Joseph, Guadalupe. "Psicología de la mujer mexicana." *Nuestra Ciudad* 1 (April, 1930), 38.

Guzmán, Martín Luis. *Academia*. México: Compañía General de Ediciones, 1959.

———. *La querella de México, a orillas de Hudson, y otras páginas*. México: Compañía General de Ediciones, 1958.

Hernández, Julio S. *La sociología mexicana y la educación nacional*. México: Librería de la Vda. de Ch. Bouret, 1916.

Hernández Luna, Juan, ed. *Conferencias del Ateneo de la Juventud*. México: Universidad Nacional Autónoma de México, 1962.

Horcasitas, Fernando. *De Porfirio Díaz a Zapata: memoria náhuatl de Milpa Alta*. México: Universidad Nacional Autónoma de México, 1968.

Humboldt, Alexander von. *Political Essay on the Kingdom of New Spain*. 4 vols. London: Longman, Hurst, Rees, Orme, and Brown, 1811. New York: AMS Reprint, 1966.

Instrucciones que los virreyes de Nueva España dejaron a sus sucesores. 2 vols. México: Ignacio Escalante, 1873.

Konetzke, Richard, ed. *Colección de documentos para la historia de la formación social de Hispanoamérica, 1493–1810*. 3 vols. Madrid: Consejo Superior de Investigaciones, 1962.

Lamicq, Pedro. *Madero*. México: Chamber of Deputies, 1958.

List Arzubide, Germán. "Propósito." *Horizonte* 1 (April, 1926).

López Velarde, Ramón. *Poemas completas y el minutero*. 3rd. ed. Edited by Antonio Castro Leal. México: Porrúa, 1963.

———. *Prosa política*. México: Imprenta Universitaria, 1953.

Loyo, Gilberto. XYZ. Orizaba, Vera Cruz: Edición de la Sociedad de Estudios Filosóficos, 1928.

Machorro Narváez, Paulino. *La enseñanza en México*. México: M. León Sánchez, 1916.

Madero, Francisco I. Speech published in *Nueva Era*, November 1, 1911.

————. *La sucesión presidencial*. México: Secretaría de Hacienda, 1960.

Maqueo Castellanos, Esteban. *Algunos problemas nacionales*. México: Eusebio Gómez de la Puente, 1910.

Martínez Estrada, Ezequiel. *Radiografía de la Pampa*. Buenos Aires: Babel, 1933.

Martínez Ulloa, Enrique. "Dimensión de lo mexicano." *Bandera de Provincias* 1 (October, 1929), 1.

————. "Guadalajara: fragmentos de una interpretación." *Bandera de Provincias* 1 (July, 1929), 1, 6.

Medellín, Roberto. "Informe del rector al H. Consejo universitario." *Universidad de México* 6 (May–June, 1933), 1–30.

Mendieta, Gerónimo de. *Historia eclesiástica indiana*. México: Porrúa, 1971.

Mendieta y Núñez, Lucio. "El renacimiento del nacionalismo." *Ethnos* 1 (January–February, 1925), 3–5.

"Mexicanización." *Nuestro México* 1 (August, 1932), 7, 79.

Mier, Servando Teresa de. *Carta de un americano al español sobre su número XIX*. London: W. Lewis, 1811.

————. *Escritos inéditos*. Edited by J. M. Miguel Vergés and Hugo Díaz-Thomé. México: El Colegio de México, 1944.

Moheno, Querido. *Sobre el ara sangrienta*. México: n.p., 1922.

Molina Enríquez, Andrés. *Esbozo de la historia de los primeros diez años de la Revolución agraria de México*. 5 vols. México: Talleres Gráficos del Museo Nacional de Arqueología, Historia, y Etnografía, 1932–1936.

————. *Los grandes problemas nacionales*. México: Ediciones del Instituto Nacional de la Juventud Mexicana, 1964.

Monteverde, Armando. "El don juanismo mexicano." In *El desastre moral de México: la bancarrota del pudor*, by Armando Monteverde and Rodrigo Cifuentes. México: Graphos, 1924.

Mora, José María Luis. *México y sus revoluciones*. 3 vols. México: Porrúa, 1950.

Motolinía [Fray Toribio de Benavente]. *Memoriales o libro de las cosas de la Nueva España y de los naturales de ella*. Edited by Edmundo O'Gorman. México: Universidad Nacional Autónoma de México, 1971.

Nieto, Rafael. *El imperio de los Estados Unidos y otros ensayos*. Jalapa, Vera Cruz: Biblioteca Popular, 1927.

————. *Más allá de la patria: ensayos económicos y políticos*. México: A. Botas e Hijo, 1922.

"Nuestros propósitos al comenzar Crisol," *Crisol* 1 (January, 1929), 2–4.

Obregón, Álvaro. *Discursos del General Alvaro Obregón.* 2 vols. México: Biblioteca de la Dirección General de Educación Militar, 1932.

"Oración que para abrir los exámenes públicos de las niñas que se educan en la Casa de Misericordia de la Ciudad de Cádiz . . ." *Gaceta de México,* September 13, 1803.

Orozco, José Clemente. *El artista en Nueva York: cartas a Jean Charlot y textos inéditos, 1925–1929.* Edited by Luis Cardoza y Aragón. Appendices by Jean Charlot. México: Siglo XXI, 1971.

Ortega, Joaquín R. "El verdadero plan." *Revista Positiva* 12 (August, 1912), 404–418.

Ortega y Gasset, José. *El espectador.* Madrid: Biblioteca Nueva, 1950.

———. *El tema de nuestro tiempo.* 15th ed. Madrid: Revista de Occidente, 1963.

Otero, Mariano. *Obras.* Edited by Jesús Reyes Heroles. 2 vols. México: Porrúa, 1967.

Ortiz de Montellano, Bernardo. "Esquema de la literatura mexicana moderna." *Contemporáneos* (July, 1931), pp. 195–210.

Pacheco, José Emilio, comp. *Antología del modernismo, 1884–1921.* 2 vols. México: Universidad Nacional Autónoma de México, 1970.

Palafox y Mendoza, Juan de. *Ideas políticas.* México: Universidad Nacional Autónoma de México, 1946.

Palavicini, Félix F. *Mi vida revolucionaria.* México: Ediciones Botas, 1937.

Pani, Alberto J. *Apuntes autobiográficos.* 2nd ed. 2 vols. México: Porrúa, 1950.

Parado León, Ricardo. "Después de la Revolución." *Crisol* 2 (February, 1929), 38–39.

Parra, Porfirio. "División del carácter." *Revista Positiva* 5 (December, 1905), 550–553.

———. "Etología o ciencia del carácter." *Revista Positiva* 5 (December, 1905), 546–549.

Paz, Octavio. *The Labyrinth of Solitude: Life and Thought in Mexico.* Translated by Lysander Kemp. New York and London: Grove Press, 1961.

———. *Posdata.* 3rd ed. México: Siglo XXI, 1970.

———; Alfonso Medellín Zenil; and Francisco Beverido. *Magia de la risa.* México: Secretaría de Educación Pública, 1971.

P. Cano, Vicente de. "Las misiones culturales del PNR." *El Nacional,* June 30, 1930.

Pereyra, Carlos. "Una obra maestra de la literatura patria." *Revista Positiva* 3 (November, 1903), 471–480.

———. "La sociología abstracta y su aplicación a algunos problemas fundamentales de México." *Revista Positiva* 3 (August, 1903), 351–386.

Pérez Martínez, Héctor. "Escaparate: I: La influencia francesa." *El Nacional*, November 22, 1930.

————. "Sobre el psicoanálisis del mexicano." *El Nacional*, September 4, 1932.

Pimentel, Francisco. *La economía política aplicada a la propiedad teritorial en México.* México: Ignacio Cumplido, 1866.

————. *Memoria sobre las causas que han originado la situación actual de la raza indígena de México y medios de remediarla.* México: Andrade y Escalante, 1864.

Pruneda, Alfonso. "Discurso." *Revista Positiva* 5 (September, 1905), 416–422.

Puig Casauranc, José María. *Páginas viejas con ideas actuales.* México: Talleres Gráficos de la Nación "Editorial," 1925.

R., Carlos Félix. "¡Mexicanos! ¿Por qué somos rebeldes y gritones?" *La Antorcha* 1 (January 24, 1925), 10.

Ramos, Samuel. "Antonio Caso." In Antonio Caso, *Obras completas*, vol. 1. 8 vols. México: Universidad Nacional Autónoma de México, 1971–1975.

————. "Antonio Caso." *Ulises* 1 (May, 1927), 12–20.

————. "Antonio Caso: (Conclusión)." *Ulises* 1 (June, 1927), 5–6.

————. "El caso Strawinsky." *Contemporáneos* (1929), pp. 1–22.

————. "Un concepto de cultura." *La Antorcha* 2 (August, 1925), 7–8.

————. "Una confesión absurda." *La Antorcha* 1 (May 30, 1925), 7.

————. "La cultura criolla." *Contemporáneos* (1931), pp. 61–82.

————. "El espectador." *La Antorcha* 2 (September, 1925), 18.

————. "El evangelio de la inteligencia." *La Antorcha* 1 (April 18, 1925), 3.

————. "La evolución de Giovanni Papini." *La Antorcha* 1 (January 17, 1925), 11–12, 30–31.

————. "El genio desconocido." *Sagitario* 9 (February 15, 1927), 9–10.

————. "A guisa de prólogo." *La Antorcha* 2 (August, 1925), 5–7.

————. *Historia de la filosofía en México.* México: Universidad Nacional Autónoma de México, 1943.

————. "Ideas filosóficas en México después de la Reforma." *México Moderno* 2 (August, 1922), 35–38.

————. "Incipit vita nova." *La Antorcha* 1 (June 13, 1925), 5.

————. "El irracionalismo." *Ulises* 1 (August, 1927), 5–13.

————. "José Torres: el primero y el último positivista." *La Antorcha* 1 (June 20, 1925), 6–7.

————. "Mi experiencia pragmatista." In Agustín Basave Fernández del Valle, *Samuel Ramos: trayectoria filosófica y antológica de textos.* Monterrey: Centro de Estudios Humanísticos de la Universidad de Nuevo León, 1965.

————. "Motivos para una investigación del mexicano." *Examen* 1 (August, 1932), 7–11.

————. "Nacionalismo y cultura." *Bandera de Provincias* 1 (January, 1930), 1, 6.

————. "Notas editoriales." *La Antorcha* 1 (May 16, 1925), 3–4; (May 23, 1925), 4; and (June 27, 1925), 3–4.

————. "El ocaso de Ariel." *La Antorcha* 1 (July 4, 1925), 14, 15.

————. "El pecado original de la Universidad Mexicana." *La Antorcha* 1 (January 31, 1925), 13–14.

————. *El perfil del hombre y la cultura en México.* México: Imprenta Mundial, 1934.

————. "Plotino." *La Antorcha* 1 (March 7, 1925), 16–19.

————. "Del siglo XIX, líbranos señor." *La Antorcha* 1 (February 21, 1925), 13.

————. "El simposio." *La Antorcha* 2 (October, 1925), 5–9.

————. "El sueño de Diego." *Contemporáneos* (1930), pp. 113–126.

————. "La tercera dimensión del conocimiento." *La Antorcha* 1 (February 14, 1925), 4–6.

Ramos Arizpe, Miguel. *Discursos, memorias, e informes.* México: Imprenta Universitaria, 1942.

Refugio Azores, María del. "Las mujeres mexicanas." *La Antorcha* 1 (February 14, 1925), 33–34.

Revilla, Manuel G. "Provincialismos de expresión en México." *Revista Positiva* 10 (January, 1910), 1–2, 53–66.

Reyes, Alfonso. *Obras completas.* 18 vols. México: Fondo de Cultura Económica, 1955–1962.

————. "Pasado inmediato." In *Universidad, política y pueblo.* México: Universidad Nacional Autónoma de México, 1967.

————. "Treno para José Ortega y Gasset." *Cuadernos Americanos* 15 (January–April, 1956), 65–67.

Riva Palacio, Vicente. *Los ceros: galería de contemporáneos por Cero.* México: Imprenta de F. Díaz de León, 1882.

———— et al. *México a través de los siglos,* vol. 2. 5 vols. Barcelona: Espasa y Cía., 1886–1889.

Rodríguez Prampolini, Ida. *La crítica de arte en México en el siglo XIX.* 3 vols. México: Universidad Nacional Autónoma de México, 1964.

Romano Muñoz, José. "Ni irracionalismo ni racionalismo, sino filosofía crítica." *Ulises* 1 (October, 1927), 4–10.

Rubio Siliceo, Luis. "Nuestra pasión." *La Antorcha* 1 (November 8, 1924), 41.

Rubio y Lhuck, Antonio. "Necesidad de la fraternidad literaria hispanoamericana." *Revista Positiva* 3 (July, 1903), 329–336.

Ruiz Díaz, Rafael. "Restalla el cohete: ¿cuál es el problema fundamental de la literatura mexicana?" *Bandera de Provincias* 1 (May, 1929), 1.

Sáenz, Moisés. *México íntegro.* Lima: Torres Aguirre, 1939.

Salazar, Rosendo. *México en pensamiento y acción.* México: Editorial Avante, 1926.

Salazar Mallén, Rubén. "Conocimiento del mexicano." *Revista de Revistas* No. 1164 (September 4, 1932), p. 42.

Sierra, Justo. *México: su evolución social.* 2 vols. México: J. Ballesca, 1900–1902.

———. *Obras completas.* 14 vols. México: Universidad Nacional Autónoma de México, 1948–1949.

———. *Prosas.* México: Universidad Nacional Autónoma de México, 1963.

Simmel, Georg. "On the Nature of Philosophy." Translated by Rudolf H. Weingartner. In *Georg Simmel, 1858–1918.* Edited by Kurt H. Wolff. Columbus, Ohio: Ohio State University Press, 1959.

Solís Cámara, Fernando. *La reconstrucción de nuestra patria.* New York: n.p., 1915.

Solórzano y Pereyra, Juan de. *Política indiana.* 5 vols. Madrid: Compañía Ibero-Americana de Publicaciones, 1930.

Sorondo, Javier. "Necesitamos mexicanizarnos." *Revista de Revistas* No. 1166 (September 18, 1932), p. 3.

Soto, Jesús S. *Aspectos de la nueva ideología mexicana.* México: Talleres Gráficos de la Nación, 1929.

Teja Zabre, Alfonso. "Tópicos de actualidad: la campaña cultural." *El Demócrata,* July 15, 1924.

Tejera, Humberto. "México y el indolatinismo." *Repertorio Americano* 8 (March 31, 1924), 17–20.

Torres, Tranquilino. "La cuestión social mexicana." *Crisol* 3 (May, 1930), 336–339.

———. "El genio de la raza." *Crisol* 4 (August, 1930), 112.

Torres Orozco, José. "La crisis del positivismo." Reprinted as "Prólogo," in *Filosofía, psicología y ciencia.* Edited by Juan Hernández Luna. México: privately printed, 1970.

Trejo Lerdo de Tejada, Carlos. *La Revolución y el nacionalismo.* Havana: Imprenta Maza, 1916.

Uribe Romo, Emilio. "Oportunidad de Hispano-America." *Crisol* 4 (December, 1930), 407–410.

Urueta, Jesús. *Obras completas.* México: Compañía Nacional Editorial "Aguilas," 1930.

Urquizo, Francisco L. *Recuerdo que: visiones aisladas de la Revolución.* México: Editorial Cultura, 1946.

Valderrama, Jerónimo. *Cartas del Licenciado Jerónimo Valderrama y otros documentos sobre su visita al gobierno de Nueva España, 1563–1565.* México: Porrúa, 1961.

"Vamos entrando . . ." *Crisol* 5 (January, 1931), 3–4.

Vasconcelos, José. "Discurso." *Repertorio Americano* 5 (January 8, 1923), 216–218.

———. *Discursos.* México: Ediciones Botas, 1950.

———. "¿En dónde está la salvación?" *La Antorcha* 1 (October 11, 1924), 1–2.

———. "El genio en Ibero-América." *Repertorio Americano* 17 (July 7, 1928), 8–9.

———. "Mensaje a Norte América." *Repertorio Americano* 9 (September 15, 1924), 17–19.

———. "El nacionalismo en la América Latina." *Repertorio Americano* 12 (March 1, 1926), 129–132, and (March 8, 1926), 148–150.

———. "El nuevo escudo de la Universidad Nacional." *Boletín de la Universidad* 2 (July, 1921), 91.

———. *Obras completas.* 4 vols. México: Libreros Mexicanos Unidos, 1958.

———. *La raza cósmica.* Barcelona: Agencia Mundial de Librería, 1925.

———. *Ulises criollo.* México: Ediciones Botas, 1935.

Velásquez, Gregorio A. "El carácter nacional constituye la fuerza de los pueblos." *El Pueblo,* August 23, 1918.

———. "Los intelectuales." *El Pueblo,* May 22, 1918.

Vetancurt, Agustín de. *Teatro mexicano.* México: Porrúa, 1971.

Vigil, José María. "Boletín del Monitor." *El Monitor Republicano,* August 9, 1878; September 7, 1878; October 15, 1878; November 5, 14, 1878; January 11, 15, 1879; February 20, 1879; March 21, 1879; April 19, 1879; May 5, 1879; June 10, 11, 12, 13, 20, 27, 1879; July 11, 19, 1879; January 14, 1880; February 6, 1880; April 21, 1880; June 25, 1880; August 18, 1880.

———. "Colonización." *El Siglo Diez y Nueve,* December 3, 1870.

———. "Necesidad y conveniencia de estudiar la historia patria." *El Sistema Postal de la República Mexicana,* June 9, 15, 22, 29, 1878.

Villalpando, Jesús. "Lo nacional, lo mexicano, lo pintoresco." *El Nacional,* November 18, 1917.

Villaseñor, Eduardo. *Memorias–Testimonio.* México: Fondo de Cultura Económica, 1974.

Vivanco, Javier. "La integración nacional." *Universidad de México* 1 (November–April, 1931), 42–46.

Yáñez, Agustín. "Notas criollas." *Bandera de Provincias* 1 (April, 1929), 1–5.

Zárate, Julio. "La raza indígena." *El Siglo Diez y Nueve,* December 2, 1870.

Zavala, Lorenzo de. *Ensayo histórico de las revoluciones de México.* 3rd ed. 2 vols. México: Oficina Impresa de Hacienda, Depto. Editorial, 1918.

Works Cited

Abreu Gómez, Ermilio. "¿Existe una crisis en nuestra literatura de vanguardia?" *El Ilustrado,* April 28, 1932, pp. 48–49.

Aguilar Camín, Hector. *La frontera nómada: Sonora y la Revolución mexicana.* México: Siglo XXI, 1977.

Arciniegas, Germán. *Latin America: A Cultural History.* New York: Alfred A. Knopf, 1973.

Azuela, Salvador. "Samuel Ramos abrió el camino a los trabajos que se han hecho sobre la filosofía cultural de México." *El Sol de Puebla,* July 25, 1959.

Bailey, David C. "Revisionism and the Recent Historiography of the Mexican Revolution." *Hispanic American Historical Review* 58 (February, 1978), 62–79.

Barker, Nancy N. "Monarchy in Mexico: Hare-brained Scheme or Well-considered Prospect?" *Journal of Modern History* 48 (March, 1976), 51–68.

Bataillon, Marcel. *Erasmo y España: estudios sobre la historia espiritual del siglo XVI.* Translated by Antonio Alatorre. 2 vols. México: Fondo de Cultura Económica, 1950.

Bockus Aponte, Barbara. *Alfonso Reyes and Spain: His Dialogue with Unamuno, Valle-Inclán, Ortega y Gasset, Jiménez, and Gómez de la Serna.* Austin and London: University of Texas Press, 1972.

Bourricaud, François. "The Adventures of Ariel." *Daedalus* 101 (Summer, 1972), 109–136.

Brading, David A. *Los orígenes del nacionalismo mexicano.* México: Secretaría de Educación Pública, 1973.

Brandenburg, Frank. *The Making of Modern Mexico.* Englewood Cliffs, N.J.: Prentice Hall, 1964.

Britton, John A. "Indian Education, Nationalism, and Federalism in Mexico, 1910–1921." *The Americas* 22 (January, 1976), 445–458.

Calvert, Peter. *The Mexican Revolution, 1910–1914: The Diplomacy of Anglo-American Conflict.* London: Cambridge University Press, 1968.

———. "The Mexican Revolution: Theory or Fact?" *Journal of Latin American Studies* 1 (1969), 51–68.

———. *Mexico.* New York and Washington: Praeger, 1973.

Cardiel Reyes, Raúl. *Del modernismo al liberalismo: la filosofía de Manuel María Gorriño.* México: Universidad Nacional Autónoma de México, 1967.

Cardoza y Aragón, Luis. *Orozco.* México: Universidad Nacional Autónoma de México, Instituto de Investigaciones Estéticas, 1959.

Careaga, Gabriel. *Los intelectuales y la política en México.* México: Extemporáneos, 1971.

Carrillo, Roberto. "Comentando a Samuel Ramos." *Letras de México* 2 (December 16, 1940), 9.

Chávez, Leticia. *Recordando a mi padre.* 2nd ed., rev. México: Asociación Civil: "Ezequiel A. Chávez," 1967.

Chevalier, François. *Land and Society in Colonial Mexico: The Great Hacienda*. Translated by Alvin Eustis. Berkeley: University of California Press, 1963.

Chiappelli, Fredi, ed. *First Images of America: The Impact of the New World on the Old*. 2 vols. Berkeley: University of California Press, 1976.

Cockcroft, James D. *Intellectual Precursors of the Mexican Revolution, 1900–1913*. Austin and London: University of Texas Press, 1965.

Collingwood, R. G. *The Idea of History*. Oxford: Clarendon Press, 1946.

———. *The Idea of Nature*. Oxford: Clarendon Press, 1945.

Comas, Juan. "Razas, mestizaje y clases socialies en la obra de Andrés Molina Enríquez: 1909." *Cuadernos Americanos* 72 (March–April, 1966), 122–141.

———. "La vida y la obra de Manuel Gamio." In *Estudios antropológicos publicados en homenaje al doctor Manuel Gamio*. México: Dirección General de Publicaciones, 1956.

Córdova, Arnaldo. *La ideología de la Revolución mexicana: la formación del nuevo régimen*. 3rd ed. México: Ediciones Era, 1974.

Cosío Villegas, Daniel. *Historia Moderna de México*. 10 vols. México: Hermes, 1955–1972.

———. "Del Porfiriato a la Revolución." *Novedades*, November 2, 1952.

Cumberland, Charles C. *Mexican Revolution: Genesis under Madero*. Austin: University of Texas Press, 1952.

Del artesanado al socialismo: artículos de José María González. México: Secretaría de Educación Pública, 1974.

Díaz Thomé, Hugo. "El mexicano y su historia." *Historia Mexicana* 2 (October–December, 1952), 248–258.

Diccionario Porrúa de Historia, Biografía y Geografía de México, 2 vols. 3rd edition. México: Porrúa, 1971.

Elliott, J. H. *Imperial Spain, 1469–1716*. New York: St. Martin's Press, 1964.

———. *The Old World and the New, 1492–1640*. London: Cambridge University Press, 1970.

Evans, Arthur R., Jr. "Ernst Robert Curtius." In *On Four Modern Humanists: Hofmannsthal, Gundolf, Curtius, and Kantorowicz*. Edited by A. R. Evans, Jr. Princeton: Princeton University Press, 1970.

Fernández-Santamaria, J. A. *The State, War and Peace: Spanish Political Thought in the Renaissance, 1516–1559*. London: Cambridge University Press, 1977.

Ferrer Mendiolea, Gabriel. "Año de Carranza: actividades de la 'Confederación'." *El Nacional*, October 18, 1959.

Finkelman Morgenstein, Maty. "El pensamiento de Justo Sierra y el sentido de sus aportaciones historiográficas." Licentiate thesis, Universidad Nacional Autónoma de México, 1966.

Franklin, Wayne. "Speaking and Touching: The Problem of Inexpressibility in American Travel Books." *Exploration* 4 (December, 1976), 1–15.

Fuentes, Carlos. *Tiempo mexicano*. México: Joaquín Mortiz, 1971.

Gallegos Rocafull, José M. *El pensamiento mexicano en los siglos XVI y XVII*. México: Universidad Nacional Autónoma de México, 1951.

Gaos, José. *Sobre Ortega y Gasset*. México: Universidad Nacional Autónoma de México, 1957.

Garrido, Luis. "Un censor inoportuno." *Mástiles* 1 (September, 1928), 7–8.

Gerbi, Antonello. *The Dispute of the New World: The History of a Polemic, 1750–1900*. Translated by Jeremy Moyle. Pittsburgh: University of Pittsburgh Press, 1973.

Gibson, Charles. *The Aztecs under Spanish Rule: A History of the Indians of the Valley of Mexico, 1519–1810*. Stanford, Calif.: Stanford University Press, 1964.

Gilmore, Myron P. *The World of Humanism, 1453–1517*. New York: Harper and Row, 1952.

Glacken, Clarence J. *Traces on the Rhodian Shore: Nature and Culture in Western Thought from Ancient Times to the End of the Eighteenth Century*. Berkeley: University of California Press, 1967.

Gómez Quiñones, Juan. "Social Change and Intellectual Discontent: The Growth of Mexican Nationalism, 1890–1911." Ph.D. dissertation, University of California at Los Angeles, 1972.

Gómez Robledo, Antonio. "La conciencia mexicana en la obra de Francisco Xavier Clavijero." *Historia Mexicana* 19 (January–March, 1970), 347–364.

Góngora, Mario. *Studies in the Colonial History of Spanish America*. Translated by Richard Southern. Cambridge, Eng.: Cambridge University Press, 1975.

González, Luis. "Humboldt y la revolución de independencia." In *Ensayos sobre Humboldt*. México: Universidad Nacional Autónoma de México, 1962.

————. *Invitación a la microhistoria*. 3rd ed. México: Secretaría de Educación Pública, 1973.

————. "Microhistoria para multi-México." *Historia Mexicana* 21 (October–December, 1971), 225–241.

————. "El optimismo nacionalista como factor de la independencia de México." In *Estudios de historiografía americana*. México: El Colegio de México, 1948.

————. *Pueblo in vilo*. México: El Colegio de México, 1968.

————. "En torno de la integración de la realidad mexicana." In *Estudios históricos americanos: homenaje a Silvio Zavala*. México: El Colegio de México, 1953.

González Navarro, Moisés. *Población y sociedad en México, 1900–1970*.

2 vols. México: Universidad Nacional Autónoma de México, 1974.

————. *Sociología e historia en México: Barreda, Sierra, Parra, Molina Enríquez, Gamio, Caso.* México: El Colegio de México, 1970.

González Ramírez, Manuel. *Las ideas—la violencia.* Vol. 1 of *La Revolución social de México.* 3 vols. México: Fondo de Cultura Económica, 1960.

Grajales, Gloria. *Nacionalismo incipiente en los historiadores coloniales: estudio historiográfico.* México: Universidad Nacional Autónoma de México, 1961.

Green, Otis H. *Spain and the Western Tradition: The Castilian Mind in Literature from El Cid to Calderón.* 4 vols. Madison: University of Wisconsin Press, 1965.

Hale, Charles A. *Mexican Liberalism in the Age of Mora.* New Haven and London: Yale University Press, 1968.

Hall, Linda B. "Alvaro Obregón and the Mexican Revolution, 1912–1920: The Origins of Institutionalization." Ph.D. dissertation, Columbia University, 1976.

Hamill, Jr., Hugh M. *The Hidalgo Revolt: Prelude to Mexican Independence.* Gainesville: University of Florida Press, 1966.

Hanke, Lewis. "El significado teológico del descubrimiento de América." *Diálogos* 12 (January–February, 1976), 21–26.

————. *The Spanish Struggle for Justice in the Conquest of America.* Boston: Little, Brown, 1965.

Hansen, Roger D. *The Politics of Mexican Development.* Baltimore and London: Johns Hopkins University Press, 1971.

Harris, Marvin. *Patterns of Race in the Americas.* New York: Walker and Co., 1964.

Hart, John M. "Agrarian Precursors of the Mexican Revolution: The Development of an Ideology." *The Americas* 29 (October, 1972), 131–150.

————. "Nineteenth Century Urban Labor Precursors of the Mexican Revolution: The Development of an Ideology." *The Americas* 30 (January, 1974), 297–318.

Heath, Shirley Brice. *La política del lenguaje en México: de la colonia a la nación.* México: Porrúa, 1972.

Henríquez Ureña, Pedro. "El hermano definidor." *Repertorio Americano* 7 (October 29, 1923), 81.

————. "El positivismo independiente." In *Horas de estudio.* Paris: P. Ollendorff, 1910.

Hernández Campos, Jorge. "La crítica como pecado original: México ante la crisis de la cultura universal." *Excélsior,* April 30, 1972.

Hernández Luna, Juan. *Antonio Caso: embajador extraordinario de México.* México: Sociedad de Amigos del Libro Mexicano, 1963.

————. "El gran *Pacotillas.*" *Historia Mexicana* 1 (April–June, 1952), 517–540.

————. *José Torres Orozco: el último positivista mexicano.* México: privately printed, 1970.

————. "Primeros estudios sobre lo mexicano en nuestro siglo." *Filosofía y Letras* 20 (October–December, 1950), 327–354.

————. "Prólogo." In Antonio Caso, *Obras completas,* Vol. 1. México: Universidad Nacional Autónoma de México, 1971.

————. *Samuel Ramos: su filosofar sobre lo mexicano.* México: Universidad Nacional Autónoma de México, 1956.

Historia General de México. 4 vols. México: El Colegio de México, 1976.

Hodgen, Margaret T. *Early Anthropology in the Sixteenth and Seventeenth Centuries.* Philadelphia: University of Pennsylvania Press, 1964.

Hofstadter, Richard. *Social Darwinism in American Thought.* Boston: Beacon Press, 1955.

Huddleston, Lee E. *Origins of the American Indian: European Concepts, 1492–1729.* Austin and London: University of Texas Press, 1967.

Hughes, H. Stuart. *Consciousness and Society: The Reorientation of European Social Thought, 1890–1930.* New York: Vintage, 1958.

Innis, John S. "The Universidad Popular Mexicana." *The Americas* 30 (July, 1973), 110–122.

Israel, J. I. *Race, Class, and Politics in Colonial Mexico, 1610–1670.* London: Oxford University Press, 1975.

Izquierdo, José Joaquín. *Montaña y los orígenes del movimiento social y científico de México.* México: Ciencia, 1955.

Jones, Howard Mumford. *O Strange New World: American Culture, The Formative Years.* New York: Viking, 1964.

Jorrín, Miguel, and John D. Martz. *Latin American Political Thought and Ideology.* Chapel Hill: University of North Carolina Press, 1970.

Keen, Benjamin. *The Aztec Image in Western Thought.* New Brunswick, N.J.: Rutgers University Press, 1971.

Korn, Peggy Ann. "The Beginnings of Mexican Nationalism: The Growth of an Ideology." Ph.D. dissertation, University of Pennsylvania, 1965.

Korn, Peggy K. "Topics in Mexican Historiography, 1750–1810: The Bourbon Reforms, the Enlightenment, and the Background of Revolution." In *Investigaciones contemporáneas sobre historia de México: memorias de la tercera reunión de historiadores mexicanos y norteamericanos.* Austin: University of Texas Press, and México: El Colegio de México, 1971.

Krauze, Enrique. *Caudillos culturales en la Revolución mexicana.* México: Siglo XXI, 1976.

————. "Datos personales." In *Extremos de México: homenaje a don Daniel Cosío Villegas.* México: El Colegio de México, 1971.

Krauze de Kolteniuk, Rosa. *La filosofía de Antonio Caso.* México: Universidad Nacional Autónoma de México, 1961.

Ladd, Doris M. *The Mexican Nobility at Independence, 1780–1826.* Austin: Institute of Latin American Studies, 1976.

Lafaye, Jacques. *Quetzalcóatl et Guadalupe: La formation de la conscience nationale au Mexique, 1531–1813.* Paris: Gallimard, 1974.

———. "La utopía mejicana: ensayo de intrahistoria." *Diógenes* 20 (April–June, 1972), 28.

Leonard, Irving A. *Baroque Times in Old Mexico: Seventeenth Century Persons, Places, and Practices.* Ann Arbor: University of Michigan Press, 1971.

Lester, C. Edwards, and Andrew Foster. *The Life and Voyages of Americus Vespucius.* New York: Baker and Scribner, 1846.

Levin, Harry. *The Myth of the Golden Age in the Renaissance.* Bloomington: Indiana University Press, 1969.

Lévi-Strauss, Claude. *Tristes Tropiques: An Anthropological Study of Primitive Societies in Brazil.* New York: Atheneum, 1972.

Lewis, Archibald R., and Thomas F. McGann, eds. *The New World Looks at Its History.* Austin: University of Texas Press, 1962.

Liss, Peggy K. "Jesuit Contributions to the Ideology of Spanish Empire in Mexico." Part 1, *The Americas* 29 (January, 1973), 314–333; part 2, *The Americas* 29 (April, 1973) 442–448.

———. *Mexico under Spain, 1521–1556: Society and the Origins of Nationality.* Chicago: University of Chicago Press, 1975.

List Arzubide, Germán. *El movimiento estridentista.* México: Secretaría de Educación Pública, 1967.

Maciel, David. "Nacionalismo cultural en México, 1867–1876." Unpublished paper. Copy in possession of the author.

McLean, Malcolm. *El contenido literario de El Siglo Diez y Nueve.* México: Mundial, 1938.

———. *Vida y obra de Guillermo Prieto.* México: El Colegio de México, 1960.

Manrique, Jorge Alberto. "El pesimismo como factor de la independencia de México." In *Conciencia y autenticidad históricas: escritos en homenaje a Edmundo O'Gorman.* México: Universidad Nacional Autónoma de México, 1968.

Manuel, Frank E. *Shapes of Philosophical History.* Stanford, Calif.: Stanford University Press, 1965.

———, and Fritzie P. Manuel. "Sketch for a Natural History of Paradise." *Daedalus* 101 (Winter, 1972), 83–128.

Martínez Leal de Helguera, Margarita. "Posibles antecedentes de la intervención francesa de 1862." *Historia Mexicana* 15 (July–September, 1965), 1–24.

Maza, Francisco de la. *Enrico Martínez: cosmógrafo e impresor de Nueva España.* México: Ediciones de la Sociedad de Geografía y Estadística, 1943.

———. Introduction. In Enrico Martínez, *Repertorio de los tiempos e*

historia natural de Nueva España. México: Secretaría de Educación Pública, 1948.

Méndez Plancarte, Gabriel, ed. *Humanistas del siglo XVIII*. 2nd ed. México: Universidad Nacional Autónoma de México, 1962.

Meyer, Eugenia W. de. "Del ser mexicano y de la historiografía de la Revolución." In *Conciencia y autenticidad históricas: escritos en homenaje a Edmundo O'Gorman*. México: Universidad Nacional Autónoma de México, 1966.

Meyer, Lorenzo. "Continuidades e inovaciones en la vida política mexicana del siglo XX: el antiguo y el nuevo régimen." *Foro Internacional* 16 (July–September, 1973), 37–63.

Meyer, Michael C. *Huerta: A Political Portrait*. Lincoln: University of Nebraska Press, 1972.

————. "Perspectives on Revolutionary Historiography." *New Mexico Historical Review* 18 (1969), 167–180.

Michaels, Albert L. "Mexican Nationalism from Calles to Cárdenas." Ph.D. dissertation, University of Pennsylvania, 1966.

Miranda, José. *España y Nueva España en la época de Felipe II*. México: Universidad Nacional Autónoma de México, 1962.

————. *Las ideas y las instituciones políticas mexicanas, 1521–1820*. México: Instituto de Derecho Comparado, 1952.

————. *Vida colonial y albores de la independencia*. México: Secretaría de Educación Pública, 1972.

Mörner, Magnus. *Race Mixture in the History of Latin America*. Boston: Little, Brown, 1967.

Mullen, Edward J. "*Contemporáneos* in Mexican Intellectual History, 1928–1931." *Journal of Inter-American Studies and World Affairs* 13 (January, 1971), 121–130.

Muñoz Cota, José. "El mirador de la Revolución: Revolución y mexicanidad." *El Nacional*, June 13, 1962.

Navarro, Bernabé. *La introducción de la filosofía moderna en México*. México: El Colegio de México, 1948.

Needler, Martin C. *Politics and Society in Mexico*. Albuquerque: University of New Mexico Press, 1971.

Noreña, Carlos G. *Studies in Spanish Renaissance Thought*. The Hague: Martinus Nijhoff, 1975.

Novo, Salvador. "Nota de la provincia." *Nuestro México* 1 (July, 1932), 6.

Ocampo, Javier. *Las ideas de un día: el pueblo mexicano ante la consumación de su independencia*. México: El Colegio de México, 1969.

Ochoa, Guillermo. "El gobierno debe mantener el avance." *Excélsior*, November 29, 1971.

O'Gorman, Edmundo. *The Invention of America*. Bloomington: University of Indiana Press, 1961.

————. "Justo Sierra y los orígenes de la Universidad Nacional de México, 1910." *Filosofía y Letras* 17 (April–June, 1949), 221–250.

Ortega y Medina, Juan Antonio. *Humboldt desde México.* México: Universidad Nacional Autónoma de México, 1960.

————. "Un olvidado ensayo histórico de don José María Vigil." *Estudios de Historia Moderna y Contemporánea de México* 3 (1970), 67–74.

Palacios, Emmanuel: "Bandera de Provincias." In *Las revistas literarias de México.* México: Bellas Artes, 1964.

Palacios, Guillermo. "La idea oficial de la Revolución mexicana." 2 vols. Master's thesis, El Colegio de México, 1969.

Parry, J. H. *The Age of Reconnaissance.* New York: Mentor, 1963.

————. *The Spanish Seaborne Empire.* New York: Alfred A. Knopf, 1966.

Peña, Rafael Angel de la. "Reseña histórica de la academia mexicana." In *Obras de Don Rafael Angel de la Peña.* Edited by V. Agüeros. México: Imprenta de V. Agüeros, 1900.

Penrose, Boies. *Travel and Discovery in the Renaissance, 1429–1620.* New York: Atheneum, 1971.

Pérez Marchand, Monelisa Lina. *Dos etapas ideológicas del siglo XVIII en México: a través de los papeles de la Inquisición.* México: El Colegio de México, 1945.

Pescatello, Ann M. *Power and Pawn: The Female in Iberian Families, Societies, and Cultures.* Westport, Conn., and London: Greenwood Press, 1976.

Phelan, John Leddy. *The Millenial Kingdom of the Franciscans in the New World.* 2nd ed. Berkeley: University of California Press, 1970.

————. "Neo-Aztecism in the Eighteenth Century and the Genesis of Mexican Nationalism." In *Culture in History: Essays in Honor of Paul Radin.* Edited by Stanley Diamond. New York: Columbia University Press, 1960.

————. "Pan-Latinism, French Intervention in Mexico (1861–1867), and the Genesis of the Idea of Latin America." In *Conciencia y autenticidad históricas: escritos en homenaje a Edmundo O'Gorman.* México: Universidad Nacional Autónoma de México, 1968.

Pike, Fredrick B. *Hispanismo, 1898–1936: Spanish Conservatives and Liberals and Their Relations with Spanish America.* Notre Dame, Ind.: University of Notre Dame, 1971.

————. *Spanish America, 1900–1970: Tradition and Social Innovation.* New York: Norton, 1973.

Pizano Aguilar, Julio. "Ezequiel A. Chávez y su contribución a la psicología del pueblo mexicano." Master's thesis, Universidad Nacional Autónoma de México, 1965.

Portal, Magda. "Panorama intelectual de México: la literatura mexicana." *Repertorio Americano* 16 (March 10, 1928), 157–158.

Porter, Katherine Anne. "The Mexican Trinity." In *The Collected Essays and Occasional Writings of Katherine Anne Porter*. New York: Delacorte Press, 1970.

Pozas A., Ricardo. *Juan Pérez Jolote: biografía de un tzotzil*. México: Fondo de Cultura Económica, 1968.

Quirarte, Martín. *Historiografía sobre el imperio de Maximiliano*. México: Universidad Nacional Autónoma de México, 1970.

Quirk, Robert. *The Mexican Revolution and the Catholic Church, 1910–1920*. Bloomington and London: Indiana University Press, 1973.

Raat, William D. "Agustín Aragón and Mexico's Religion of Humanity." *Journal of Inter-American Studies and World Affairs* 11 (July, 1969), 441–457.

―――. "Ideas and Society in don Porfirio's Mexico." *The Americas* 30 (July, 1973), 32–53.

―――. "Positivism in Díaz's Mexico, 1876–1910: An Essay in Intellectual History." Ph.D. dissertation, University of Utah, 1967.

Reyes Heroles, Jesús. *El liberalismo mexicano*. 3 vols. México: Universidad Nacional Autónoma de México, 1957–1958.

Rivera, Agustín. "Dialogue between A. R. and Florencito." In *Readings from Modern Mexican Authors*. Edited by Frederick Starr. Chicago: The Open Court Publishing Co., 1904.

Romanell, Patrick. *Making of the Mexican Mind*. Notre Dame, Ind.: Notre Dame University Press, 1967.

―――. "Samuel Ramos on the Philosophy of Mexican Culture: Ortega and Unamuno in Mexico." *Latin American Research Review* 10 (Fall, 1975), 81–102.

Ross, Stanley R. *Francisco I. Madero: Apostle of Mexican Democracy*. New York: Columbia University Press, 1955.

―――. "Imágenes de la Revolución mexicana." *Latinoamérica* 1 (1968), 37–48.

Ruiz, Ramón Eduardo. *Labor and the Ambivalent Revolutionaries: Mexico, 1911–1923*. Baltimore and London: The Johns Hopkins University Press, 1976.

―――. *Mexico: The Challenge of Poverty and Illiteracy*. San Marino, Calif.: The Huntington Library, 1963.

Ruiz Gaytán, Beatriz. "La Facultad de Filosofía y Letras y sus postulados." *Historia Mexicana* 30 (April–July, 1970), 574–581.

Sanford, Charles E. *The Quest for Paradise: Europe and the American Moral Imagination*. Urbana: University of Illinois Press, 1961.

Simpson, Lesley Byrd. *The Encomienda in New Spain*. Rev. ed. Berkeley: University of California Press, 1966.

Spengler, Oswald. *The Decline of the West*. 2 vols. New York: Alfred A. Knopf, 1926–1928.

Stabb, Martin S. *In Quest of Identity: Patterns in the Spanish-American*

Essay of Ideas, 1890–1960. Chapel Hill: University of North Carolina Press, 1967.

Stevens, Evelyn P. "Mexican Machismo: Politics and Value Orientations." *The Western Political Quarterly* 18 (December, 1965), 848–857.

————. *Protest and Response in Mexico.* Cambridge, Mass., and London: M.I.T. Press, 1974.

Tannenbaum, Frank. *The Mexican Agrarian Revolution.* New York: Macmillan, 1929.

————. *Mexico: The Struggle for Peace and Bread.* New York: Alfred A. Knopf, 1950.

————. "Some Reflections on the Revolution." In *Is the Mexican Revolution Dead?* 2nd ed. rev. and enlg. Edited by Stanley R. Ross. Philadelphia: Temple University Press, 1975.

————. "Spontaneity and Adaptation in the Mexican Revolution." *Journal of World History* 9 (1965), 80–90.

Tavera Alfaro, Xavier. *El nacionalismo en la prensa mexicana del siglo XVIII.* México: Club de Periodistas de México, 1963.

Toynbee, Arnold. *A Study of History.* 13 vols. London, New York and Toronto: Oxford University Press, 1939.

Turner, Frederick C. *The Dynamic of Mexican Nationalism.* Chapel Hill: University of North Carolina Press, 1968.

Uranga, Emilio. "El significado de la Revolución mexicana." *Novedades,* November 19, 1950.

Valle, Rafael Heliodoro. "Ideario mexicano." *Repertorio Americano* 13 (September 4, 1926), 143.

Vázquez de Knauth, Josefina. *Nacionalismo y educación en México.* México: El Colegio de México, 1970.

————. "Sobre la síntesis de la historia de México." *Historia Mexicana* 21 (October–December, 1971), 217–224.

Vázquez, Josefina Zoraida. *La imagen del indio en el español del siglo XVI.* Jalapa, Verucruz: Universidad Veracruzana, 1962.

Villaseñor, Eduardo. "Intenciones sobre la cultura en México." *La Antorcha* 1 (January 17, 1925), 16.

Villegas, Abelardo. *La filosofía de lo mexicano.* México: Fondo de Cultura Económica, 1960.

————. "El liberalismo mexicano." In *Estudios de historia de la filosofía en México.* México: Universidad Nacional Autónoma de México, 1973.

Villoro, Luis. *Los grandes momentos del indigenismo en México.* México: El Colegio de México, 1950.

————. *El proceso ideológico de la revolución de independencia.* 2nd ed. México: Universidad Nacional Autónoma de México, 1967.

Warman, Arturo. . . . *Y venimos a contradecir: los campesinos de Morelos*

y el estado nacional. México: Instituto Nacional de Historia e Antropología, 1976.

Weatherhead, Richard Whitney. "Justo Sierra: A Portrait of a Porfirian Intellectual." Ph.D. dissertation, Columbia University, 1966.

Weingartner, Rudolph H. *Experience and Culture: The Philosophy of Georg Simmel.* Middletown, Conn.: Wesleyan University Press, 1962.

Weinstein, Michael A. *The Polarity of Mexican Thought: Instrumentalism and Finalism.* University Park: Pennsylvania State University Press, 1976.

Wilkie, James W.; Michael C. Meyer; and Edna Monzón de Wilkie, eds. *Contemporary Mexico: Papers of the IV International Congress of Mexican History.* Berkeley: University of California Press, 1976.

Wolf, Eric. *Sons of the Shaking Earth.* Chicago: University of Chicago Press, 1959.

Womack, John, Jr. *Zapata and the Mexican Revolution.* New York: Alfred A. Knopf, 1969.

Yáñez, Agustín. *Don Justo Sierra: su vida, sus ideas y su obra.* México: Universidad Nacional Autónoma de México, 1950.

―――. "Estudio preliminar." In J. Joaquín Fernández de Lizardi, *El pensador mexicano.* México: Universidad Nacional Autónoma de México, 1962.

Zea, Leopoldo. *Conciencia y posibilidad del mexicano.* México: Porrúa y Obregón, 1952.

―――. *La filosofía en México.* 2 vols. México: Libro-Mex, 1955.

―――. "Humboldt y la independencia de América." In *Ensayos sobre Humboldt.* México: Universidad Nacional Autónoma de México, 1962.

―――. *The Latin-American Mind.* Translated by James H. Abbott and Lowell Dunham. Norman: University of Oklahoma Press, 1963.

―――. "Ortega el americano." *Cuadernos Americanos* 15 (January–April, 1956), 132–145.

―――. *El positivismo en México: nacimiento, apogeo y decadencia.* México: Fondo de Cultura Económica, 1968.

Index

Index